Advanced Acclaim for Lo

Lore Reich Rubin, MD, has written a fascinating case history of a little girl, the daughter of psychoanalytic luminaries, who grew up to become a psychoanalyst herself. If that weren't enough, the little girl described is also the author of this case history. If you read it as a book about her well-known parents, Annie Reich and Wilhelm Reich, you'll not be disappointed, but in truth this is a book about another Reich, their daughter Lore. *Memories of a Chaotic World: Growing up as the Daughter of Annie Reich and Wilhelm Reich* is an extraordinary accomplishment, a psychoanalytically sophisticated self-analysis. We learn of Reich Rubin's love for her mother, her fascination with her father, and her disappointments with both.

The ambivalence is held and elaborated in all directions. Reich Rubin demonstrates how theoretical issues, clinical technique, and institutional power dynamics are sometimes more clearly revealed in the first-person narratives of psychoanalytic history than in the official or party-line books and journal articles dedicated to these topics.

Living a thoroughly psychoanalytic life, she has contextualized theory and technique in personal, social, political, and economic contexts. She navigates the exciting years in Vienna, the rise of Nazism, the emigrations, the hardships, the changing directions of psychoanalysis, and the changing trends in European and North American left-wing politics. Emigration is a planned psychological trauma, and Reich Rubin captures the developmental turmoil of a pubescent girl on the run from Hitler and the coming war who then arrives in a new land with a changing body, a new language to learn and a mother from the old country who is trying to adapt. She then launches a career in psychoanalysis, studying with the émigré analysts in New York City who were not only giants in the field but also family friends since her childhood. This is an extraordinary book. It is autobiography. It is analysis. It is history.

—DANIEL S. BENVENISTE, PHD, author of *The Interwoven Lives of Sigmund, Anna, and W. Ernest Freud: Three Generations of Psychoanalysis*

Memories of a Chaotic World

Memories of a Chaotic World

Growing Up as the Daughter of
Annie Reich and Wilhelm Reich

Lore Reich Rubin

IPBOOKS.net
International Psychoanalytic Books
International Psychoanalytic Books (IPBooks)
New York • IPBooks.net

Published by IPBooks, Queens, NY 2021

Online at: www.IPBooks.net

Previously published in German by Psychosozio-Verlag, Giesen Germany 2019; translated into German by Lilith-Isa Samer.

Cover Design by Kathy Kovacic, Blackthorn Studio.

ISBN: 978-1-949093-96-4

Library of Congress Control Number: 2021917853

To the Grandchildren of Wilhelm Reich:
Renata, Katie, Toby, Erica, Nick, and Cecelia

My Parents in Love, Climbing in the Alps, 1926

Contents

Foreword
by Wolfram Ratz

First and foremost: Lore Reich Rubin, "the other daughter," has remained in the shadow of her father, her mother, and her sister Eva. Yet, she has to tell highly interesting and very touching stories. Lore is presently 93 years old—high time for her to share the history of her life, so we can experience it with her.

Vienna witnessed the best and the worst moments of the 20th century. It was an epicenter of the achievements of a rich social life and a dark nightmare after the end of the great empire, the global economic crisis and the takeover of power by the National Socialists. During that process, entire cultural landscapes were destroyed.

After the devastating, ever-recurring armed conflicts in Europe—driven by the longing for a bearable life—psychoanalysts launched, a search for their causes in the wake of World War I. The course of events could not be stopped, but their background could be explained (see, e.g., Wilhelm Reich, *Massenpsychologie des Faschismus*).

It was "the century of the self," of the genesis of psychoanalysis with its tremendous importance for the understanding of the subconscious. The psychoanalysts saw themselves at the time as an elite and as part of a larger endeavor. In 1928, Lore was born in Vienna into one such family, as the daughter of Annie Reich and Wilhelm Reich. "Everything was grey, even the food," according to her description of her life at that time. The parents saw themselves as pioneers starting their professional lives and, at times, relegated the upbringing of their children to grandparents and children's homes. Due tb the relocation of Wilhelm Reich to Berlin and the increasing alienation between their parents, the children were frequently left to their own devices. The mother was in charge of the children, the father—hounded by the political, professional and personal turmoil of the pre-war years—disappeared more and more from the family. After their emigration to the United States, rejections and emotional outbursts on the part of Lore's father alienated him more and more from her—a situation that was to last until his death.

Only after Wilhelm Reich had died in the year 1957—"[which] was as if an evil spirit had been banished"—did the scattered family, enlarged by Reich's second wife, [Ise Ollendorf], and their son Peter, reunite again. Eventually, after struggling to understand his personal development and the tragedy of his life, Lore came to reconcile with her father.

Reich Rubin's book is a very personal and authentic account of her life as Wilhelm Reich's daughter, adding a new perspective to his personality. May this perspective not serve to cast a shadow on his achievements, his great mind and his efficacy. I am very pleased that Lore Reich Rubin's memoires are now available in book-form and that we were able to contribute to the translation of a German edition.

—WOLFRAM RATZ,
Wilhelm Reich Institute; Vienna

Acknowledgements

This book took a very long time to be created and I have so many people to thank for their help. I started writing it without any idea of publication, just as a creative expression of some vivid early memories. I have to thank my children for growing up enough so I could find quiet times to sit at my typewriter. Many of these early writings were lost over time and are here recreated, unfortunately often in much less poetic form. I read some of these pieces that pertained to vignettes about early psychoanalysis to my study group at the Pittsburgh Psychoanalytic Institute. They were so enthusiastic that I realized that my story may be interesting to others. So, after I retired from practice I started working on a memoir.

Many of my friends read parts and offered critique and corrections to my work. I wish to thank Brig Alexander, Audrey Schoenwald, Helen Tauster, and especially Virginia Carter for helping to make the first chapter readable. Above all I thank Janice Gibson who proof-read and edited about six early chapters.

I also am grateful to many people who sent me documents like the FBI files, Prison Record, and STASI files of my father Wilhelm Reich. And also, the many people who sent me information on my stepfather Thomas, his ex-wife Ruth, and their daughter Ruth. And I especially want to thank Andreas Peglau both for his very informative book on my father in the early 30's in Berlin and his help with fact checking on my book.

Cynthia Adcock was very creative in helping me with the title of the book and with summarizing it in a precise manner. Laureen Nussbaum did an amazing amount of work both correcting missed mistakes in the German edition (unfortunately it needs a second printing to be useful) and proofreading this English version. My thanks to both of them.

Special thanks go to the Wilhelm Reich Institute in Vienna whose members, especially Wolfram Ratz, Günter Reissnert and Thomas Harms, who pushed Psychosozial-Verlag into agreeing to publish the book, and hired and paid for the translation into German by Lilith Saner. And I also thank the editors of the Verlag for all their help.

I want to give a special thanks to Wolfram Ratz. Without his enthusiasm, energy and dedication this book would never have reached publication. He became an unofficial consultant to the Verlag, who had him arbitrate many decisions. He was in constant communication with me and a great support.

Thanks also go to Arnold Richards, Tamar and Lawrence Schwartz at International Psychoanalytic Books for all their help for publishing my English version of my memoir.

And last of all I want to thank my family, especially my daughter Erica, brother Peter, and niece Renata for their helpful comments, patience, and listening, and for their great help in sorting of photographs.

—Lore Reich Rubin

Chapter 1

VIENNA (2000): RECALL OF EARLY CHILDHOOD

In the autumn of 2000, after an absence of sixty-four years, I returned with my husband to Vienna. I had avoided this visit because it seemed strange to visit one's old home not knowing anybody there. But, as a last chance before problems of aging overcame us, I decided I had to make the pilgrimage.

Austria seemed, at that time, to have developed a poor reputation as a travel destination. Everyone we knew reacted negatively to our planned trip, telling us that Austria had become fascist and anti-Semitic, and that many travelers were avoiding Vienna. Nevertheless, we decided to go and were pleased to find the atmosphere very friendly and antifascist. Also, a huge holocaust memorial statue had been erected in a central part of Vienna.

There was a big uproar about the Neo-Nazi Heider, whose political base was in Carinthia, not Vienna, with demands that the government resign in order to force him out. As it turned out, I discovered that I had a distant cousin living there, whose family had returned right after the war. Her sons described with great enthusiasm the demonstrations held every Thursday in downtown Vienna, blocking traffic, and causing great inconveniences. None of the people we spoke with, however, were much put out by these demonstrations; at least in Vienna, Heider did not have much popular support.

Vienna, in recent years, has also reversed its attitude toward Freud. This famous Viennese has been honored by city sponsored meetings. The city has dedicated a small triangular park to him, and maintains a Freud Museum, even though most of Freud's possessions are in London.

What surprised us most was the reception we received from followers of my father, Wilhelm Reich, and from practitioners of offshoot schools of body therapy. After my father's rather ignoble routing out of the comforts of Vienna, it was amazing to learn that not only Freud had been rehabilitated in Vienna. The city had even held a ceremony for my father and offered the keys of the city to my sister, Eva, on one of her earlier visits. My father, after his expulsion from psychoanalysis, turned more and more to the idea that psychic conflict is expressed by rigidification of the musculature of the body, as a defense against libidinal energy, turning it into body armor. Out of this theory, after his death, developed numerous modes of body therapy, some closely resembling his work and some very far removed from the "psychy." Just a couple of years ago all these different groups held an international congress of body therapists in Vienna. It was a huge success and showed what a large movement it has become. My sister made numerous visits to Vienna. She wanted to return to live there and established a network of friends and connections. Because of her I met a number of body therapists, some enthusiastically calling themselves Reichians, who welcomed us, wined and dined us, and took us on a tour of all the places I had lived in, and where I had gone to school. They showed me a plaque in my father's honor that they had erected on the wall of the building where I was born. It was dedicated to him on the celebration of the 100th anniversary of his birth. On it they first quoted him quoting Freud, "Liebe, Arbeit und Wissen die Grundlage unseres Lebens'—sie sollen es auch bestimmen" [my father's comment added] (Love, Work and Knowledge are the basis of our life— and should also guide it"). The sign follows this quote with Reich's Orgone symbol and then continues "In diesem Haus lebte und wirkte Dr. Wilhelm

Reich (1897–1957) Psychoanalytiker, Grundlagenforscher, Begründer der Körperpsychotherapie. 1929 eröffnete er hier die este Sexualberatungsstelle Österreichs" (In this house lived and worked Dr. Wilhelm Reich, Psychoanalyst, Scientist, Founder of Body Therapy. In 1929 he opened here the first Sexual Clinic of Austria)

So, my homecoming was suitably friendly and welcoming.

Vienna has gone through a lot in the twentieth century: the first world war, the revolution that deposed the Habsburg monarchy, the starvation and economic plight after the war, the rise of and take over by Austrian fascists, the occupation by Germany, the second world war, followed by the Allied occupation with a quarter of the city occupied by the rampaging and looting Russians. So perhaps it is not surprising that the Viennese cling to the grandiose baroque architecture of the Habsburg monarchy. We were struck by the pretentious baroque grandeur of the city, its huge ornamental public buildings, their vast scale. It showed how the city of my birth had been dominated by the Habsburg dynasty, which even set the tone, long after they were gone. Vienna suffered some damage during World War II and has been carefully restored to the same architecture and design. However, the Viennese are unreasonably attached to their baroque Habsburg heritage. For instance, they rebuilt their damaged opera house as an exact replica of the one destroyed, even though it is horseshoe shaped and one can only see a fraction of the stage from the expensive loges and director's circle. Only the bridges over the Danube could not be rebuilt to their original state. They are now drably modern, leaving the city without a grand waterfront. Even the apartment houses which all seem to be over a hundred years old, had only their facades renovated as they had been damaged by the bombing, but the interior remains unchanged, except of course they now have elevators. The ceilings still are about twenty feet high and frescoed with angels and fruits. The windows are huge and overlook gray treeless and grassless streets and courtyards. That is what I remember best of my years, especially the earliest years, in Vienna. All was gray; the buildings, the sidewalks, the weather, the rain. It rained often and it was bitter, damp and cold. There was no central heating in the high-ceilinged rooms. Instead, there were coal-fed tiled stoves. The tiles were beautiful, the stoves warm when one huddled right in front of them, so that one's front was comfortable and one's back froze, and they required a lot of work. But on this November return to Vienna, it was sunny, bright, warm and comfortable.

We lived in the Blindengasse opposite a women's prison. The street was narrow, and the prison was windowless, oppressively gray and huge. Some of the kind Reichian therapists drove us around and showed us this street. The building of the women's prison is still there and still windowless and overwhelms the street. But the stone has been cleaned so the building is now gleaming white. It is on this street, where on the corner of our apartment building, these therapists have erected the plaque commemorating my father.

We went inside the building. The window in the staircase looks out upon the courtyard, which is tiny and all concrete. This is the view I had out of my window as a child. The building now has an elevator, but in those days only stairs and I wondered how they got the baby carriage up and down those stairs. We saw the upstairs corridor with two apartment doors per floor. This is exactly as I remembered it, for our family had two apartments made into one, so we had two doors. Once a beggar came to one of those doors, and then when he knocked on the second door, was totally startled to see the same people come to the door. This is a screen memory, a true memory, but it stands for something much deeper. It is after my parents' marriage was falling apart and my father left for Berlin, and I missed him. The knock on the door seemed to me, the two-year-old, that maybe he had returned, and I was excited by the beggar's appearance and then second appearance.

I have a double set of memories of my early Vienna years: mine and the home movies that my father took and showed us repeatedly. In my memory Vienna is gray, our house is gray, even our food is gray. In the movies, we

4

smile, it is sunny, we eat cherries, people play with us. In my memory our room has no window or sometimes I see a window that looks upon a gray wall. In the movies we are swimming, we laugh. Which is truth for me? Both are. They are two memory streams. I have seen them both of course; I have seen the movies. In my memory, life is dull and lonely with little to do. In the movie I am at a lovely nursery school at age 2, earnestly washing the dishes. This I do remember. I said I liked washing dishes. It was a Montessori nursery school and these were real breakable dishes. The water was warm and sudsy. So, is my memory gray only after my father left?

I adored my mother, I thought of her as an angel. She was always kind and soft-spoken with us, endlessly patient, she never showed anger. If in these memoirs she comes out un-maternal, one must never forget how deeply I loved her, how I saw her so pure, so kind, so supportive—actually, she left the childcare to our nanny. I don't have any memory of her tending to my needs, washing me, dressing me, feeding me, or even holding me. Later observation shows she is really two people. An excited professional, intellectual, cultured woman who always stands with pelvis thrust forward, legs astride, feeling important; and a depressed withdrawn woman who slumps in her chair. This second type appeared after my father left. So, I think Vienna turned gray early in my life, but I clung to happy images that saw me through.

Our nanny's name was Mitzi. Actually, she did everything; cooking, cleaning, and childcare. Our family speaks of her always with warm and glowing love. I remember her coldness when I do not wish to go to bed. "You can stand next to your bed all night" she says. It feels very cold out there. That is my only true memory of Mitzi outside the movies and the photographs. In the photographs she is pushing my older sister in the baby carriage, while I, the toddler walk next to them. My sister Eva, five years old, snuggled in a coat with a fur collar, and a tightly fitting wool hat. I am about 1½ years old, or maybe closer to two. My sister had diphtheria and was in a hospital for a long time, after that her legs became paralyzed, so she had to ride. This condition lasted about six months (Today I do wonder; did Mitzi carry her down those stone stairs of our apartment house?) We take long walks in the cold Vienna Winter. I do remember people stopping us, outraged that the older child is riding and the younger child walking. I guess the Viennese, like the Russians, don't hesitate to interfere if a child is being mistreated. I don't think we explain the situation, but just keep walking. Mitzi visits her mother and takes us along. I think the walk is several miles. On the way we always stop at the Stephanskirche (now named Stephansdom) to warm up. Mitzi in later years has confessed that she took us there and had us christened. My parents were atheists, my mother an apostate ex-Lutheran, my father a non-religious Jew. Atheism was their religion and firmly dedicated belief. How they would have shuddered had they known of our sprinkling. Would they have fired Mitzi? I don't know. This christening left a strange memory trace in my subconscious, as I do not remember it consciously even after my sister told me about it recently. But every time I entered a religious institution, be it for a Bar Mitzvah or a church funeral, I would have a compulsion, that was irresistible, to cross myself. Knowing that this was unacceptable especially in a synagogue, I would shield my right hand with my left, and then perform a tiny motion of a cross. I thought this was most strange and had no idea where it came from, but I *had* to do it. Only after the story of my christening was finally told to me was I able to abandon this compulsion.

About thirty years ago my sister visited Mitzi in Vienna. Did Mitzi have a last name? Did my sister know it? Actually, I think Mitzi was my sister's nanny and I was added to this twosome. Mitzi told my sister how busy our parents were, how important and bustling. But they left a mere pittance for Mitzi to run the house and feed us with. Mitzi tried to make us warm and cozy, she says, she felt sorry for us, our life was so gray. And this is true, I remember our dinners—farina, with a little milk, chocolate shavings and sugar. These dinners make me shudder even now. It is like Oliver Twist getting porridge. I must have yearned for some protein or some vegetable or fruit. Years ago, Edith Jackson experimented in Vienna with letting toddlers choose whatever they wanted to eat. After a day or two of candy, these little children chose a balanced diet. Even as I write this I yearn for fruit. Of course, in those days, in winter, Vienna had no fruit and barely any vegetables.

Our parents felt themselves to be very important, very much part of a great intellectual and social revolution. They were psychoanalysts, they were intellectuals, they were Marxists. They went to meetings, gave or took classes (Father gave, Mother took), wrote books, organized the working class. My parents had so many friends, all of whom were part of something important. They consorted with psychoanalysts but also artists, movie directors, writers, and people in the labor movement. Vienna was just the right size for the intelligentsia to be able for all to know each other. In 1929 when I was one years old, they traveled for four months in the Soviet Union to see the revolution at first hand. Of course, this was when Russia was undergoing a huge famine because of forced collectivization, but of that they saw nothing. We were left in the charge of Mitzi.

As Mitzi remembers it, and I also, we sit in our gray house and eat porridge, while our parents have consultations with patients. We, the children. live in a back room. We are not unhappy, we just are. That is, I just am, my sister has temper tantrums. She is considered neurotic. My mother cuts my sister's hair to look like a boy. Was this haircut related to the diphtheria? Or was she having tantrums at hairbrush time? I have seen the photograph—a terribly sad child. My sister resents that haircut to this day. My hair is curly, and I smile. My mother never expressed anger at my sister's tantrums; she had a martyred patience, or a paralyzing inhibition of her own affect. This forbearance I think was part of my angelic image of her. In 1930 my father decides, for complicated reasons which I was not privy

7

to at the time, to move to Berlin. My mother remains in the apartment in Vienna. Then Berta Bornstein, my mother's best friend, moves in to share the space my father vacated. Around Easter time my mother joins him on a ski trip, leaving us in charge of Berta and Mitzi. And then we are on a train, I am so excited, we are to join our father in Berlin. How I look forward to him, how I can't contain myself, so that I shake with anticipation. But when we get there, he is changed, all is changed. He is changed and now the grayness returns.

Chapter 2

BERLIN (1931–1933): FAMILY AND POLITICAL CHAOS

We arrive in Berlin by train. I am all excited about seeing my father again though I do not verbalize this to myself. I just feel it. But next I remember a long walk on a hard, paved path around a huge reservoir. My parents are arguing, and I suddenly feel it is too far to walk, I want to be carried. My mother says I am too old to be carried, but basically, they are locked in some kind of battle. What I later realize is that they are arguing about getting rid of the children.

How easily Father could combine his personal needs with ideology. "Getting rid of the children" could be combined with societal progress; both a communist goal and a "psychoanalytic" goal. Children should be raised in a commune, away from their family, so that they won't have an Oedipus complex and at the same time will have socialist communal values (Reich Rubin 2008). These ideas were not unique to him. In fact, the Soviets had invented children's Crèches, the Zionists on the Kibbutz separated the children into children's homes, and without ideology there were many group homes for children. Even the psychoanalysts in Vienna developed children's pensions so that children could stay in Vienna, away from their parents, and be psychoanalyzed.

So just after we arrived in Berlin, we were sent to a children's commune, run by the Communists. I was barely three, my sister seven.

9

We arrive by train, at a country place near Berlin (Fronau). There is a huge field of grass where there are children and counselors, and strangely in this outdoors a woman is washing a girl's hair in a bucket. I get a sinking feeling; as if it dawns on me that I may be left there. My mother looks nervous. (Hair washing later becomes a symbol for impending disasters.)

How does one describe a communist children's commune? My sister and I are segregated by age groups, so I am all alone. There are of course other children and counselors—do I even know their names? My mind becomes a frozen fog. I do not cry for my mother, I do not even think of my mother, I wander about in a daze. I don't talk to anybody. I know there are other children, gray shadows hovering about me, but I hardly notice them. In later years, as a grown up, I am approached and introduced to women who were my counselors. When one laughs "with" me about how I did not wish to use the woods as a toilet on a walk, this memory comes back. I think I had just recently learned to use the proper facilities when this novel idea was proposed to me. Another woman laughs and says don't I remember that I was jealous of her baby. I remember this also, but quite bitterly. Apparently, she is breast feeding and I am looking. It may be the first time I have ever seen a baby breastfed. She laughs in my face and says, "Don't you feel 'Eifersucht,' ha, ha" (envy). I experience her as hostile and enjoying herself at my expense. I come away with a lasting idea that I am not entitled to the comforts others experience. These are the only memories of interactions with grown-ups, perhaps because they have been later recalled to me. No, there is another: I have soiled the bed at night and go to find help from a grown-up. The counselor, probably young, is flirting with a man and more than a little annoyed at me. Otherwise, I remember terrible food that I don't want to eat, and a funny, bewildered, bereft feeling for which there are no words. I am walking next to a river on rough round pebbles that hurt the feet. Also, it is hot and suddenly, like a curtain opening, I know I don't want to be there. But this last memory may be from a later camp experience.

We sleep in a dormitory with stacked bunks. My sister later tells me that she was envious of me because we had sheets, while she slept on burlap covered straw pallets. I don't remember this, but apparently, I stopped talking at all, and also developed rickets. I know my mother removed me, after about six months. My sister stayed longer. Her bitterest memory of the commune is that her father —she never thinks of him as *our* father—came to visit in his newly bought automobile. He looked happy and excited, and she was immensely proud of her father. He read to the children of her group and then offered a ride in the car to a few. My sister's great chagrin was that she was not selected as one of the children to ride in the car. I am sure that he believed in communal sharing and that she was just one of the children.

My mother looks worried; I am standing in front of a man with a stethoscope, my bare chest exposing the bony bumps running down on each side of my sternum, where the ribs are attached. I have rickets. A disease brought on by malnutrition. I have not been eating since the communist children's commune, and I have not been drinking milk, a disgusting thin brew that is boiled to prevent bovine tuberculosis and has a thin scummy skin covering it. Even disguised as cocoa it is undrinkable. I get plenty of sun in the summer, but this is a cold winter. Cod Liver Oil is prescribed. A tablespoon of oil, chased by a bite of salted bread, is given me every day. Do I cooperate in taking this horrible medicine? I remember later, at age six, tasting its oily nothingness chased by the salted piece of bread—but at age four? Or am I three?

I want to describe the lasting effect of living in the commune. From then on it confirmed what I had already experienced in various ways in Vienna— one can't rely on family; it may disappear at any time, and one has to be prepared to be abandoned and that one can only be rescued by self-reliance. The fact that total abandonment happened to so many children in the next few years, only reinforced these ideas. However, our abandonments were never total; they just hung over our heads. Years later my ex-kindergarten

11

teacher came to visit me and brought me a story she had transcribed from my dictation and that she had saved and brought all the way to America. In it I travel in a boat I have created out of a night-potty, using a wooden cooking spoon as an oar, alone over the ocean, showing I can take care of myself. Is this also a fantasy of escape from danger? It is quite possible, by then I know about concentration camps (not death camps, just starvation camps) and political people having to flee. I know the Nazis have won in Germany and that we have had to flee.

When I was eighty years old, I returned to Berlin for a visit and to see the city I had lived in. I was befriended by both Reichians and Psychoanalysts, wined and dined, and was present while both groups cooperated, for the first time, to hang a plaque about both our parents on our former apartment house.

I was taken on a trip, in the pouring rain, to Fronau to see the old house of the children's commune. On the way I was told with enthusiasm how wonderful this commune had been and how the children—probably adolescents—loved it. We arrived, still in heavy rain in a most fashionable pricey suburban setting with huge villas and large lots of land. No one seemed to acknowledge the irony of a communist commune placed in the middle of all this bourgeois affluence. Is it possible that there had been no fashionable surroundings seventy-seven years ago? But the commune's house was still there in its original shape and seemed to fit well into its neighborhood. Shocking to me was the realization that the huge grass field I had seen on first arrival was actually just a side lawn of proper dimension for the locale. Small children see the world differently.

My memories of Berlin and my family life there are impressionistic. We have a radio, and it is booming a threatening sound of a man shouting or screaming, getting more and more excited. Then the crowd chimes in, it must be a huge crowd, and they chant in a threatening way. Later, I know they are chanting "Sieg Heil;" a great roaring kind of noise. At the time I am about 4 years old, and I can't make out the words. But it is frightening, or it seems frightening because my father seems so tense listening to this. Is my mother also listening? I don't know; or is she tense because he is tense? That makes more sense to me. Because the screaming, shouting man on the radio who gets more and more and more excited, actually sounds a little like my father, who can also escalate into more and more anger. The quality of my father's voice does not have the screechy quality of the man on the radio, but probably the tension of listening to the escalation is the same for me, perhaps for my mother. Though, of course, she understands who the screechy man on the radio is and what it means to have this huge crowd chanting, "Sieg Heil."

I do know something of what is going on. I know that there are Brown Shirts, who go around beating people up, though I have not actually seen this. And I know they are the "bad" ones. Again, I think I confuse the tension in society and the tension in my home. Or to put it another way, I understand the tension in society because I see the tension in my home.

I am on the subway, or it has become an elevated train by this time in the trip, and there are two Brown Shirts in the car. They make me feel as if I should be frightened of them. I had already heard that last night they pulled the flag (was it red?) from my school and mounted the Swastika. But I am not frightened of these men; they actually look fine and friendly at me, the little girl. This is confusing to me; it has to do with values. These people have been labeled "bad" and "dangerous" so I should hate them, but they look ordinary and benign, so the hate in me is fake. But that makes me immoral. One can see that the pressure to be "politically correct" is quite severe.

This pressure later transfers to the "correct behavior" in the face of the Nazis. One must never give in to them, one must be brave, and one must die rather than obey. So, as I grow up, I can't understand or condone those who obeyed or cooperated; the Jews who willingly packed their bags and presented themselves at the depot to be deported. Or my friend Klaus, who joined the Jewish Committee and helped the Jews pack for their trip, thus saving his own skin. All this is immoral. And yet deep inside myself I know that I am a coward and God knows how I would behave if faced with the same situation. But that is the important fact of our life. We grow up constantly knowing of the threat, but are never actually personally faced with it.

The threats are more personal, later to be conflated with the bigger picture. My parents are both working, and my parents are not getting along. Let us start with the "both working." To most modern people, that evokes the picture of either a nanny or day care, but I remember it as much more chaotic. There was a maid of all work, who incidentally did not like children, but in my memory she is not there all the time. She did feed me a piece of bread spread with butter and liver paste once—a disgusting delicacy that was not unusual—but she certainly was not a babysitter in the usual sense. I do remember playing with my sister in the room that served as children's bedroom, playroom, and family dining room—though I don't think the family ate many meals together, as I don't remember a single one. We were playing quietly while my parents were down the hall, in separate rooms, analyzing patients. (The habit of Psychoanalysts practicing in their own homes was common throughout Europe.) There was no maid in the house. Suddenly my sister let out a howl, and for the first time and only time, both parents came rushing into the room. She had stuck her finger in the electric outlet. I was four and she was eight. Certainly, someone must have told her in eight years not to touch the outlets. Electricity was not new. This is the twentieth century; in fact, the house was modern. I even believe it had central heating—radiators. So, did she stick her finger in there out of boredom, or to get attention? I don't know, but she got attention. We were

14

expected not to ever disturb our parents, when they were with patients; we were to be quiet and we were not to be seen by the patients, this sometimes involved a game of hiding if we needed to use the bathroom or had to go through the hallway for some other reason. I think my poor eight- year-old sister was supposed to be the babysitter.

My parents busily and importantly practice psychoanalysis in the home, but what I conceive they are doing through four-year-old eyes is a different matter. I know their activities are of world-shaking importance, much more important than my sister and I are. Psychoanalysts are very brave, are disapproved of by the majority of people, so one must be proud and defiant when people ask, "what one's parents do?" To investigate what they really do I decide to listen at my mother's analytic door, on one of those lonely, unsupervised days. I edge up to the door, but my clumsy, high shoes, which we are forced to wear, bump against the sill and I make noise. The door opens and my mother comes out and scolds or frowns, but I am amazed, I see a man lying on the couch. What a strange thing. Nobody ever really explains this to me, but through snatches of conversation I gather that psychoanalysis is very concerned to encourage sex. Especially there seems to be a concern with "Aufklärung." This entails explaining sexual processes to children.

I have my own version of "Aufklärung." One afternoon I hear noises in the bathroom and push open the door, already somewhat ajar. There are my parents in the bathtub standing up. Now this is strange already because part of our lifestyle is that somehow, I never see my parents using the bathroom for anything, neither bathing, tooth brushing, nor using the toilet. Nor do they ever dress or undress or lie a bed in the morning. In fact, they each use their analytic couch as their bed, so of course it is always cleared of bed clothes early in the morning. My father was a firm believer in separate bedrooms. So here I am with the amazing sight of my parents, nude, standing up, and so called "caught in the act." My mother, looking

15

embarrassed, tells me to leave the room, but my father orders, "No! Let her look." and so I do at their genitalia, all engorged. Now I have had part of my "Aufklärung" without however an explanation. I am in awe, I guess, but also a little put off by the obvious disagreement between them and my complicity with either one if I stay or go. The one thing I don't experience is penis envy; the sight of my father's member is far too strange. So, I guess I am a witness to the fact that Freud is wrong, it neither occurs to me that "I want one" nor that "I have nothing." In later years I view the whole experience as my father being aggressive to my mother and to me.

But on the lighter side, I feel free to ask and answer questions. I am paraded out in front of their friends the way other children are to show off a poem they have memorized. I am asked, "Where do babies come from?" "Girls come from mothers' bellies and boys come from fathers' bellies," I proudly proclaim. Nor am I shy about asking questions. I run up to a total stranger, a woman, on the street. "Do you have babies?" I ask. When she denies it, I ask "Why not" which totally flummoxes her.

One has to remember that the 1930's was still a time when the question of "where do babies come from" was studiously avoided, and the stork was still considered a very active procreator of humans. Not till I was clearing out closets recently did I come across two pamphlets written at that time by my mother on this topic. One was "Wenn dein Kind dich fragt," ("When your Child asks you") directed at parents, and "Das Kreidedreieck" (The Chalk Triangle) directed I think to teenagers.

The other idea I understood about psychoanalysis was that it consists of recovering forgotten traumatic memories—especially the "primal scene" (the experience of parental intercourse). I now understand of course, that both these concepts, Aufklärung and traumatic memories, were emphasized as rebellious conceptualizations by my father against the Freudian establishment—that had turned away from trauma and repressed memories, placing their emphasis onto fantasies, and they did not wish to encourage sexuality in children. Instead they used the concept of childhood sexuality to understand childhood sexual conflicts in adults. Later, in my own work as a psychoanalyst, I always found that real trauma, that was repressed, presented a much more hopeful outcome in treatment than muddled guilty conflicts, and that it was a shame how far psychoanalysts had turned away from the realities of people's childhoods. On the other hand, the current non-psychoanalytic tendency to ferret out "forgotten" sex abuse by the father and pressing people to "recall" these abuses has done much harm to the genuine recollection of repressed trauma.

In the mornings my sister was to take us both to school. This involved the subway and then a change of trains and then the second ride became an elevated train. The school must have been in the suburbs on the other side of the city. Now this may seem like an unusual responsibility for an eight-year-old child. But from my reading of other memoirs, I believe that making children travel long distances by themselves was done by other people as well. I think it was done by other working women—part of the feminist ideology of the day. The memoirs I remember were that of Karen Horney, whose six-year-old child or children traveled alone by tram to school. This was also in Berlin. And then there was Muriel Gardner who sent her, I believe, eight-year-old daughter, to America alone on a boat accompanied by a man who was a total stranger to the child. All this so Muriel Gardner (1983) could stay in Vienna and be "Code Name Mary," rescuing political refugees while her daughter was to be safe from the fascists.

Anyway, my sister is running to catch the second train, and I am too slow. So, there she is on the train and the door closes, while I, age four, am left howling on the platform. Then the system kicks in, authority rescues me. How they know where I am to go, I don't know. But there I am on the

17

next train, proudly bragging to fellow passengers how I can travel all alone. However, in the funny way memories have, I often merge this memory with that of the Brown Shirts on the same train on another day. Thus, in my unconscious, using memory, I acknowledge the sense of danger that my conscious mind has blocked out.

My parents are not getting along. At first this is not clear to me at all. There is the memory of a car trip from Vienna to Berlin. I cannot exactly place the time, but it belongs to a time when I believe, as all children do, that we are a family and I belong. I am sitting between my mother and father in the front seat, my sister is not with us—is she still in the children's commune? It is nighttime; we are driving on a dark country road through woods with swaying tall trees. There seem to be no moon or stars. My father has raised his voice. I can feel my mother's tension through the touch of our bodies in the narrow front seat. I get nervous, but don't acknowledge the source of my nervousness. Suddenly I pipe up in ungrammatical German, "sind da Bärs da?" (Are there bears here?) I have projected the danger inside the car onto the dark swaying trees outside. A perfect place it seems to me for hiding bears. My mother assures me there are no bears. My father has quieted down. But I have no conscious knowledge about the tension inside the car and remember this trip for years only in terms of dangerous bears.

In 1930 my parents had separated in Vienna; he had gone to Berlin, and she had stayed with the children in Vienna, sharing the apartment with Berta Bornstein. But then, as I read in Sterba's memoirs (1985) (Memories of a Vienna Psychoanalyst), my parent got together on an Easter vacation ski trip, where if one looks at a photograph Sterba published, they fell in love again. So, we, the family, in 1931 when I was barely three, moved to Berlin to be with my father. Unfortunately, he also had another woman, Elsa, one without the burden of young children that tied her down to babysitting. Of course, I did not know this till many years later. (Elsa is not to be confused with Ilse, my father's wife, later New York.) I only saw that my mother was desperately unhappy, and, as we say in German, "verzweifelt" (not easily translatable, but it means desperate and not knowing where to turn). In the beginning my father tried to solve the problem, I now realize, by getting rid of the children. Then my mother could be again free to be joyously abandoned and help him in his great anti-fascist tasks—he had met Elsa on an antifascist parade.

To get back to Berlin. Both children, in due course, are returned and the family reconstituted, but to what a dreary, isolated existence. Amidst terrifying political times, with private armed gangs fighting, and general strikes, as well as the "decadence" of the Weimar republic, the children live in the bleak, all-purpose room, in a state of suspended animation while the parents work. There are a few highlights of course. The "Dreigroschenoper" (*Three Penny Opera*) is played on the gramophone, and I learn all the words by heart. Also there is an album of Marlene Dietrich, very sexy, which I also learn by heart. My sister is given a bicycle, very exciting; unfortunately, it is stolen the next night. I seem to have a tricycle with which I play alone on the street. But then identical twins come to play with me—Ursula and Brigitte. But they only want to ride the tricycle and as a self-contained unit they don't need me. I feel more alone. It does appear that on the rare occasions when my father interacts with the family there is life there. He is full of life, though often full of rage. My mother seems to be "dead." In grown-up parlance one would say she is depressed. As she later explained to me, he was running around doing all kinds of exciting things while she was "stuck at home with the children."

In a rare good mood my father decides to take the family skiing in Arosa Switzerland. But at age four I cannot yet ski; so I am left in Berlin in the care of the maid, who, as already mentioned, had no interest in me. How I survived that isolated week I don't remember, but I did not fog myself out as I had done in Fronau. I actually suffered acutely for being the only one who did not "belong" in the family. At some time after this the maid was leaving us to get married. Strange as this seems to me now, my mother hung a rope full of pots and pans on her suitcase, as one might hang on a car currently. Trolling these pots as she hauled her suitcase down the stairs, the maid disappeared from our life forever.

My parents were psychoanalysts and communists; my mother more of a psychoanalyst than a communist. Both parents were certainly soon totally disillusioned by the carrying-on of the Communist party in Germany whose slogan was "after Hitler our turn." This meant that in the election the Socialist party defeat was more important than defeating the Nazis. Mothers only contribution to "the cause," she told me shamefacedly much later, was to pour tar into the streetcar tracks during the general strike.

My father was a rebel both as a communist and as a psychoanalyst.

My father was in Germany to "defeat the Nazis" and very active, but never one to accept authority so a poor Communist party follower. But he had a huge following in the mental-hygiene movement which the Communist Party wanted to use as a front organization. They used him and he used them, till they decided to kick him out. The Soviet Union was turning more and more reactionary about sexuality, while my father's whole purpose in being a communist was to rescue the world from totalitarianism and fascism by freeing human sexuality from authoritarian control. His thinking was based on the idea that only the complete orgasm could undo character armor and neurosis, including the tendency to fascism. It was authoritarian society that suppressed sexuality and caused fascism. He had a publishing house called Sex-Pol which published a journal called "Zeitschrift für Politische

Psychologie und Sexualökonomie" as well as books and pamphlets The party wanted control of these activities and my father refused.[1]

Despite my father's growing disillusion with the Communist Party and the Soviet Union, he remained a strict party-liner at home. The children are also to be communists. For my sister this means joining something like the young pioneers. One wears a red kerchief and a white shirt, goes to meetings, and participates in parades. Recently she told me that at age eight she quit being a communist, refused to wear her uniform and go to her group meeting. My father shouted at her, and unbelievably to me, she shouted back and refused to go. My role is much more confusing. I actually don't comprehend it. I come home from preschool one Christmas time singing the new song I have learned "Oh Tannenbaum." My father is there, I am singing to both parents. Suddenly my father shouts at me or my mother or both, "Why is she singing that song, why can't she sing the Internationale?" (The Soviet National Anthem and the leading song for communists.) I am chagrinned and baffled. I was just moments ago so proud. My mother must have said something because the next thing I know there is a horrible argument, and he is shouting louder and louder and I get frightened. When he shouts like that he always looks as if he will lose control completely any minute and get physical. Then he bangs out the door, and my mother sits on the settee crying. I stand quietly there confused, frightened, and hurt. She says, "Why do you just stand there, why don't you comfort me?" I go over, but don't know what to do, and in some non-expressed way I think, she should be comforting me.

My father was also a very active rebel psychoanalyst. Besides a full practice, he was, with Otto Fenichel, a leader of the left-wing rebel Marxist group of psychoanalysts within the German Psychoanalytic Society. Some

---

1 Andreas Peglau has written an extensive research on Reich's activities in Berlin "Unpolitische Wissenschaft. Wilhelm Reich und die Psychoanalyse im Nationalsozialismus"

of the members of this group were Erich Fromm, Edich Gyömröi, Edith Jacobson and my mother. In addition, according to Peglau, he was the only worldwide psychoanalyst who came out publicly against the Nazis prior to 1941. He was one of four psychoanalysts whose books were burned on May 10, 1933 by the Nazis in Berlin. Most of the other German Psychoanalysts wanted to keep a low political profile so not to offend the Nazis

One can see that my father was involved in a whirlwind of activities. For instance, after a full day of practice, meetings, and giving talks and lectures he also wrote three books in three years and numerous articles. (Two of these books, *Character Analysis* (1933) and *The Mass Psychology of Fascism* (1933, 2020), are still being sold today.) I wonder now if he was a man who needed little sleep. As children we did not know about all these activities, but we understood that he was a psychoanalyst and a communist, that we were to be proud about psychoanalysis and communism, and that we were special because of these parental activities.

My father thought family is a bourgeois institution and one should not be connected to someone just because they are family. This obviously included children who should not cling to their parents and also, in his mind, extended to wives who should not be possessive of their husbands. In the 60s this anti-possessive ideology came back. So, the connections formed through mutual enthusiasms and work were the important thing to him. As in Vienna, my parents were part of a closely knit in-group of dedicated pioneering psychoanalysts of the Marxist persuasion. These people never came to the house, but on Sundays and vacations the group materialized in our lives as we went on hikes, to lakes, skiing, or to Grundlsee together. This in-group was centered on grown-ups, we children were only part of it because they were our parents—a very different feeling than belonging to a large family.

Both being communist and psychoanalysts meant defying conventions, being advanced, even bohemian, and not always acceptable to ordinary

22

people. We understand that psychoanalysis is disapproved of by many people so one learned to be very proud of this status and at the same time defiant and special. My parents are revolutionaries, and we bask in their filtered glory. Of course, being a communist fades out before one really knows what it is; knowing only at first that they are the "good guys" vs. the "bad guys." Confusingly the communists soon become the "bad guys" without any explanation (such as the Moscow trials, the purges, the social rigidity against abortion, divorce etc., of the Stalinists). But we are still the "good guys" because secretly—secretly because it becomes dangerous—we are still Marxists now disconnected from the Communist Party. [the Marxist phase fades away quietly within two years].

As a child I have no idea at all what it is all about. When I am about ten, I am on a school outing talking to another child, while our teacher is intensely listening. The child is saying, "The Bolsheviks are very bad "and I am saying, "Oh yes, and the Communists are very good." The teacher must have been amused. My mother would have been horrified as by then the Communists were considered "very bad." I just had not been informed of the change.

A social trend current since the 1970's is feminism. For some reason this current feminist movement believes that it invented a radical new idea. But actually, feminism has had several reincarnations. My maternal grandmother was a housewife, perhaps even a compulsive one, but she was a suffragette and regretted all her life that she had no career. She raised my mother to be Victorian in her sexual behavior but to never be a housewife; she was to be a career woman. Unfortunately, this grandmother died in the 1918 flu epidemic and never saw my mother's achievements. My mother went to medical school in 1921, at the age of 19, one of a small class of women, so when she met my father, she already fit into one of his ideals. My father was a feminist believing that women should be equal to men, have careers and carry their weight in a marriage. The Communists, Socialists, Zionists had similar ideas. The problem then and now had to do with children. As already mentioned, these political movements wanted to solve the problem by having separate children's communes. What the Zionists discovered is well documented. It was the women who ended up working in the children's communes, as well as in the communal kitchens and communal laundries— that is women's work. My mother, on the other hand, had another solution. She intended to have servants and nannies to take care of the despised lowly tasks of housework and childcare. Unfortunately, this solution never worked out as planned. She never had enough money to pay for more than one all-around maid, and that solution was not even available to her at all times because there was no money, and later there were servant shortages as other jobs opened up. In later years she solved this problem by marrying a man who could not learn English, could not work, and in effect became a house-husband, but in typical male fashion, was a gourmet cook. In Berlin, after we left the "wonderful" Mitzi in Vienna, Mother made do with a maid who did not care for children and was probably a terrible cook. However, as my parents, or at least my father, rarely ate at home, this did not really matter, save for contributing to my eating disorder. As far as I remember my mother never went near the kitchen, never even boiled an egg, certainly was not observed by me washing dishes, laundry, or doing any other household task. The one exception to this was sewing. She sewed by hand, though later we had a machine, but I think that was used by a seamstress who came twice a year to make our clothes. My mother could embroider, mend, and do all kinds of alterations. She did a lot of this work while sitting behind her patients—this was quite usual in those days. As I understand it Anna Freud would shell the family's peas for supper, while doing analysis and Berta Bornstein would knit her child patients sweaters while analyzing.

24

One has to understand that sitting still all day while doing analysis is too difficult, so men smoked incessantly, and women analysts did these hand chores. In America where these activities are considered unprofessional, analysts write on notes compulsively that get too lengthy to be useful and, in my estimation, interfere with proper listening.

Part of my father's feminism was the belief in what is now called family planning. Recognizing that having children is what makes women less equal than men, he felt that children should be limited. At the same time, he believed that to free the women so she could have a complete sex life, full orgasm, one had to remove the fear of pregnancy from the sex act. So, a large part of his work with the sex clinics was preaching and arranging for birth control. The diaphragm had not yet been invented, or was just being invented, but there was a silver cup that fit over the cervix which could be inserted by a doctor and removed once a month for menstruation. Alternatively, there was abortion. Abortion was probably the most prevalent form of birth control, apart from withdrawal during coitus, which Freud already noted caused anxiety and sexual inhibitions. My mother too had to use abortion as her form of birth control and undergone seven abortions in her life. Much of my fathers' political thought and actions revolved about making and keeping abortion legal. It was part of his eventual split with the Communists that the Soviet Union started outlawing abortion under Stalin, and so the Communist party was not happy with my father's propaganda for the legalization of abortion in Germany.

What people don't seem to know today is that in Hitler's Germany abortion was also illegal. German women in fact were encouraged to create blond, Arian, future soldiers for the Reich. It is only in the concentration camps that the Nazis forced abortions on women. When Poland finally freed itself from the Soviet yoke in the 1990's, it turned out that the Communist regime had not provided birth control and that women were having multiple abortions.

My father's feminism was more extreme and though well sociologically defended, was self-serving. He certainly never went near the kitchen or did any other household task. This is in great contrast to the current feminist movement which made one great innovation. Men are to share the household tasks completely and to some extent they are to be equal parents as well. Both my brother—16 years my junior, so young enough to grow up during the 1960's new feminist movement—and my son, are great contributors to household tasks and childcare. I really think the feminist movement had great success there. But my father believed in equality in working by men and women. Unfortunately to him that meant that each partner in a marriage would contribute equal amounts of money to the household and the rest were personal funds. But because my mother's earning capacity was much less than her husband's as she was less established, less experienced, did not teach and had no fame, had to take out time for pregnancy and recovery from childbirth, she never earned much money when we were young. My father would only contribute a share equal to hers. So, we children and Mother often lived in poverty. In the meantime, my father bought a car, a novelty in the late 1920's and 30's, ate in cafes and restaurants, bought clothes or sports equipment as needed, movie cameras and projectors, victrolas and records.

This leads to a frightening experience for me. I am walking on the street with my mother, itself an unusual occurrence. There are ugly, gray, frozen heaps of snow piled near the curb, making a dismal urban winter picture. There is a street vendor who is offering green and red gummy snakes for sale for a penny. I ask my mother to buy one for me and she refuses. I plead; she says, "I have no money." I say, "Not even a penny?" The way she says that she has not even one penny is very frightening, because I believe her, and I believe her despair. Having grown up so far surrounded by beggars and wounded World War I veterans I understand that there are people who have absolutely no money and see that they have the same look on their face as my mother. In a very separate compartment in my brain, from the same time,

I have kept the memorized lyrics of the Dreigroschenoper, which idealizes these same beggars and also thieves. So, I am frightened by my mother, and our situation. What I learned years later is that my mother had absolutely no money. I think it was the beginning of the worldwide depression, and that that day she sold her inheritance from her dead mother for just enough money to buy our supper. For me that supper is probably unnecessary as I am going through a phase where I often refuse to eat, or I only want to eat Palatschinken (a sort of crepe rolled with jam). Perhaps this desire is motivated by the fact that not only does it taste sweet, but it requires some work in cooking and therefore represents some kind of loving care, if only by the maid. The money my mother inherited was in bonds. My grandmother had scrimped and saved to buy Turkish Railroad bonds, which after World War I and Turkey's defeat became utterly worthless. One can conjecture that Mother's bad mood was a combination of worry and chagrinned hurt at my father who, after all, had money at this time and could have bought our supper, and disappointment at her own mother for her tightness with money in order to make this foolish investment.

Children know nothing of the economy; what adults can put into a larger picture and to organize their experience, presents itself to children as a kaleidoscope of disconnected pieces. This is 1932, the bottom of the worldwide depression. So is my mother walking on the street with me, instead of seeing patients in her office because the economy has affected her practice? Or has she lost the maid because she can no longer afford her, and she needs to run an errand? Children can notice the poverty around them but do not know of their own as they take whatever situation they are in for granted. This incidence then, when my mother complains to me that she has no money, opens a wedge in this oblivion and for a moment an abyss of fear appears to me. Poverty would mean starvation, homelessness and death. The fact that I am already starving, partly from poor food and partly from my own refusal to eat, has nothing to do with this primordial fear.

Starvation is a big general topic. My sister and I are surrounded by memories and mementos of starvation. There was the starvation in Austria after the World War I defeat. My mother has told us many times how she ate absolutely nothing but turnips for a year, and therefore will never eat another turnip. And she tells us how the America Quakers came on rescue missions and fed her and other Austrian children and youth. Starvation is also on the walls of our apartment hung with Käthe Kollwitz charcoal drawings of starving mothers and children. Starvation is in the folklore, the Grimms' Fairy tales like Hansel and Gretel where the parents are too poor to keep their children and so abandon them in the woods, only to be rescued by the cannibalistic witch with the wonderful edible gingerbread house. Starvation is in the faces of the many beggars who are begging for food. And just a couple of years later starvation is in the concentration camps. So, for instance, when we are told to eat our supper and to think of the starving children of Europe, we know what is meant, but that does not mean we can eat. At the same time that I do not eat I have a memory of a long hot hike with some summer camp. I am thirsty and somehow alone amidst the company. I survive the hike by daydreaming of a land, like the fairy story Schlaraffen Land, which I alter from the greedy eating, to where you just drink and drink and drink as much and as long as you want. This daydream sticks in my memory till as an educated adult I realize it is a daydream of the suckling child who can drink and swallow to its heart's content, a kinesthetic memory of a time when I was an infant before the age of five months when I was weaned to the cup. I don't know if bottles existed then.

Everything is falling apart around us. The marriage is in crisis, the economy is failing, the political situation has deteriorated, the anti-Nazis are losing, the idealized communists turn out to be a rigid totalitarian outfit, the psychoanalysts are about to extrude my father for being a communist, and my parents have lost their emotional stability. My father reacts to the stress by getting an ugly, raised red rash all over his body.

Quite late one evening my mother takes us two children into the bathtub and washes our hair. This is already ominous as my first glimpse of the communist children's camp was a hair wash. It is even more ominous as my mother, perhaps only in my faulty memory, has never given us a bath. It is also an unusual hour. She is very quiet and frowning and gives us no explanations whatsoever. After this bath *we are dressed*, bizarre to me, as it is obviously bedtime. Then my mother, without my father, takes us to the railroad station—and supposedly in the care of the conductor—we are put on the night train to Vienna. (Of this more later) This involves crossing borders, I think two, and therefore passports. What has happened? Only years later do I find out that the Reichstag has been set on fire by the Nazis, Hitler has taken power, Hindenburg has suspended civil liberties. My father thinks he is in imminent danger of arrest and so they have decided to ship the children to their grandfather for safety. I don't think they planned or thought of it as the end of the family, but that is what it turned out to be.

The denouement in my parent's marriage came on a mountain top. As certainly roads would be blocked and trains searched, my parents decided to walk out of Germany. They hiked over the mountains with only rucksacks full of possessions. As my mother described it, my father was terribly anxious. Suddenly on top of the mountain she felt contempt for him and for his anxiety. At that moment she was able to rid herself of the thralldom in which he had held her. Therefore, she turned around, abandoning him on top of the mountain, reentered Germany and Berlin and was able to arrange for a proper removal of the furnishings of the apartment.

Chapter 3

IN VIENNA WITHOUT PARENTS (1933)

Some events are memorable, they stick with us in vivid underlining whether in black and white or color. Such is the memory of my trip with my sister from Berlin to Vienna in February of 1933. I am four years old, soon to be five, she is eight. We are in a second-class sleeping compartment on the night train. There are two double-decker wooden bunks, in beautifully shellacked smooth wood, but no bedding or pillows. We lay head to foot together on the forward-facing lower bunk. The rest of the compartment is empty. It is the middle of the night, way past my bedtime, which I think is rather early, typical for European children, and there is that eerie feeling one gets when deprived of sleep late at night. I am frightened, not of the obvious things like the sudden separation from my parents, but of the details of border crossing. There will be demands for passports, there will be officialdom. We travel from Germany through Czechoslovakia on our way to Austria. In reality we are in charge of the conductor who will take care of all this. My sister has similar worries. She is scared that someone else will come and share our compartment. Her idea is that if "they think we are asleep" they will not come into the compartment. So, she starts kicking me to make me quiet, and the more she kicks, the more I howl. I howl, she kicks; we are all alone. Of course, no one wants to share the compartment with a howling child, but this we don't understand. So not only are we all alone, but we are alone from each other. I have no idea if she knows why we are on this train; certainly nothing has been made clear to me. We arrive in Vienna; it seems also in the middle of the night, though this cannot be possible. I remember the platform, glistening with dots of mica in its stone flooring. It is a dull and dirty floor, so the mica pieces stand out. My grandfather is there to meet us; his face is grim, and he does not look grandfatherly pleased to see us. I don't think I understand that he is worried.

We are ensconced in my grandparent's apartment. A large dining room with a great oriental rug, with geometric designs of blue, red, and gold colors. One can sit for hours looking at it and dreaming unconscious fantasies. There are also a piano and one comfortable chair, or is it two, where my grandfather relaxes after work. On the garden side of the room are two large bright alcoves overlooking the garden downstairs with the lilac bush and the walnut tree. In summer one can open the windows and pick a walnut. In one of these alcoves my sister sleeps. On each side of the dining room is a door leading to bedrooms. The right-hand door leads to my grandparents' room with their large double bed, at the foot of which is a couch on which I sleep. I have understood that my mother slept on this same couch till she was 14. The other door leads to my bachelor uncle Lutz's room, which is really out of bounds, but which we occasionally use. It has a very large radio cabinet with speakers and even though I have known all about radios in the past, I sit in front of it imagining that a little, talking man lives inside the box. There is also a corridor that leads to a toilet, a bath chamber, a kitchen, and, I am not sure, is there a maid's room? I recall and don't recall that sometimes there is a maid. This is the first house I have lived in that has a true "Hausfrau." In the morning my grandfather takes the trolley to his "Bureau" and a wild activity ensues after he leaves. Feather beds are hung out to air over windowsills, the parquet floors are waxed by skating over them with brushes and wax, cakes are beaten by hand till the dough bubbles, and strudel dough is stretched over the large walnut dining table till it is paper thin. Everything is cleaned and scrubbed and cooked, the table set by one o'clock when my grandfather returns for his midday meal. After the frenzy of the morning work the house is calm, my grandmother serving a magnificent five-course meal, starting with soup and ending with a truly delicious desert, which obviously took several hours to create. Then after his rest my grandfather returns to work, and my grandmother, dressed up for the afternoon, becomes a lady who visits others and who on Wednesday has her day "at home" when people come to call. I find out I have relatives, a Tante Eugenie and a Tante Maya, and a cousin, once removed, named Mitzi. Also, I am taken on walks and brought along on calls. My first religious education is extended to me when my grandmother explains the ubiquitous Austrian shrines of the suffering Christ on the cross. I hear the story of Calvary.

This household is so strange to me, after the haphazard domestic arrangements of my working mother. The childcare is especially strange. I am returned to infancy, bathed every day, dressed, nose wiped, fed. I am told that I am too hot or too cold, to put on a sweater or take it off. My shoes are tied for me—though somebody must have done this for me before—and every day I am forced to take a nap, whether I am sleepy or not. No one, as far as I remember, has ever taken care of me like this. I instantly regress to babyhood. I lie in bed, luxuriating in its warmth, too lazy to get up, and urinate in bed. I do this repeatedly till I am told that I am too old for this. This reprimand is my first inkling that I distrust this domestic so-called caring grandmother. Other incidents follow; I am being bathed and confide in her my fantasy that there are two me the good Lore and the bad Erol. But she receives this confidence in the wrong spirit because the next thing I know she makes use of Erol when she corrects me. She has in my mind abused the privilege of confidences and that is the last one she gets. So not only do I wish to regress to babyhood, but I want to have a perfect caretaker, the slightest fault leads me into distrust.

Lying at the foot of their bed, behind their foot board, am I exposed to primal scenes? I was asked this by my first adult psychoanalyst, who laughed when I said, "Oh no, they were too old" and when he asked me how old, I thought about fifty. (Actually, they were in their late sixties) This laughter was not good for my transference trust. But I truly don't think I ever heard or saw anything that could be construed as sexual. Once I peeked as my grandmother was dressing and saw her put on what only later, I realized was a sanitary belt. My mother, however, who slept in that bed till age 14, was exposed to quite a bit of her parent's sex lives which, she said, caused much repression in her. It is important to mention again, that the real grandmother had died before I was born and mine, called Malva, was a substitute. She had been a virginal businesswoman, a friend of my real grandmother, Therese, till Therese died, so perhaps the conditions of the marriage contract were "no sex"? But it is important to realize that putting the child to sleep at the foot of the bed below a footboard was probably an acceptable Viennese custom. So, Freud's preoccupation with the significance of primal scenes leading to repression was probably a very vital contribution to understanding hysteria in that culture. I once saw a movie about the imperial, pre-WWI Austria, "Colonel Redl," and remember that his whole family slept together in one bed.

In my uncle and grandfather, I sought to find the ideal male, the father figure to replace the one I was deprived of. These men were much kinder, did not yell or have temper tantrums. My uncle Lutz was a bachelor in his early thirties, seldom home, and I don't remember him eating the Mittagessen with us. He was idealized by me as a very tall, blond, handsome man who skied and rode a motorcycle. He became my idealized masculine figure. I don't know that he paid particular attention to me. I remember I am put into his room and bed for one of my forced naps, feeling uncomfortable because, as I have said, his room is off limits. I force myself into a hypnagogic state

34

of sleep, open my eyes and see a wooden-Indian-type figure standing over me. (Of course, we have no wooden Indians in Vienna, so this is a later explanatory memory for a figure standing over me that seems to be made of wood.) Am I afraid? I don't quite remember. Finally, I wake up fully and see it is my uncle. I think, "he is so still so he won't wake me." I do worry because I am lying in his forbidden room. But I don't think he is angry. Am I thinking of the forbidden psychoanalytic rooms in our Berlin apartment? Am I expecting my father's anger and explosion?

As I begin to distrust my grandmother, I put all my affection into my grandfather. I see him as the ideal kindly gentleman, both paternal and maternal. I remember he takes me up the street and buys me fruit ices in a cone. He teaches me cat's cradle; I think he reads or tells me stories. He probably represents what to all children is the ideal grandfather. Born in 1866 I believe, he is 67 years old, and still working in his cocoa importing business. In his old-fashioned way he goes to work twice a day, coming home for the main meal and his siesta. Exercise for him consists of taking walks, brisk and far, what is known as Spaziergang. He has strong Victorian values of honesty in business and believes in strong family ties, proper homes run by proper wives, the belief that all people should be honorable in their dealings. Up to recently I would have said that he was absolutely honest and honorable in his business dealings, that a handshake was as good as any contract. I have had to possibly revise my ideas in reading a 1940's letter from my uncle to my mother, which seems to indicate that the business cheated on its taxes by fancy bookkeeping. However, in other letters it is quite clear that after my uncle forced a business partner to pay a debt by threatening a lawsuit, my grandfather, behind my uncle's back, repaid the money to the partner, though by this time he was short of money. Born into a period of European stability my grandfather believes in stability and peace, despite the world war, the collapse of the Austro-Hungarian Empire, the death of his son and first wife, the current depression, the past starvation. (I think that this belief in stability and his sense of family obligations prevented him a few years later from leaving Austria in a timely fashion.) He likes children and is kind to them, puts them on his knee and tells them stories. He plays the piano and likes chess. His office is in a building in Vienna that has a continuous elevator. One car after another, like a giant chain, that keeps moving. One steps into it as it moves. A second chain of elevator cabins goes down. As far as I can tell, he does not drink, certainly not beer, which is probably considered lower class. I am told he is a Free Mason, but I see no sign of this, and I don't remember him in male company. Mostly he seems surrounded by his wife and her visitors and the "Tanten" who might be his first wife's sisters, but I am not sure.

Living with my grandparents I begin to feel I belong. But then cracks appear in this ideal picture. He is listening to music (gramophone or radio I don't know). I am in front of his chair and am dancing in my clumsy lace-up high shoes. Accidentally I step on his toes. He gets angry and snaps at me. I am abashed, deeply hurt, he does not try to comfort me in my hurt. Only years later do I understand this memory. Actually, I was making love to him and flirting, and he rejected me. This little episode seems to begin the eroding of trust with him too and soon events prove me right.

We've been staying at my grandparents since February. They have put me in the Montessori school at the Rudolphplatz, a school I already attended at age two, prior to our sojourn in Berlin. I am very comfortable there; the teachers are lovely and the place feels like a familiar home. Somebody obviously transports me there every day I go and calls for me, but I have no memory of that. Now it is June and school is over. In hindsight, I the grown up, myself a grandparent, know that caring for two children feels too much for my late sixties' grandparents. But I am basking in this well-run home where I am paid attention. However, now we are sent to a "sleep-away" camp in Carinthia. This is at the other end of Austria. From that camp I have two memories. The first is significant as it shows my state of mind. I am happy, I feel my oats, I even feel aggressive. We are swimming at a narrow canal. I push another child into the water. Luckily someone catches her, and I am scolded because I pushed her into the deep water. In the other memory we go swimming at a lake, and I put on my wool bathing suit, which however is all moth-eaten at the crotch. I doubt that I owned two bathing suits so I must have been nonchalantly wearing this one all along. I don't think my grandmother would have let the bathing suit pass, so my mother must have sent my or my sister's old bathing suit at the last minute. Anyway, I notice the holes, but it is hot, so I put it on anyway. An older girl camper looks at me and says, "you can't go in that" and so I take it off and sit in the heat while all others go swimming. I feel shamed and inferior. This episode sticks in my mind all these years because it is a reminder what things are really like in my family and points out that the so-called Eden at my grandparents is just an interlude. Being sent to camp should already remind me, but I guess it needs a more forceful symbol. The incident seems to be one of those seminal turning points where I wake up from what seems to be my natural state of happiness to what is actually going on around me.

I have no memory of contact with my parents, or news of them during the months in Vienna. But I am told that my mother came to visit several times. I wonder, if I acted like the toddler in Bowlby's wonderful evocative movie "A Two-Year-Old Goes to the Hospital." Where the child is ignoring his mother while she visits in the hospital because it is angry about being abandoned, and I think it takes three days for him to forgive her. And of course, in that case the mother made a determined effort to overcome her child's mood. I believe my mother did come for occasional days, after all she was busy working, but we could not get over the hump. So, I have blocked her out.

Where were my parents? As already recounted, they separated on the mountaintop, while fleeing Germany. My mother had returned to Berlin, where she was able to pack up the furniture and then, for many reasons but none completely convincing, she ends up living in Prague. Why Prague when she has her two children and her father and brother and apparently aunts and a cousin as well in Vienna. Her own explanations, given to me years later, are as follows. While in Berlin she was in analysis with Frances Deri, a training analyst there. Mrs. Deri left Berlin for Prague, so she followed her there. She went to Prague to look it over, very worried how about to make a living, and on the "Rathaus" steps she met the Loewenfelds, psychoanalyst friends of hers from Berlin, who also intended to move to Prague. The Loewenfelds offered to refer her a five-times-a-week patient so she could start her practice and survive in Prague. My personal theory adds to this: She did not wish to return to her family, especially her stepmother. She did not wish to depend on her father, though having him take in her two children was a different matter. She could not return to Vienna because by joining the psychoanalytic pariah, my father, she had put herself somehow outside the charmed inner circle of Anna Freud and they might not have made it easy for her to re-establish her practice there. Henry Loewenfeld had also been a member of the Berlin Psychoanalytic Kinderseminar. As many of those younger analysts were probably in analysis themselves it is hard to believe that their anti-psychoanalytic establishment views were not known to the establishment. Confidentiality about what was heard on the couch had never been very secure. So no doubt Anna Freud knew all about the Kinderseminar and its rebellious atmosphere. As was the custom at that time, my mother had had several brief psychoanalytic treatments. She seems to have left these without guilt, but perhaps with Mrs. Deri she had established a proper psychoanalytic process. The above reasons why I think my mother went to Prague instead of returning to Vienna are my speculations and will never be able to be verified. But it is also possible that my mother understood that Austria was not as safe from fascism as Czechoslovakia. The Czechs, under Mazaryk, had a vibrant democracy. The Austrians were on the verge of fascism. Besides this, Hitler had written in *Mein Kampf* his full intention of uniting Germany and Austria. It was remarkable to many how much the Freuds and their circle seemed oblivious of the impending doom in Austria, concentrating instead solely on the development of psychoanalysis as a movement. But having lived through the struggles against the Nazis in Germany, seen the defeat, and its consequences my mother could not indulge in this oblivion as did the Viennese psychoanalysts.

Prague was just a few hours from Vienna by train, so it is quite possible that my mother came to visit and that she even dug out old children's clothes from the furnishings she had rescued from Berlin and sent them to my grandmother. I vaguely remember a beautiful white gauze summer dress that my mother had wonderfully embroidered for me and that I wore the summer I was five. But I have blocked out any picture of her giving it to me, trying it on, or otherwise being connected to it. As my mother and father were wont to spend some time in the summer at Grundlsee with Mädi Olden, it is very possible that I spent some time there that summer, but I have no memory of it.

My father's attempts to settle after Berlin are more tragic. Again, I knew nothing of his travails till very recently. My sister remembers that he appeared one day at my grandparent's house, wearing hiking clothes and a rucksack and that my grandfather turned him away angrily. When he returned to Vienna at some point that spring of 1933, he gave a public lecture which was very radical and which outraged Anna Freud who wrote about it very irately to Ernest Jones (Riccardo Steiner 1989). She felt strongly that psychoanalysts should keep a low political profile—showing that the so-called obliviousness to the politics of Austria was more of an ostrich policy, hoping that if they made no noise they would not be noticed. There is much evidence (Fallend, K. Nitzschke, B. 1997) that the Freuds hoped that psychoanalysis could get along with the Nazis and fascists if they were totally apolitical. My father must have noticed that he was not welcome to return to Vienna. He next tried to feel out Ernest Jones in England to see if he would be welcomed there. From the painful correspondence published by Riccardo Steiner (1989) it is clear that Anna Freud got there ahead of him too. There is a lengthy correspondence between Anna Freud and Ernest Jones, carefully preserved by the British Psychoanalytic Society, in which Anna slowly convinces Jones that Reich is evil and dangerous to psychoanalysis and should be kicked out. Jones, who had the power to decide who could come to England and practice psychoanalysis there decided that my father would not do. He actually thought that the Soviet Union was the proper place for my father to settle. Had he done so he would have been dead within two years, the Soviets having killed all their analysts by 1936.

My father then did move to Denmark, where two events conspired to have him kicked out within the year. One was a secret conversation that Jones had with his "friend the Danish ambassador about Reich," (Steiner, R 59), the other was a newspaper uproar against Reich "the sex maniac." Finally, my father was able to settle in Oslo Norway, for a few years, till 1939 when the war broke out.

The family was scattered, the children placed with grandparents who felt overwhelmed by the responsibility.

I have a repetitive dream, the only element I remember, or the only constant element is a trolley riding by below me while I am on a path above. I finally figured the dream out as representing two elements. It condenses two short memories which together represent the wish to stay with my grandparents and the degree of comfort I have there, as well as the distrustful feeling that they wish to get rid of me. This was subsequently born out in fact. The path above is the path I have walked with Malva the step-grandmother, who in her best afternoon frock is walking with me to visit Tante Maya. On the way as already mentioned she explains the story of Christ on the Cross, as we pass several shrines. These shrines are ubiquitous in Austria, but I have never seen them anywhere else. This walk represents belonging to a family. The trolley down below represents a trolley ride I took with my grandfather. He and I, but I don't remember my sister, go on the trolley to an apartment in a house. There is a bare wooden floor, unpolished and grim looking, in a largish room and several children are standing about, boys I think, looking unhappy. My grandfather has his Victorian disapproval look on his face, the same look he has when he encounters beggars who in the cold weather are begging with their little child in arms, the child having no underwear and looking cold. Abruptly we leave again. He tells me that he was examining an orphanage for a charity he belongs to. I believe him but wish he hadn't taken me along. It is really many years before it occurs to me that he was looking the place over for me. And I have to give him credit that he rejected it.

But then on a cold November day of 1933, one of those gray, blustery, damp days that Vienna is notorious for, my grandmother takes me, probably on the same trolley, to a park. There are several children playing there and I play happily with these children. I look up and my grandmother is gone, and I am left with the children and the grown-up lady the children are with. I understand immediately, with that same sinking feeling that overcame me when we arrived at the communist children's commune, that I have been abandoned, dropped off, deposited in the care of the strange lady. I stay with her and the children for three years.

I never in the future liked Malva, the grandmother, but I had no understanding of why. She was prim and she was proper, and she used my daydreams about Lore and Erol against me, she reprimanded me for peeing in the bed, but she was an extremely good caretaker, the only experience of this type of care I ever had. The memory of my unceremonious drop-off at Grete Fried's, as the lady in the park turned out to be named, was totally repressed and all that remained was a slight negative affect. When years later my mother cried and told me Malva was dead, had a stroke—mother left out that this happened after two Black Shirt Nazis looked over her home

41

for possible confiscation—I had no emotion, just that tinge of negative affect and a slight feeling of "so what?" "What is mother crying about?" The memory of Grete Fried and the park returned to me years later, like a real "aha" during psychoanalysis. It has convinced me that repressed memories truly exist, and they do not need to be about sexual molestation.

Grete Fried ran a "pension" for children. Up to ten children from other countries lived with her in Vienna because they were undergoing psychoanalysis. At that time there were no, or almost no, child psychoanalysts, so if a parent thought a child needed this treatment they had to come to Vienna. Actually, a rival group of child analysts existed in London under the leadership of Melanie Klein. The leading child analyst in Vienna was Anna Freud and all the others, mostly women analysts who dealt with children, were or had been her pupils. Dorothy Burlingham (Burlingham, M 1989) came to Vienna with her four children so one of them could be psychoanalyzed, but Anna Freud eventually had all four in analysis. Then she felt the children needed a school and a place to stay, and this was organized under the auspices of Eva Rosenfeld. Erik Erikson and Peter Blos were the teachers in the school and of the ten to twenty or so children in it most were in psychoanalysis. Peter Heller (1990) has given descriptions of this venture. But by 1933 Eva Rosenfeld no longer ran this children's "pension" and Erikson had left for America. The school was replaced by an unusual Montessori School which had close connections to the child psychoanalysts. The school was run by Emma Plank whom everyone called Nushi. Then Grete Fried was drafted to run a new "pension" for children, I am sure under detailed and close supervision by the analysts of the children who were placed there. So in order not to be separated from my sister, I was placed there as a favor, as I was not in analysis, and also a year younger than was thought proper for the "pension." My sister was seeing the child analyst, Berta Bornstein, who was in supervision with Anna Freud.

Grete Fried rented several apartments during our three-year stay with her, though we seem to have lived on the Köstlergasse near the Naschmarkt for almost two years. All the apartments were similar, located in 19ᵗʰ century old buildings with stairs and no elevators, with large, high rooms, dried up parquet floors, un-waxed and gray from washing, and angels and other frescoes on the ceilings. Also, there were cracks in the ceilings which could be made into many shapes and stories. There was a huge homemade board, covered with light blue linoleum, which served as a dining room table, sometimes used as a common room for homework, large tiled stoves to heat the common rooms, gas boilers in the bathroom to make hot water, and a kitchen which was never entered or seen. I think there was a maid with whom we had no contact, and I don't know if she was there only sometimes or always. One night she fell over a pail and broke a rib, and this was indeed a topic of conversation. There were many bedrooms for all the children. I believe Grete moved when her "pension" expanded and she needed more rooms, and also when after the political upheavals in Austria, the "pension" shrank, and she needed fewer rooms.

I remember some of the children who were there for some of the time. Two American brothers, Frankie and Gar, made a very favorable impression on me. I believe, but will never know, that they were part of the Johnson and Johnson fortune. They had an electric train that ran on a battery. It was a wonderful set up, even if Grete Fried later complained that the acid from the battery ate up part of the rug. The brothers shared a room, as did my sister and I, but they got along as far as I know, whereas there were times when my sister teased me mercilessly. Sometimes another child would also share our room. One, I remember, could only fall asleep by rocking her head, or was it his head, over and over again. We seemed to have accepted this peculiarity. One Polish boy came briefly who spoke not a word of German and was utterly miserable. (I can relate to this misery as I later entered camp in America without a word of English.) He did not last very long. The daughter of Margaret Ribble, a well-known British psychoanalyst, stayed a few months. (Her mother was in analysis with Freud, but whether that was at the same time is unknown to me.) The son of Sergei Eisenstein the film director of "Potemkin" also was with us at some time. A most memorable child for me was Sieva Trotsky, the grandson of Leon Trotsky.

Sieva and I went to the same Montessori school and walked there together. Having recently revisited the site of where we lived, I realize we must have taken some trolley cars to get to school. After the trolley, Sieva and I had a very long walk in the cold, raw, damp Vienna winter. He would point to a miserable and poorly clad man across the street and say, "Da is ein Spion" (there is a spy). Naturally I took this to be part of his admirable boy imagination. Later I understood that Sieva was serious and that he was probably right. Stalin was out to kill his grandfather as well as other members of his family and was probably spying on the grandson as well. While Sieva was with us his mother committed suicide. Sieva was taken by his uncle to Paris. But then his uncle had appendicitis in Paris, called an ambulance but instead of the ambulance Stalinist agents came and took the uncle away and murdered him. Sieva's grandparents found him in a Paris orphanage—though in a very recent newspaper interview with Sieva, the orphanage is not included—and he lived with them till both were dead.

He was present when Trotsky was killed in Mexico in 1939, but also had been present when machine guns were shooting into their bedroom in a previous unsuccessful murder attempt. Both these attempts were organized by Soviet agent Naum Eitingon. It is claimed that Sieva's mother was in analysis with Max Eitingon, whose cousin, Naum, was a general of the NKVD, the Soviet equivalent to the CIA, and further, that the money given by Max Eitingon, so generously to the Berlin Psychoanalytic Institute, was really Soviet money. In my mind, it is most likely that Max Eitingon reported the contents of Trotsky's daughter's analysis to Stalin's agents. Did she commit suicide because she understood the conspiracy that was going on around them? I don't know. Did she think that the situation was hopeless?[2] Was Sieva in analysis while staying in Vienna? Presumably, but I don't know with whom. What is written by Etkind (1997) and later Martin (2000) discussions between individuals without the supervision of the state. It is known that many analysts were killed by Stalin in his purges.

Sieva made a lasting impression on me. One day he honored me by showing me a trick that I did not know about. He showed me his penis could grow from a small stump into something much longer. I had never seen this before or known about it, so of course I was very impressed, and it made an indelible mark on me. So it will be no surprise that I was very hurt when in 1958, as a grown-up professional woman, I looked him up in Mexico City and he did not remember me. However, he was very polite and invited us over. We arrived at a high, gray-walled fortress-looking place with a red flag flying in the courtyard. What I remember best of the visit was Mrs. Trotsky, the eighty-year-old widow of Leon, rushing out to shake my hand and asking me in French—I knew no Spanish or Russian, she knew no English or German—saying, "How do you do, why do you prefer Freud to Fromm?" My French unfortunately was not up to this question, whereupon she wheeled about and returned inside the house.

As can be seen from these memories of the children at Grete Fried, they were a rather interesting and nice bunch. However, Mrs. Fried had a seventeen-year-old daughter, Riddy (short for Margaret), who was not so pleasant. I was the shortest being only five and she the tallest, being the oldest. A new mirror was to be hung in the hallway so we could see to comb our hair. If it was hung for me, she could not see, if it was hung for her, I

---

2 This story about Max Eitingon is controversial. Well researched by Martin, J., 2000 Elkin, A.,1997, and believable, but hotly contested by psychoanalysts e.g., Schröter, M., 1997.

could not see. I don't think she had any sympathy for my predicament, as she could have bent down, but I could not bend up. It must have been hard for her to share her home with all these children. The mirror was hung for her. As I grew, I remember looking into it and putting my thumb to my nose. Just then Riddy came along, saw the gesture, and decided it was meant for her; she slapped me hard. I think I never forgave her, though I met her years later as an adult. This not forgiving of minor figures was probably my way of preserving the major ones and keeping them in my life.

In winter we would sit around a coal-burning Kachelofen (tiled stove), which unfortunately did not heat the whole room, so it could be quite cold. I remember sitting there with all the older children who were reading, and I had a thick book of the Grimm's Fairy Tales in old fashioned, German Gothic print. I could not read yet, so I sat there pretending to read, so as to be part of the group.

The person I never warmed up to was Grete Fried herself. I thought she was cold with a fake caring voice she did not mean. There was nothing personal between her and the children, she was a caretaker, but she was not a lover of children. She was strict in certain ways, forcing us to eat our food, which often seemed disgusting to me, or telling us about another place where children who poked their elbows out at the table were made to hold books under their arms while they ate; but she certainly saw to it that we had baths and had our toenails cut. She had despite her supervision by the various child analysts, no sense of how children felt about being placed with her. I now understand that the child analysts themselves could not admit how the children felt about being placed, as they were the cause for the placement. Grete Fried complained bitterly to me that my mother had sent no new underpants for me, as if I could do something about this. She had communal baths for us with no understanding that little girls did not wish to be seen naked by boys.

I remember serious travails every morning. It was bitter cold, the only heat being in the common rooms. I would put one thumb out of the feather bed, grab a garment and put it on in the bed, then another and another. But my high lace-up boots defeated me. Apparently, not learning from experience, I would slip out of these shoes without properly untying the laces, and in the morning I would be confronted with a tight knot in the laces. It is a symbol of how alone and on my own I was, after the careful babyish tending at my grandparents, that I had no one to ask for help with my bootlaces. Slowly and with extreme difficulty I would get the knot undone and then put on my shoes, only to be confronted every cold morning with the same frozen knot. I never asked anyone for help. It was an atmosphere created by Grete Fried that one would not ask for help, yet I cannot convey how she created that atmosphere. I have one concrete instance, but it seems unlikely that an atmosphere is created by this one episode. One night, when my sister was teasing me unbearably, I went to complain to Mrs. Fried. Her light was on, but she was already in bed with her husband, who incidentally played no role whatsoever in the running of the "pension." Mrs. Fried made it quite clear, that it was after hours and she was off duty, I was on my own. I think her duty consisted of feeding us the best she could manage, bathing us, and seeing that we went to school. It apparently did not include our emotional life. I always conceived of her as not having an emotional life of her own. I never saw her angry or disturbed or grim or sorrowful, nor can I remember her laughing or being charmed. I see her as implacable, determined, humorless, and totally lacking in empathy. Years later, in America, we once sat near her in a resort hotel restaurant where she was exhorting Riddi's maybe ten-year-old son to drink a glass full of gelatin that would strengthen his nails. He refused and she insisted—the whole scene brought the atmosphere of her "pension" forcefully back to me.

All the experiences at Grete Fried's were in sharp contrast with my daytime experience of school. Here under Nushi (Emma Plank) I could expand and feel at home. Nushi was a most remarkable woman, devoted to children and their needs, full of understanding and empathy and capable of conveying to each child that it was special, and cared for. Was she my teacher? Or the school director or both? She ran the Montessori schools I attended, first the Rudolphsplatz Nursery and Kindergarten and later in the Grünetorgasse where there were four elementary grades, divided into two rooms. This school was a very special Montessori school that combined, as Nushi explained to me when I was grown, Montessori techniques with concepts garnered by child analysis. When in recent years I visited the Montessori nursery school of my grandson I was shocked to learn that there was no doll corner, no block building, no paint corner, just materials that would create learning. The teacher told me that the children had plenty of time for creativity and fantasy play at home, school was to create skills. Nushi's school had the sandpaper letter outlines of Montessori, the practice in pouring liquids into a glass from a pitcher, the washing of real dishes, the method of correctly carrying a chair or a pair of scissors, but it also had all the appurtenances of a play area and paints. This was the nursery school. In grade school each child worked at whatever it wanted to; reading, writing, arithmetic, from workbooks carefully arranged on shelves. But also paints and other equipment for creativity were provided. At times there were group activities where we sat in a circle for story telling or danced about the room in eurhythmics. While we were working on workbooks, children could sit where they wanted at little tables with a few chairs and talk to each other. How Nushi did it I don't know, but there was an atmosphere of calm and dedication to work in these classrooms, no rowdiness or noise and yet no feeling of forced attention or forced sitting still. I remember only two occasions when any kind of discipline was exerted. Once I was late to school, and instead of walking into the hall coat closet directly, I had to walk through the classroom where the children were already busy at work. I felt very self-conscious having to walk through the class, but nothing was said to me. The other occasion was the one time I did not feel like doing work and just wanted to color all morning. The teacher gently asked me did I not wish to do something else, and again I felt self-conscious and complied. When I left the school at the end of second grade I was far ahead in skills when compared to the public school third grade I entered.

Every June the whole Montessori school traveled to Altausee for a month of camp. This camp I loved and remember especially for the picking of wild strawberries by the bucketful. Anybody who has ever eaten wild strawberries— fraises de bois—will forever be disappointed in the cultured variety. We also picked mushrooms and learned about toadstool vs. edible mushrooms. We learned about other poisonous and edible plants and the name of the flora about us. We planted radishes, or maybe that was in Vienna. It was Nushi who created this wonderful atmosphere of kindness, interest, involvement and belonging. If a child had a problem or was upset, she would take them aside and have a good talk and the child would feel better. I remember no teasing or fighting amongst the children. It is perhaps ironic, that I later learned that Nushi had been an analytic patient of my mother.

By Christmas 1933 my parents began to reappear in my life—first my mother and later my father, a transformed father, charming, amusing, exciting minus psoriasis. We would sit in the back hallway of Grete Fried's where the telephone was located and the cat litter box, usually dirty, and wait for his weekly phone calls, long-distance all the way from Denmark or Norway. These phone calls, one can imagine, were a bit of a strain: an artificial exercise in relationship. What was one to talk about? But still it represented attention being paid. I think my mother also had a weekly phone call.

Christmas 1933 was the most exciting event of all. The doorway to the common room at Grete Fried's was mysteriously closed all day. Then at midnight (but this must be a misremembering) the door was flung open and there was a resplendent, ceiling high evergreen tree with live candles, decorations all over, and an angel on top. And underneath were hundreds of presents. I don't think in those days that presents were wrapped. Many of them were for me, amongst them a Steif Teddy Bear, which was to be treasured by me above all else. I never liked dolls with their cold porcelain faces, but this Teddy one could hug and sniff and love and feel cozy with. I vaguely remember a toy baby pram; one could wheel the teddy around in. Ah, the wonder of that Christmas tree, it felt like our first Christmas, though I was five. Next to the tree was a bucket of water in case the candles set the tree on fire. It was so festive and so surprising. I had not known what was being accomplished behind that closed door. After this festivity we took the night train with my mother and went skiing for a week. Did my father come on this ski trip also, or the next one over Fasching (Mardi gras)? I don't remember or was it Easter that he came. There were a lot of ski trips that year after the Christmas one. How I loved skiing. Children are so close to the ground; they do not fear to fall. I did have lessons, I remember, as the first thing they taught us was how to fall down properly and how to get up again. There were no lifts, so one had to walk up the hill, children towing their skis on a cord attached to a hole in the tip. Grown-ups either had seal skins, which were strapped to the bottom of skis to prevent backward slides, or they herringboned up the hill, or carried their skis on their shoulder. One spring a little friend and I took all morning to climb the hill, and then when we were at the top it was so late the sun had melted the snow away. In general, it took a long time to get up and a very short time to get down. Skiing was hard work; I loved the downhill but not the uphill, nor the cross-country. While on skis if one fell into the deep powder, it was almost impossible to get up, one felt helplessly engulfed. In later years when we were in America and there were lifts, I loved the downhill and never wanted to go cross-country ever again.

My grandparents also remained in my life. Once a week, after school, I dutifully visited them. My sister perhaps had longer school hours or was seeing her psychoanalyst because she was not with me. As it was afternoon my grandfather would be working, and I had a long and strained visit with the now disliked and distrusted grandmother.

My life seemed divided between the exciting times when I saw my parents or was with Nushi, and the dull times when I was with Grete Fried. I thought of my time with her as being "in the ice chest." How I chose this symbolism I don't know, since, as far as I remember, we never had an ice chest in Europe, using instead pantries and shopping fresh every day

Chapter 4

THE SUMMER OF 1934

IN DENMARK WITH MY FATHER

My father was actually not settled. He had been kicked out of Denmark and Sweden but had snuck back into Denmark for the summer. Nevertheless, he invited us to spend the summer of 1934 with him on the beach in a lovely little house, where apparently, he was residing under an assumed name. With him lived Elsa, the woman who had had the affair with him in Berlin. This father seemed totally turned about from the Berlin father. He was charming, jovial, elegant in white duck summer trousers, and very interested in his children. As far as we could see he was not at all nervous about his dubious residency status. The only time he showed any nerves was on a day trip to Sweden when we had to pass a border and he admonished us over and over not to mention his name. I realize that in these memoirs I am repeatedly thinking about the strains of border crossings. At that time European countries took identity papers and passports extremely seriously. Not only did they have lists of undesirables, but they felt free to arrest people on their lists. The passport control officers always looked grim and threatening. When one arrived at a hotel in the new country one had to give up one's passport so that hotel could notify the police of one's presence. People like my father and later my stepfather, who had traveled under assumed names, always exuded a tension that was transmitted to the children.

Our trip to Denmark was a bit of an adventure; in retrospect I don't understand how our parents let us embark on it. My sister aged ten, and I aged six were sent again all alone by train, from Vienna to Berlin where we were picked up by their friend Edith Jacobson and stayed the night with her. (A detailed description of this visit to Edith and my relationship to her can be found in Rubin, L 2005.) The next morning we went by train to Denmark. We had arrived in Berlin without incident, noticing only on the dining car that Germany had a shortage of butter, and it was not served on the train. Later I learned that civilians were not getting butter, part of an austerity measure to prepare for military strength and war. Edith indulged us and we had a delightful visit. But when we traveled further, we were suddenly reminded that we were in Nazi Germany. At a small station there was a troop of Hitler Youth in uniform. One of them suddenly pointed somewhere on the train and shouted "look a Jew" in the most horrible tone of voice as if the whole troop would attack this person. Luckily the train moved out. But it was a very unpleasant reminder of what was happening in Germany and that we should not have been traveling through it. Now one might wonder how I understood this. I can only say that by age six I knew that the Nazis were persecuting the Jews. Earlier in Berlin I had not heard of this. As far as I knew the Nazis were fighting the labor movement, the Socialists and the Communists. And this makes some sense, as obviously the Nazis had to fight their political opposition before they could turn their attention to their agenda.

Our summer in Denmark was memorable. We lived right on the beach and went swimming all the time. We danced with Elsa, who was a dancer, while my father worked. I think he was writing, not seeing patients. Denmark was a dairy country; we ate vanilla ice cream, something that did not seem to exist in Vienna, had butter and cheese in quantities unheard of in austere Austria. It was in Denmark that I lost my first tooth while biting into a large kohlrabi that we had picked up in a field. This was a truly exciting event. I don't think I knew about losing baby teeth and so did not expect this. Of course, there was no tooth fairy—I think the tooth fairy is an American invention—but I did realize that I was growing up. We played the record of Ravel's Bolero over and over again and danced to it, pretending to be tigers. We went to Tivoli in Copenhagen, the famous amusement park and went on rides, and of course it was remarkable that it stayed daylight till eleven o'clock at night. Elsa would do calisthenics with us on the beach and taught us eurhythmics. I remember the surprise I felt, when my father fished me immediately out of the water as I fell off the dock. I was slowly floating toward the algae covered rocky bottom when a hand grabbed the back of my bathing suit and lifted me up as slowly as I had been drifting down. This was before I had learned to swim but I was too startled to feel fear. I was deeply pleased by my father's attention; I don't think I had experienced so much caretaking from him before. Altogether he was child-oriented and pleasant.

My father was sociable and entertained visitors, something he never did in Vienna or Berlin. I remember we served them meals on the vine covered verandah. This felt like a normal family activity, so we must also have eaten meals together when there were no guests, though I have no recollection. Of the visitors, I remember two. The first was a wonderful afternoon with the Otto Fenichel family; his then-wife Claire, also a dance and eurhythmics teacher, and I believe in touch with eastern rites like Tai Chi, their daughter Hanna, aged two or three, a lovely golden-haired little girl, who grew up into a professor at Berkeley. The afternoon was very pleasant. The Fenichels were familiar to me from many "Ausflüge" (hiking excursions) in Vienna and Berlin and it made me feel a sense of continuity. There was absolutely no sign of tension between the two men as would appear a year later, leading to a lasting split in the friendship.

The other visit that I remember was such a horrifying experience for me that it left an indelible mark. We entertained a man, on the same verandah, who had just been released from a concentration camp. (I was told it was a concentration camp but reading the book about Edith Jacobson makes me wonder whether it wasn't a regular prison which had regulated length of sentences, but some very inhumane conditions.) He was very quiet and had a very strained expression on his face. I don't remember his name. But his arms were so thin that they resembled a bone without flesh. He had been starved. His face was all hollows and big eyes, and he resembled a skeleton. Starting with this vision, and compounded by later experiences, skeletons became an active part of my terrified imagination.

Elsa and my father seemed a very compatible couple at the time. Though she was a little subdued and perhaps subservient. She was extremely nice to us children and I have fond remembrance of her. My father seemed relaxed in the relationship. However, there were some things in Denmark that mar this perfect time. They have to do with nudity. Elsa and we children would dance topless on the beach, attracting boats that had come to watch. The beach was private and seemed isolated from other houses. As I recall, my father when he was with us was always dressed. We children did not think anything of this, but I guess the boats hovering about made us know that what we were doing was not quite conventional. At one point my father decided that he would repeat a charming photograph he took of his children when I was an infant and my sister four or five. In that photo I sit on my sister's lap, and we are both nude. He wanted to repeat this with us now ages six and ten. I did not wish to have my photo taken in the nude, but he insisted, and he won. So there is now a photo of me, at age six, sitting on my sister's lap with the most miserable expression on my face. This incident was a reminder of his domineering ways in Berlin. I know that nowadays in America we would call the nudity and the photographs voyeurism and sex abuse, and I do feel that way; but in some defense of my father, he was influenced by a German movement, where nude bathing and lack of shame were considered better and normal, anti-bourgeois and in contrast to Victorian morality. I am not convinced that he had conscious salacious thoughts as he took these pictures. On the day trip to Sweden, for instance, we saw a lot of nude people sunning on rocks, too far away to see too much, and my father was very pleased with the ease and naturalness of the Swedes. Also, as we know, currently women in France and perhaps elsewhere in Europe are quite comfortable being topless on the beach. So, in this sense my father was part of the ideology and ambiance of his times. However, the episode of the nude photo left a bad taste in my mouth—less of shame than of being overpowered and forced. Years later a patient, with triumphant glee, showed me pictures of Elsa, bare breasted, and my sister, then aged eleven, with developing bosoms, dancing on another beach. Undoubtedly my father was the photographer. These photos had been printed in an Italian magazine, amazingly submitted by my sister. The picture of us in the nude with my miserable expression, from the previous year was included. This was one time when it was hard to keep a professional "analytic stance."

At the end of July, it was time to travel to Lucerne Switzerland for the International Psychoanalytic Association's congress, which is held in the summer every two years. Of course, my father could not traverse Germany the way we children had on the way to Denmark. So we, Elsa, children and my father took his auto and boarded a boat to Belgium and from there we drove through France to Switzerland. Of the boat trip I only remember that I had an upper bunk and at one point woke up on the floor, having evidently fallen out of the bunk. I must have had a concussion, but I never mentioned my fall to anybody.

Of the trip I have two unpleasant memories. I think my father was transforming himself back slowly to his Berlin personality as he approached his colleagues as well as his ex-wife and her friends. He may have anticipated some difficulties with the psychoanalysts at the congress.

According to the Fenichel Rundbriefe there was some awareness that there would be conflict.

The first incident happened in a campground on route. We did not have much money, so we stayed in campgrounds that supplied tents, rather than in country inns. We arrived at dusk in one of these camps and my father declared that the tent was too small and that I would have to sleep in the car. I was six years old, in a strange place, and I was to be extruded from the family. I think he said something to the effect that I was not to be a whiner. So my sister, Elsa and he entered the tent and I lay down across the back seat of the car. I looked up against the gray sky at the swaying ominous trees, and stared at them frozen with fear, it seemed to me all night, afraid to close my eyes. Whether it reminded me of the trees on the trip when I was two or three where my parents were arguing and I projected my fear onto bears outside amongst the trees, I don't know. The trees in the dark looked similar. I think something bitter and silent arose in me, the seed for a growing deep antipathy. I read somewhere that in Japan when young children are bad, they are placed outside the family home for a night which cures them of their misbehavior. So indeed that kind of experience must make a deep impression. Do these Japanese children also develop this silent hostility? My father and I never referred to this incident again, and I am sure he entirely forgot it. In later years I also developed a fantasy that something sexual was going on in the tent and that is why I was excluded. Should I have made a grand scene, a temper tantrum? I don't know why I did not, but perhaps his slowly lessening good mood might have made me feel afraid.

The other incident was less scary but fed in me a strange sense of contempt, perhaps in revenge for the night alone in the car. We were driving on a steep, narrow, winding alpine road in the middle of a horrendous thunderstorm. Lightning, rain, wind and hail were all about us. To "protect me" from a possible rock fall from the cliffs above, Elsa put her hands over my head. My father became very anxious. He kept saying "Nur keinen

Axelbruch, Nur keinen Axelbruch" (just no break of the axle). To see him so anxious and out of control of the situation diminished him in my eyes. In my child view he was to be strong, the protector, the man who could handle any situation, not someone falling apart with anxiety.

All these feelings together, shame of giving in to him, silent deep antipathy, distrust of his moods, and contempt for his anxiety, were never cured. They festered and though there were several later attempts to get close again, and even at times he pleased me, I think it was the beginning of a lasting rift in the relationship. However, I was not aware or so clear at the time about these inner feelings.

LUCERNE

We arrived in the small Swiss town of Lucerne, my sister, father and Elsa and I, and camped in the park on the beautiful lake. My father's mood was sunny again as he prepared to attend the International Psychoanalytic Association (IPA) congress of 1934. It was wonderfully bright, and the lake glimmered. We camped in a tent and cooked our food outdoors. It amazed me years later to learn that our camping had raised snickers amongst the Viennese psychoanalysts who told each other broad humorous tales about my father camping in front of the hotel with his mistress and sporting a knife on his belt—using these circumstances to illustrate how crazy he was. Humor has always been the way the Viennese deftly assassinate character. By making it humorous the victim has no defense. Humor, of course, was also a very good method to ward off unpleasant affects of anxiety, anger, and rage, and was later used successfully to deal with the unpleasant situations of the invasion of Austria by the Nazi Germans. It may be remembered that Freud would not take the Austrian Gestapo seriously but remarked that the Austrians were too "schlampig" (hard to translate, a cross between sloppy and inadequate) to be taken seriously, that is till Anna Freud was kept at Gestapo headquarters. Only then did he agree to emigrate. But our little family was totally oblivious of the impression we were making and the stories circling around us. We happily camped and basked in the sun. When the Congress started my father hired a nursemaid to babysit so he and Elsa could attend functions. Hiring this young, kind Swiss Fräulein, despite his shortness of funds, was an act of kindness in sharp contrast to both his frequent stinginess and my mother's habit to always stick us in a camp, when we needed watching in the vacations or during the later congresses. And I was very pleased with the arrangement.

Then suddenly the whole atmosphere changed drastically. We are in a hotel room with my father, mother, and Berta Bornstein, the close friend of my mother's. My father is shouting and screaming at my mother just as in Berlin, and Berta is *washing my hair* in a basin in the room apparently in an attempt to shield me from the uproar, or to distract me from what is happening. Hair washing has already been associated by me with disasters, so Berta does not succeed in sparing me. In fact, she etches it further into my consciousness. More scenes follow, always with my father shouting. One seems to be in the presence of my grandfather who sounds stern and disapproving as I have only seen him before, when he has scolded the beggars in Vienna. My mother again just seems to be in despair. At one point we are driving with Father and Mother in his car, and I ask in all innocence—or is my unconscious more aware than I am—what other professions there are besides Psychoanalysts, and this brings my father to another state of shouting at my mother and frightening me. I think about his contradiction that we are encouraged by him to ask him about anything, but when one asks, he blows up. I am confused by this. As an adult, I realized that he was protesting my ignorance of the workers of the world and blaming my mother for not being politically correct. But now as I write this, I also surmise that he may very well have been worried about his own future and what he was going to do. We are told not to mind my father, that he is *crazy*. This sinks in, I believe it absolutely. In the turmoil created by his shouting I become defiant and possibly obnoxious. There is some evidence that my sister and I turn unruly and misbehave quite brazenly.

We are told that our father is crazy and we ourselves see that here is a man who was in a good mood yesterday and then out of no apparent reason starts to rant and rave. Nobody, of course, explains to us what has happened, or why he is so angry. So "crazy" is used as a form of dismissal, like a name calling. It is very effective. Now I don't have to deal with this scary man who will suddenly turn wild and angry for no reason, is unpredictable and has offended me recently; though he also pleased me recently when he so thoughtfully hired a Fräulein instead of dumping us in a camp. By thinking of him this way I can get into the good graces of my mother, who is dealing with her separation and pending divorce by using this form of total rejection.

I must digress: the word "crazy" was thrown around a great deal in the psychoanalytic movement: surprising when one considers that psychoanalysis was a field dedicated to helping people with problems. When the attacks were not about loyalty to Freud or his theories and heresy, they centered on character assassination. The label of "crazy" has been applied repeatedly against analysts. To mention only a few: Rado, Rank, Jung, Adler, Tausk, Ferenczi, Federn, Melanie Klein and her daughter Melitta Schmiedeberg. In Vienna these name callings were done with expert techniques of witticism, jokes, and subtle put downs. The person was thus dismissed and not to be taken seriously. As my father offended people, especially his own psychoanalysts, he was frequently labeled crazy; the label was enough to discount all his ideas and points. Even long after his death in the 1970' the French analyst Chasseguet-Smirgel (Grunberger, B. & Chasseguet-Smirgel, 1984) found the "crazy" label a sufficient reason with which to fight the ideology of the French student movement for using Reich as a Guru in their protests.

What has happened? Why is my father so upset? Of course, nobody explains. I am an adult reading the Fenichel Rundbriefe before I know that my father finds out, on his arrival in Lucerne, that he has been kicked out of the IPA. He then expects the old members of the Berlin Kinderseminar to support him and to demonstrate on his behalf, but they keep silent for good reasons, afraid that they too would be kicked out. The grounds for the expulsion are well documented in letters by Anna Freud and have to do with my father's radical politics and the fear this engenders in the psychoanalytic establishment, that wants to placate the various governments of Europe and portray itself as non-political. As is clear in a letter by Anna Freud to Max Eitingon (1984) the IPA did not wish to open itself up to accusations that the expulsion was about politics; so they settled on the fact that Wilhelm Reich "had resigned" from the German Psychoanalytic Association, thus was not a member of a regional group and therefore not a member of the IPA. That is, the expulsion was based on a technicality. The only problem was that Reich had not resigned from the German group, in fact he had been expelled, but nobody had notified him about this. (I wrote extensively about this expulsion and its background (Reich Rubin, L 2003). Furthermore, it turned out that many other German psychoanalysts had to flee Germany and therefore give up their membership in the local German Psychoanalytic Association, so that red-faced, the IPA soon had to reverse its rules or be in the position of having to rescind membership of a number of refugees.

The rationale for the expulsion, that my father represented a threat to the psychoanalytic movement because of his radicalism, had some notable flaws. There were many other radical psychoanalysts. My father, in a letter to Anna, even pointed out the case of Nic Hoel, a Norwegian national and a currier for the anti-German underground, who was welcomed by Anna Freud. But most notable of all was Muriel Gardner, the heiress of a huge American fortune, who was very active in the Austrian anti-fascist movement. Anna Freud had no intentions of cutting herself off from the potential financial support that Gardner could give to psychoanalysis. Anna Freud had a number of other motives for the expulsion of Reich (Reich Rubin 2003). Just to summarize, she had conducted a behind the scenes vendetta against my father for many years. Reich was a "favorite son" to Freud and Anna was "the daughter" and wished to be the only power behind the throne. There were quite a number of other victims of this power struggle. For instance, Helene Deutsch had to be extruded from power as soon as Anna was ready for her role. Besides power Anna had some more "neurotic" motives for the struggle against Reich. She, who was a virgin, nicknamed "the iron maiden" by her colleagues, could not tolerate my father's theories that only the ability to have a complete orgasm represented mental health. Furthermore, she was my mother's analyst and very aware of my mother's agonies about my father's unfaithfulness. She was adamant that my mother should leave him and become part of her adoring circle. Altogether Anna Freud was a much more skilled infighter than my father, who could be quite naïve. It was only when the archives in London were opened after her death that some evidence emerged for her struggles against my father. (Steiner, R. 1987)

There were more personal reasons for my father's upset. My parents are in the middle of a divorce negotiation. They are arguing about the children and money. That is why my grandfather is there. As I piece it together now, it is during these discussions that my father declares that Eva is his child and Lore is my mother's and so he won't pay for me. Of course, in reality, he does not pay for my sister either, so my mother, possibly with the help of her father, is left as the sole support of her children. It is amazing to me that children, who are present during huge fights between their parents, even though they know the language, understand nothing that is being said and only feel the affect and hear the shouting. It is my teacher, Nushi Plank, who tells me later that my parents are getting a divorce. But I also believe that my father's declaration of my being solely Mother's child, had less to do with me, but is more a belated protest for her conceiving and birthing me.

He did not wish to have another child, the marriage was shaky; he wanted freedom to be with other women, to be politically active and not have any ties that interfered. At the same time, he wanted my mother's sole loyalty to him. As she decided to have another child anyway, hoping it would cement the relationship, he probably felt that this was her problem to deal with.

In the midst of all this arguing and fighting we traveled together, in his car, to Grundlsee, and spent some time there. I have no memory of this part of the summer, or how we all parted. Next, I just remember that I am back in Vienna and back at Grete Fried's.

Chapter 5

RETURN TO THE SUPERVISION OF GRETE FRIED (1934-1936)

When we returned to Vienna and to the emotional desert of Grete Fried's "pension" in the fall of 1934, I was a changed child. After the intense and fluctuating emotions of the summer—my father's vacillations in mood, my mother's disconnection to me in her preoccupation with the divorce, the violent quarrels, the repeated iteration that my father was taboo because he was "crazy," combined with the traumatic memory of the skeletal concentration camp visitor—I felt as if I had been condemned to Siberia. I became anxious, whiney, and neurotic. I reverted to the eating disorder of my early childhood enhanced by new fears. Food became disgusting as it reminded me of all kinds of disgusting things. Grete Fried, who served the most horrible concoctions of creamed cabbage or at other times old red beets, which tasted sickeningly of stale sweet, did not help this. How Grete did it I don't know, but she was able with her flat affect and flat voice to *make* us eat these things. I again became very thin. But my terror was not only at the dinner table. Ugly items on the sidewalk made me gag and I walked in terror that I would see something disgusting. At the same time, at night the shadows in the room became skeletons, like the man in Denmark, which would chase me if I closed my eyes. I would lie for hours in bed with wide-open eyes, fearful of death, I think. Skeletons seen elsewhere combined with the image and compounded the problem.

I remember I am taken to the movies—an event that probably only happened once while I lived in Vienna—either Shirley Temple or her Austrian imitator will be shown. Prior to the main feature a Walt Disney "cartoon" of King Midas is put on the screen. All he touches turns to gold; even food turns to gold, and he cannot eat. King Midas looks in the mirror and a grinning skeleton looks back at him. I "freak out" and have to be taken out of the theater. Another, but secret, fear is of going into the water closet (which is separate from the bathroom in Vienna). The tank is old-fashioned and hangs high up above one's head. A long chain is pulled to flush. Because this is so high up it makes an enormous rushing water noise and I develop a fantasy. A figure will rush out and throw a bucket of red pimples on me. So after I use the toilet, I must run out before the flush sound comes. The person with the bucket of pimples is of course a thinly disguised figure of my father with his red, angry urticaric skin. I think now how frequently when children see any kind of disorders, they are afraid of contact and contagion; even elderly relatives with prune-wrinkled lips who wish to kiss you create the same kind of anxiety.

It is unfortunate that it is amidst these anxieties that my grandfather decides to take me on an outing. We visit an art exhibition of a famous artist. I remember it well: Large, dark green and black paintings in a large set of rooms, *all of skeletons*. Wide-eyed and stiff I walk about the room. A mustachioed man angrily turns to my grandfather and says, "This is no place to bring children." Oddly he has changed places with my grandfather who usually takes the moral high tone. This outing has stuck in my memory all these years, yet I think it is the only outing I can remember. Is it possible he did not take me or us elsewhere, to the Prater (famous Viennese amusement park) for instance? I do know I went to the Prater, but I don't remember with whom. I did love the merry-go-round and admired the huge Ferris wheel, though I never was on it. But this was in an earlier happier time.

Now, only in the wonderful atmosphere of Nushi Plank's Montessori school do I feel relaxed and myself. I have entered first grade, a very important step. All dressed up for the first day I present myself in the classroom. Opposite me sits one of the children of Lampl-de-Groot, I think her name is Edith, also dressed in her best clothes. We are told what an important day this is, the first day of our formal education. Lampl-de-Groot is a child analyst. Another offspring of a child analyst is Kostya Mänchen, the son of Annia Mänchen. These children, among others, become my best friends in school. But because I don't live in a family, there is no one to arrange after-school play dates. In fact, Kostya invites me to his birthday party, but as this does not go through any adult, I never get to go. A fact I seem still to regret. This feeling of well-being in school and anxiety at Grete Fried's is like a split between two lives that are lived parallel but in different universes.

Without telling anyone about my anxieties, I ask to "also" to be in analysis. As may be remembered, all the other children at Grete Fried's are being analyzed, which is why they are living there. Adult wisdom, or perhaps financial considerations, dictate that I don't need analysis, but I am allowed to see Berta Bornstein once a week for therapy. I am six years old; all alone I take the streetcar from school and go to the Mariahilferstrasse where Berta's office is located. When I leave, I take two trolleys to get home to Grete Fried's. On certain days I take an elevated train, labeled "Döbling," from Berta's, and visit my grandmother. This is important as there are also trains labeled "Hitzing" which I mistakenly take one day, getting horribly lost and having to be set straight by a conductor.

Next to Berta's office is a minuscule store window with a baby doll and a tiny bottle hung on the doll. I have never seen such a toy before. (As most children were breastfed it is unlikely that there existed many dolls with bottles) I stand before that window and stare at that doll with such yearning, I want this toy, but again, I never mention it to a soul. It is in a dusty display case in one of those ubiquitous Viennese stores that sells only one type of item and probably has a customer once a week. The doll is about six inches high and the bottle maybe an inch tall. It probably costs a few Groschen. Had I mentioned it, it might have been produced for a birthday or Christmas. I think it was symbolic of my sense of aloneness that there was no one with whom I felt I could share this deepest wish.

Now here I lie on the couch and pretend to be in analytic therapy. Berta sits behind me knitting, always knitting. (She does this, I later read, with all her patients.) The knitted item becomes a garment for the particular child. How her fingers must have hurt. Berta is a somewhat round woman with a huge birthmark on her cheek. One would not want to touch it, but it does not rouse the disgust and fear that have been plaguing me. Naturally I tell her nothing about why I have come. And equally naturally, apparently, she never asks. This must be considered proper technique. There are no toys in her consulting room. There had, I now know, been a big disagreement between Melanie Klein and Anna Freud on child analytic technique. Melanie maintained that children's play was equivalent to free association and could thus be used for interpretation; Anna on the other had thought children were not able to free associate and that play therapy was not the equivalent of free association. Whether other Viennese child analysts had toys in their consulting rooms I don't know. Berta seems to have thought that it is possible to "talk" to a child. But of course, I have no method available to really talk and have spent a great deal of energy lately "not to talk"; though I enjoy going to her office. Instead I develop symbolic actions. I arrive on her doorstep having to go to the bathroom and can't hold it. As the door is opened by a startled Mary O'Neal Hawkins, an American studying child analysis in Vienna, who shares the office. My bladder opens, and urine runs all over the sisal welcome mat. I am six years old and horribly embarrassed. Somehow Berta and Mary O'Neal are able to dig up a pair of spare underpants. Nobody asks me how this happened. But they are very nice to reassure me that it is all right. I must have liked their solicitude because after that I start leaving their office having to pee urgently. On the long ride home, I desperately ask a fellow passenger what to do and she suggests that I stop at a store and ask to use the bathroom. This then becomes a regular practice. I do talk to my "friendly therapist" about this. It has so many secret meanings: The wish that a grown up would go with me, the wish to regain the solicitude she had expressed the day I wet my pants, the memory of my grandmother taking such care of us, and a symbolic expression of my experiences when my sister and I traveled alone from Berlin to Vienna on the train—a traumatic event that I had not mentioned to anybody. We do not delve into the meaning, however. I have always wondered was it I who was supposed to explain myself, how was it supposed to work?

Instead, to my surprise, the unforeseen happens; suddenly Grete Fried takes me aside and tells me I am not to go to stores to go to the bathroom. My therapist has betrayed me! She has talked behind my back to Grete. But she has not told me she would do this. She has not herself intervened. She has not understood the deeper meaning of my actions. Trust is again an issue. I change my tactics. I start worrying in her office that I might miss the last trolley of the day, the blue trolley—that trolley leaves at eleven at night. Anxiously I iterate "wann kommt der Blaue?" (When does the blue one come?) She neither reassures me, nor guesses out loud at my anxiety about traveling alone. I see that there will be no help for me here. It is equally possible that she understood I did not wish to travel all over Vienna alone, but that she refrained from saying anything because there was nothing she could do to rectify the situation.

I don't understand how child therapy was thought to work. I guess it worked only with very communicative children who would explain everything openly, not symbolically, and not with play dolls. Only once did

Berta make an interpretation that I heard and remember. She told me that sometimes children who like and yearn for sweets really must miss their mother, but I took this concretely as an explanation of why children like sweets. I did not associate it to myself. It might be remembered that Berta was my mother's best friend, who moved into our house in Vienna when my father first left, and who washed my hair while my parents were fighting in Lucerne. So the topic of missing my mother was "verboten" in her office. If a child misses its mother, it should go see a child therapist instead!

By now it must be clear that not only was I suffering from anxiety but also from a real split in my relationship to people. I easily distrusted people if they were not the all-giving and kind person I had fantasized about. At the same time, I held an abiding belief in the goodness of my mother. I thought of her as a blond and blue-eyed angel. She *was* blond and blue-eyed and perhaps she was sometimes kind and solicitous. To me she was an angel. My sister and I would lie abed at night talking about how we had the *best* mother in the whole world. Then my sister would announce that she was four years older and therefore had had the possession of our mother for four years longer. To this there was no answer other than that I was four years younger and therefore would die later and have mother all to myself for those four years. This belief in our angel-good-mother had sustained me for quite a few years, but later it came apart.

The worst of Eva's assaults on me was the destruction of my sleep. My sister would lie abed and drone in a dramatic frightful monotone "Die Hexen kommen und fressen deine Leiche auf, die Hexen kommen und fressen deine Leiche auf" (the witches are coming and gobbling up your corpse). I would lie with my eyes wide open staring into the dark. If I closed them large blobs of white or yellow would come toward me and begin to assume shadowy, black places like eyes. They were going to eat me. Though I remember they had no mouths. I was terrorized. I needed to keep my eyes open in order not to see them. Every night for months I saw the blobs, round and light colored with one or two dark shadowy patches for eyes.

In all the years of psychoanalysis I eventually underwent, no one seemed to understand this particular vision. But then one day I read a synopsis of Melanie Klein's theories. Suddenly I understood all. The blobs were breasts, obviously, as seen by a poorly focusing infant. The darks spots were the aureole and nipples. The breasts represented both my longing for the paradise of my early relationship to Mother, and the fear that my secret rage at her had turned her malevolent and evil, persecuting me for my destructive wishes. My fear of my father chasing me with pimples from the toilet, and the fear of the concentration camp skeleton, was replaced by an even stronger fear of the persecuting mother.

My parents considered my sister to be neurotic and in need of analysis. To this end she had to stay in Vienna, as that is where the child analysts were. I, on the other hand was not considered neurotic. Why not, I can't imagine, as I had a real anxiety neurosis. My sister's analysis meant staying at Grete Fried's. I was just somehow thrown into the pot with her. For whatever reason, both my parents agreed that my sister's analyst should be my mother's best friend, Berta Bornstein. It is certainly unacceptable to me today, from my current psychoanalytic standpoint, but at the state of knowledge of the time, it seems not to have been unusual. It is almost certain, however, that my sister was a "control case" under the supervision of Anna Freud. My father was a very trusting and naïve man to entrust the care of his favorite child to two women who had an implacable hatred of him.

While we were in Vienna at Grete Fried's, my sister never mentioned her analysis. But in later years she told me that to her mind it consisted solely of Berta haranguing her that our father was "crazy," and she needed to give him up. The analysis was carried on over to America and continues till my sister rebelled at age 20. She thought of it as "brain washing." As a grown up I met at least two other people who recalled with a shudder their child analysis with Berta and their feeling that they were being harangued.

I will return to the story of Berta Bornstein and my father but first I must digress to some important political events. While living at Grete Fried's the whole group of children seem to have been taken on a number of outings. I know we went to Eurhythmic classes. We also mysteriously went to places by car. Whose car this was I don't remember, certainly Grete owned no car. In connection with these car rides, two things occurred which were equally momentous in my child view. First someone was driving a whole bunch of us children in a car in the outskirts of Vienna when the car veered and drove into a ditch. No one but the car was seriously hurt; to me this was an incredibly exciting event. We were somehow rescued and taken to the house of someone the driver knew, who lived nearby, and there I burbled on-and-on about this experience. We were sitting in a sunny room about a dining table, and I needed to convey over-and-over again what had happened till I was told to "shut up." I was shocked into quietness, and again that sense of alienation overcame me. So, when the second momentous event occurred, I think, I kept it to myself. Yet this was a much bigger thing.

We were doing some activity in the first district of Vienna, when shooting started. We could hear the "pop-pop" of the guns. The government was overthrown. Dolfuss, the prime minister, was killed. For me it was a repetition of some of the experiences in Berlin. The streets were closed off; we were stuck in the first district, not permitted to go home. This was disorienting and frightening. Again, we were shepherded to the home of some acquaintance, sitting about their dining room table. Others held forth in excitement, but I kept quiet. Nobody really ever explained what had happened. But after this Austria lost any civil liberties it had, and became close to a fascist state. This is when Muriel Gardner—the real "Julia" of Lillian Helman's film—dedicated herself completely to helping political refugees to escape and therefore sent her daughter away to America for safety. It is also when opposition parties were suppressed; my father would no longer be safe, should he have returned to Austria.

Contrary to our sojourn in Berlin, the enormous political events that occurred in Vienna were not really known to me. There was fascism, but more of the Italian variety. Their agenda was the destruction of the free press and the suppression of the Socialist opposition. Nevertheless, I had no excited Father to emulate; he would have forced me to understand what was happening. So basically, I was blissfully unaware of the situation.

Had my father returned to Austria, he would no longer be safe from arrest.

It is a symbol of the state of disrepair inside my family that my parents could have left us children in this increasingly dangerous Vienna. Their motives were mixed. On the one hand both my mother and my father were busy trying to reconstruct their lives, which had so suddenly been wrenched asunder. My mother was trying to earn a living in Prague, get over her divorce, and was establishing a new relationship with a man. My father had been kicked out of Denmark, had to resettle in Norway, and had to also reestablish his earning ability. On the other hand, their idea was that my sister's analysis was primary and for that the children had to remain in Vienna.

On my fiftieth birthday my sister gave me copies of my father's letters to my mother as a birthday present. Of course, we never saw mother's letters to him so the story may be slightly one-sided. It turns out that there was a long correspondence mostly about the children, starting in late 1934. In this pile of correspondence was a letter from Berta Bornstein. His presence, in my sister's life, she wrote, his letters, phone calls, presents and other attempts to stay in touch were "interfering with her psychoanalysis." So he was asked to cease all contact with Eva. My father regretfully, but with dutiful adherence to psychoanalysis, complied. He had no idea that the "analysis" consisted of a droning and haranguing of my sister by Berta that our father was "crazy," and she must give him up. My sister, all her life, felt severely traumatized by the analytic experience.

It should be remembered that Berta Bornstein was a control student of Anna Freud's.

So what is even more shocking is that this whole attempt to separate a child from its love of a father had been enacted in exactly the same way with the four Burlingham children. (Burlingham, M. 1989). As has been well documented, Dorothy Burlingham left her husband who had manic episodes and came to Vienna seeking analysis for one of her children. This son was seen by Anna Freud. Soon Anna had all four children in analysis, and at the same time took Dorothy in as her best friend. She started living with Dorothy and also saw to it that Sigmund took Dorothy into analysis. This was a very cozy family situation in which Robert Burlingham, the father, had no role. The analysis of the children also seems to have revolved around getting them "to see" that their father was crazy. Some of the children resisted this severely, so the analysis took years. When Robert wished to come to Vienna and see the children and the situation for himself, Sigmund and Anna intercepted him. They explained to him that his presence was deleterious for the mental health of his children and that it was interfering in their analysis. Robert was dispatched back to the United States and later the children were discouraged from visiting him there. Further when Dorothy had sexual yearning for her husband, she was told to *sublimate* this energy with hard work. This meant that Dorothy was encouraged and prodded to give up her husband—and incidentally continue her relationship with Anna Freud. These events are so precisely what happened in my family. Anna also had pressed my mother to give up my father before she rejoined him in Berlin. One can't help but feel that both Anna and Berta where malign spirits working out their neuroses under the moral righteousness of analysis.

In his letters one can watch my father bow to the superior wisdom of the analysts. He too still believed in my sister's need for analysis and thought this was primary. He therefore withdrew from her life. But in the process, he withdrew from my life. Gone were the weekly phone calls, the letters, and the presents. My father was gone. He had simply disappeared; I knew not where. When once a picture postcard did appear in which was seen a ski slope with tiny figures slaloming down the mountain, I treasured it, thinking it was a photo of him. Of course, no one explained where he had disappeared to or why. He was obliterated, not talked about, and in my own conscious mind he went underground. At Christmas time, he sent two identical blue parkas. How I loved them, but unfortunately mine was too small so I never got to wear it. These were the only lapses in his promised silence. They were not enough for me. I simply developed a blank where he was concerned. Nor did my sister and I ever talk about him as we did when we idolized our mother.

My mother was busy restructuring her life. While we idolized her and talked of her as an angel, she rarely appeared in Vienna, and I have no memory of her doing so. At some point she must have been there because she asked me, "You don't want to visit your father this summer, do you?" I quickly and dutifully said, "No." There seemed no other answer possible, and I certainly had no time to reflect. I think that the memory of the forced nude posing played a role in my decision and as well, of course, my anxiety attacks in the water closet. However, it was not mentioned to me by either sister or mother that my sister was going to Norway that summer. I think when I finally understood that, only in the actual absence of Eva, did I feel like I had been snookered.

The summer of 1935 started off joyfully enough by our return to Nushi Plank's wonderful June school camp. This was in Altausee, very close to Grundlsee, where we had often visited Mädi Olden. The camp was so wonderfully calm and friendly, surrounded by our teachers and familiar classmates. We had school in the balmy outdoors, picked wild strawberries by the bucketful. I think this was the summer we visited the famous salt mines near Salzburg, where Hitler later stored the stolen art treasures. At camp I finally was able to talk to Nushi about my worry that my parents were separated. She sat on the edge of my bed and listened thoughtfully and sympathetically. She just had a wonderfully kind interest that made this confession possible.

GRUNDLSEE

Grundlsee was a very important part of my life. When I revisited Europe with my own family years later, we made a detour so I could see it again. Located south of Salzburg, it was the first of a chain of lakes of glacial origin, which delved deep into the Alps of the Austrian Totengebierge (Dead Mountains), so named for their high standing, treeless, rocky tors. Below were high alpine meadows called 'Almen'; cowherds would bring their cattle up to the Almen in spring and stay with them, bringing them down in fall before the heavy snow. The cows always had bells about their necks making a wonderful music. The lakes were very long and relatively narrow. The east side of Grundlsee had some houses on it; the west side was wooded and steeply mountainous, thus uninhabited. Only the first lake in the chain was inhabited. In my childhood there was no road along the lake, past a small town named, I think, Goschen. From there one walked on a pleasant dirt path. On the way to Mädi's house there was a brook and in it were glass bottles filled with different amounts of water. As the water coursed by, a little tune was played. When I returned as an adult a road had been built necessitating the moving of several houses, as the east side was just a narrow flat before the land started to rise to more mountains. Up these slopes were located small peasant huts with tiny plots of land, each field with carefully delineated boundaries. There was no electricity in any of the houses, so at night oil lamps were used, and cooking was done on wood-fed stoves. The outhouses were usually two-seaters, sometimes three-seaters. The lake, I noted in 1974, was bitter cold. But as a child I was oblivious of this. Boats on the lake were shaped like gondolas, propelled by a single oar manipulated by a standing boatman. Using this oar was a true art. These boats were called "Platten." Once a day, a passenger motorboat made a round trip from the north end to the south end of the lake.

About halfway up the east side coast, Mädi (Christine) Olden owned a house on the lake. Mädi, had been a very beautiful woman in her youth and had been an actress. Later she became a psychoanalyst. At the time of this account she was divorced from her husband, who was part of the minor nobility.

I believe that the house on the lake had belonged to Mädi's family, but in the 1920's she took it over. Soon friends of hers bought adjacent houses, so a little colony was founded; and this colony attracted many guests. Always present were psychoanalysts, artists, writers, and actors, a very bohemian, avant-garde group. Even after we all moved to New York, Mädi was able to keep up a salon, with interesting people in the arts. She befriended the music students who were to become the Juilliard String Quartet and had them give practice concerts in her living room. Other musicians such as Isaac Stern would join them there. Mädi also kept the wonderful wardrobes she had brought from Grundlsee, which were great big Austrian closets with wonderful painted folk art.

This Grundlsee colony was charmed by and idealized the peasants who lived around them. Because the area was so inaccessible, there was no local church, and the peasants abided by some very old pagan rituals. Amongst these were fertility rites and what the urbanites considered "dirty" songs. These appealed to the group's revolutionary, free-sex spirit. Marriage, by the peasants, was not undertaken till a woman had several children to prove her fertility and to secure the proper passing on of property rights. Whether an itinerant priest ever came by to legitimize the children I do not know. To Mädi's cohort the peasants seemed very sexually liberated. In 1974 I became aware that at least some of them might have been on the Nazi side after the Anschluss.

My mother was a close friend of Mädi's, and it was Mädi, who in Prague, introduced my mother to Thomas. We often stayed as guests in her house in Grundlsee; we children mingling with the horde of other children. Mädi had Salzkammergut green and white patterned pottery, a tiled kitchen, served Austrian dishes like Nocherls, Spätzle and Palatshinken, and wore the regional dirndls. When we were in residence Mother also wore a dirndl and I sometimes wore a dirndl and, above all, I had a genuine pair of prized Lederhosen.

When, in the summer of 1935, the June Montessori camp was over I went to Grundlsee to stay with my mother. Eva was absent. I think it was the first time that we were separated. That summer my stay in Grundlsee, the scene of so many happy summers, was not a happy one. My mother had a new man friend. His name was Thomas; a mustachioed, round, short man, about as opposite to my father, in my eyes, as one could be. He looked like the future

78

Russian Premier Khrushchev and behaved and moved like the actor, David Suchet, who portrays Hercule Poirot. He was not a psychoanalyst and did not have "modern" ideas of child raising; rather his ideas were closer to those of my grandmother. This led to clashes over the years, but that summer we were too new to each other. We stayed in a peasant hut about 50 yards up the mountain away form Mädi Olden's house. There was not the sense of community one usually got when staying with Mädi; with meals served in a large dining room, sun porches, the lake and lots of adults and children wandering about. In our peasant hut we seemed isolated and sequestered. Nor was my mother sunny, she seemed preoccupied and moody, though no longer in her hand-wringing despair. As an adult I can observe that she did not act like a woman in love. She also had to work, so even though she was on vacation she had a patient or a couple of patients come to see her. At such times I was to be very quiet. I have a vision of me. I sit very quietly on the stoop of the hut. My mother is working. I am totally bored. I sing under my breath, and then into my mind flashes the image of my sister and the betrayal of her leaving and my staying. I remember the wonderful time on the beach last year, the sun, the sand, the sea, and Elsa dancing. I do not think my mother and I interacted very much.

There is another picture I have. We, Mother, Thomas and I, eat at a restaurant in the town at the north end of the lake. There is a fish tank in the restaurant in which live trout are swimming. One chooses the fish and then it is prepared. I order Palatshinken. After the meal we take a walk in the garden. I do not believe my mother and I are connected. She is very silent. I start calling her name, addressing questions to her, and finally I am saying "Annie" every few seconds. There is no response, instead a withdrawal because I am misbehaving. My insistence is driving her further away. Then Thomas snaps at me, "Do you know you have said 'Annie' fifteen times in five minutes?" There is utter disapproval of me in his tone. My mother says nothing. Certainly, there is no drawing me to her and giving me a hug. I am left with the feelings of an unsocialized misfit. It is only upon recalling this incident as an adult that I figure out that she was ignoring me and that I was not such an inept neurotic being, but a normal, ignored child, asking for attention.

Suddenly my father appeared in Grundlsee with my sister in tow. With great happiness they announced their wonderful idea of the future. She will go and live with him in Norway. She was enthusiastic. My mother confessed to me years later that she was appalled and appealed for help to her friend Mädi. Together they concocted a plan. They told him the police were after him, a totally plausible thing in the new fascist Austria. He became very frightened and decided to flee immediately, leaving my sister behind. After this my sister became absolutely evil to me, the only object on whom she could unleash her disappointment at my father's sudden abandonment.

I have no memory that he and I exchanged a word or a greeting. He was hurt that I would not come that summer and he just cut me off.

After this possessive determination to keep her children from her "crazy" ex-husband, my mother strangely turned about and stated to me, "I have to go back to Prague. I must earn a living. Grete Fried is closed for the rest of the summer so you children will have to go to camp." For once I found my voice and pleaded with her not to send us. Putting on her very worried mother look, she said, "What can I do I have to earn a living." For this there was no answer. But I learned something. Earning a living was paramount; loving children was unimportant in this larger scheme of things. In fact, I think Mother did believe this. Years later, she worried in the same manner when it was time for me to have children. "How would you support them?" My one-time pleading to her was not heard. I understood with finality that I was expendable, unimportant, a mere child, who, if well-adjusted, would love to be among her own kind, that is her peers, and who should never *need* a parent. With this knowledge my idealization seems to have withered; the blond, blue-eyed angel was replaced with the image of a worried woman who could not cope with children. It took me years to recognize her for her many impressive, positive attributes and to understand that being maternal was not amongst them.

The camp we were sent to was a nightmare. It was housed in the same facility as the heavenly Montessori school camp, making a mockery of my earlier happiness. There were strangers as counselors and strangers as children. We slept in the same dormitory but in other beds. This led to a fantastical sleepwalking episode. I went to the bathroom in the middle of the night and then walked into my bed from earlier that summer. I woke up some hours later confused and disoriented, then seem to have ambled back into my current bed. In this camp I was both an angry, defiant child and a nighttime terror child who could not sleep. I am lying in bed, the shutters are drawn, and the dormitory is dark, but there is a chink in the jalousie and through it I can see the older children on the lawn running about and playing tag. We are probably put to bed at six o'clock, as in many European homes. For one momentary flash my mind opens to the thought that my sister hates me and is mean to me, she of course being one of the children enjoying themselves outside. Then I clamp down firmly and repress this thought. It is replaced instantaneously with an anxiety attack. The image of the blobs coming after me, to eat me, comes back. I can't close my eyes; only by keeping the eyes open can I avoid the terrifying image. Night after night I can't sleep. I begin to dread the dusk and my nightly terror. At the same time, I become an angry and defiant child. I don't get along with my counselor who has other children whom she openly favors. In the rain I sit on my butt, which is thinly clad in underpants—we still wore skirts, not pants, in camp—and slide down a muddy slope. A groundskeeper sees me and yells that I am going to get sick. I keep on sliding. That night I feel sick.

81

The favorite child of the counselor also feels sick and is made a fuss over. I tell the counselor that I too am sick, and she says, "You are only trying to get attention." So I go to bed. In the middle of the night, I vomit next to the bed. I must have had a high fever and I land in the camp infirmary. To me this is gratifying revenge of the "I told you so" variety against the mean counselor.

The camp doctor, a woman, has the same type of personality as the counselor. I call them 'petty Viennese,' who express petty meanness. I hear the doctor scolding an older boy who has an infected ingrown toenail. She tells him he is a pig who did not cut his toenails properly. I sleep in the next bed basking in my vengeful negative feelings.

When I get well, they notice I am too thin. The Doctor prescribes that before breakfast I am to take, as medicine, 28 sugar cubes flavored with the juice of a lemon. I might have a sweet tooth, but this concoction is sickening. I can't get it down. After I throw up, they stop giving it to me. How strange to think what the state of the medical arts was, at that time, to have prescribed sugar cubes as a nutritional supplement.

RETURN TO VIENNA

My sister was completely thrown by the abrupt departure and desertion by my father. She had always been my caretaker, the stable presence in my disintegrated family. She felt a heavy responsibility to oversee our travels, she teased me, and she did not act greatly loving, but she was the only constant family presence. Now she turned into an envious, green-eyed, vicious monster, who was out to destroy me by teasing. According to my mother's later tales, we had started out life like that and my first words were "eyea" which meant "Eva hurt me." I do not understand why my father's desertion led to her behavior towards me, but perhaps there was no one else on whom to let out her rage. She delighted in separating me from any group of children and to making me the butt of their jokes; telling my weaknesses to embarrass me, grabbing my toys and destroying them, wrestling and pummeling me, and one-upping me in every way.

In the Fall of 1935, I returned to the cold Siberia of Grete Fried. I again lived a split life, a wonderful morning in school feeling confident and productive, surrounded by friends and wonderful teachers, and afternoons and evenings at Grete Fried's, accompanied by a hostile teasing sister who made my life hell, frightened me every night, and tried to get the whole group of children to gang up on me. Gradually, also, the children were taken away. The parents apparently worried about leaving them in the fascist Vienna. Frankie, Gar and Sieva disappeared. Finally, our entourage was so shrunken that Grete Fried moved to a much smaller, cheaper apartment, so that even the comfort of familiarity was gone.

One day the most dreaded thing happened: The Montessori children decided to gang up on me. For this I was totally unprepared. My world fell apart. Luckily this only lasted a day, but that day I reached the depth of despair. It happened to be a Berta Bornstein day and I haltingly told her what happened. It was the only time I truly tried to open up to her and she could not understand it at all. I think she could not comprehend my affect or why it affected me so much. In fact, I got no sense of comforting, no advice, and no relief there. Perhaps she was simply, despite her later great New York reputation as a child analyst, an incompetent.

Grete Fried was also an incompetent in conveying other than a flat affect. At one point I needed my adenoids removed. I was taken to a very old hospital that had been a monastery. It had huge ceilings and arched doorways. There I was told, after being put in a nightgown, to sit on a man's lap. Then a mask was clamped on my nose and mouth. I struggled valiantly kicking him in the shins, but he held me tight. I saw black and white spiral circles whirling about, and then it was over. I had my wonderful Teddy Bear with me, and despite their warning that it might be too dusty, I snuggled up to it to recover.

My Teddy Bear was everything and everybody to me. Scientifically it might be called a transitional object. But this was not a transition; this was my lifeline in a seeming desert of human relationships. I loved that bear, depended on him and felt fulfilled by him. Grete brought me home and I lay in bed alone with him in a sort of dreamy daze. I expected nothing. But then she came trying to be solicitous and reassuring. A tender smile hovered on her lips, which unused to such a shape looked strained and fake. She struck me as odd and funny and totally uncalled for. Contemptuously I turned my back on her and went to sleep.

In the spring my mother suddenly swooped down on us and took Eva and me on an alpine ski trip. Grete Fried's "pension" was declining and, I think, Mother had already decided to bring me to Prague to live with her in the fall; Eva was to stay alone in an extra room rented in my grandparent's apartment house, so she could stay in Vienna and continue her analysis. Ernst Hemingway in his "A Movable Feast" (only in its first original edition), has a glorious chapter on an alpine spring ski tour he took with his wife, which evokes exactly what it was we were supposed to experience on our trip and what had been experienced in the past by my parents. He describes the glorious sunny, snowy vistas, the deep powder untouched by footprints or tracks, the movement from hut to hut, and the spring corn snow. Reading him as an adult brought a yearning to me for the wondrous alpine Austria we have left behind. Unfortunately, this trip was far from glorious.

Here we were I, close to, or just having turned eight, and my mother and sister. We hiked up some mountain, I with skis pulled behind me by a rope. The climb was steep and endless. I kept saying, "When will we be on top?" Mother kept answering, "It's just around the corner," but we would get around that corner and there was another corner. I was not enjoying this at all. My sister did not say anything, and Mother could not have been enjoying this either. There certainly was not the exhilarating aura associated with her politically defiant youth or her romantic adventures with my father. She looked grim. Of course, the hike was meant for a much older child, and she was pushing it to take me along. Finally, finally, we reached an alpine hut put there for the benefit of hikers. There were wooden platforms to sleep on; the hut may have provided blankets as I don't remember that the torture of carrying a heavy pack was added to this disagreeable hike. Was there beautiful scenery? Probably, but I was too exhausted to notice. Just as we fell asleep a group of about eight young people came into the hut with just the kind of gayety and excitement that Mother was trying to recreate. I remember they started getting undressed then whooped "one-two-three" and turned out the lights before taking their last clothes off. It was this group that must have reminded my mother about what she was missing. For she showed again that she was downhearted, and that we were "not enough" to cheer her up. I had a distinct feeling that she missed having an exciting man. She was in a permanent relationship by then with Thomas, but alas, he was no athlete; quite the contrary; I watched him once in a shallow pond of water holding on to both her hands and jumping up and down in the water like a small child. I must have said something because I was told he was afraid of the water, and this was to acclimatize him to it. So on our alpine trip Mother looked grim, depressed and disappointed. We just were not adequate company for her.

This trip might have been planned to get closer to or know her children better, but I took it to mean that we were a substitute for all her exciting previous friends, husbands and colleagues with whom she had taken such trips before. My mother's rebellious life against the Victorian ethos

85

and morals of her own mother had started in the Wandervögel, a youth movement that would wander about the Vienna Woods on Sundays, in forbidden *coed* groups. There were all kinds of political branches for this movement, from the right and from the left, but it was a youth movement very much tied to nature and naturalness. Following this, she had taken numerous alpine hikes and ski trips; my father had done the same. There are photographs of them with climbing ropes slung about their bodies-— Mother looking very "alive." invigorated and proud. I don't think they ever were true rock climbers, but skiing and alpine touring were the Austrian national sports.

There is a famous paper by Andre Greene, a French psychoanalyst, called "The Dead Mother." The mother is depressed and unresponsive to the child. The child tries desperately to entertain her and get her to connect with itself. Finally, the child gets depressed. Then the "pièce de résistance" comes when the mother completely livens up not for the child but for the man, the sex object. I do think this is what was going on between my mother and me. I have described her only as despairing, depressed, down in the dumps, silent, unrelated and withdrawn. But this really was only a small aspect of my mother. She was a great romantic, a believer in romantic love, and enlivened by this. She also had intense, long-lasting, intimate, life-long friendships with quite a number of close women friends. Alternatively, she had an active feminist image of herself which was intellectually stimulated and stimulating, culturally active, and very intensely connected and identified with her profession and the psychoanalytic movement. She would change personality completely in this latter mode; stand with pelvis thrust forward, wide based legs, seemingly feeling her oats; her face scrunched up and intense, her eyes bright and shining, her whole posture showing vigor. This was the mother I so actively sought to recreate, find or entice into interest in me. But alas, childrearing and connection to children was not part of her own ideal image.

The summer of 1936 saw another psychoanalytic congress, this one in Marienbad in the Czech Sudentenland. This congress was marked by the absence of my father, no longer amongst the members. I understand it dealt primarily with the importance of the superego and the role of unconscious guilt.

We had spent some time prior to the congress with mother at a hotel at the resort. When the congress started, my sister and I were again sent to a strange camp. This camp is marked for me by two memories. I had my trusted teddy bear with me and slept with him at night. The children were outraged by this infantile behavior and teased me mercilessly, but I clung to my bear. The other memory is my sister saying, "Shall we go and walk to the congress and meet Berta Bornstein?" This was a pleasant escape from what felt like a horrid camp. We walked along a beautifully maintained dirt path set between overhanging trees, for perhaps two miles. I was so happy, being with a newly-turned-friendly sister, on a wonderful outing, wearing one of my favorite dresses. I felt attractive and pretty. When we met Berta Bornstein, she was with a group of other women including my mother. Berta greeted us by saying, "Lore, what are you doing here, I only wanted to see Eva." This tactless greeting by the woman, who was supposed to be my therapist, was combined with my mother's absolute removal from the situation. She was in her intellectual, belonging to the important congress mood; the arrival of her children had nothing to do with her. I had seen this aspect of my mother before, but generally she had been depressed or helpless for so many years that she struck me as utterly changed. She exuded the feeling that she was with her colleagues at this great event, where important intellectual history was being made. In retrospect I understood that my mother really had undergone a change. No longer under my father's domination and more noisy intellectual achievements, she had blossomed

87

and become her own person. She took herself seriously as a psychoanalyst and felt that her colleagues appreciated her. To me this meeting with my mother at the congress was a trauma underscoring my unimportance in her life. When Berta took Eva off for her "session," I was left with my mother and her other colleagues. I became an impediment with which she had to deal. There are photographs of me with some of these adult women at that congress. I am badly slumped and look miserable but wearing my favorite dress. It is because of this photograph that the episode has stuck so forcefully in my memory.

I left my life in Vienna after Montessori camp in June and joined Mother and Thomas in Prague, while my sister stayed in Vienna to continue her analysis. Nushi made a surprising, touching goodbye ceremony for me and gave me a book for a present—an Insel Buch in beautifully decorated cover and in gothic print, which I greatly valued but never read. But I do not remember whether I ever said goodbye to Grete Fried.

Chapter 6

LIFE IN PRAGUE (1936–1938) WITH MOTHER AND THOMAS

By the time I arrived in Prague, in the fall of 1936, I thought of life as chopped into segments of two to three years, in which one moved from city to city. For me this discontinuity seemed permanent, the people left behind appeared forever gone, to be replaced by new ones. I was very surprised, years later, to learn that other people kept contact and memory of previous connections even though now separated by distance. My mother, for instance, still had friends she knew in grammar school.

I arrived in the new city a depressed, alienated, and unconsciously angry child, but also an only child as my sister stayed in Vienna. Now I had to adapt to living with my mother again as well as with her consort, Thomas. To make sure that I understood that he was part of my life and an adult authority, Thomas decided he had to take a child rearing stand right at the beginning so that I would understand "what was what." On my first day in Prague I asked, or perhaps pleaded and whined, for the purchase of a small red rubber ball costing perhaps a penny. I had come with my Teddy bear but no other toys. Thomas decided this was the time to intervene. He told me, in no uncertain terms, that I was not getting the ball, I was a *spoiled* child, and I needed to learn to behave. My mother, as was typical, said nothing. So with this intervention Thomas and I set off on the wrong foot.

Mother and Thomas were living together, though a marriage was not finalized for several years. This was part of the revolutionary ethos in which both she and Thomas traveled. Nowadays this pattern is so normal that people might not remember how "outré" and bohemian living together was at the time. Thomas was a Russian, his figure short, squat, and round, with a rather muscular upper body. He sported a handlebar mustache of which he took inordinate care, and which necessitated his wiping his mouth after every spoonful of soup. He dressed elegantly, used only the best fabrics, and there was some quality about him that led headwaiters to fall all over themselves for him. He knew wines and had long discussions with his vintner, knew good cigars, and was a gourmet cook. He was a collector of books and of political cartoons by Daumier, often clipped from their original nineteenth century newspaper edition. He spoke Russian and could speak Czech, which the rest of us never really learned—French, and German— but later when he came to America, he could never learn English. It just defeated him. I knew Thomas to be a well-informed individual, who read all kinds of newspapers and had a better grasp of what was happening in the world than anyone else I ever knew. In fact, it is because of his insistence that we emigrated to the United States. He understood before anyone else, that there was going to be war and that Germany was going to invade all of Europe. So our application for US immigration was completed earlier than others, and we were able to fit into the Austrian quota by 1938. My father, for instance, had no idea what was coming, and wrote to the Prague US consul in 1938 asking him to block our visas because he had custody of the children.

I did not appreciate Thomas' better qualities at the time because he and I started off on the wrong foot; and I did not care for his generally old-fashioned ideas of childrearing, his compulsive neatness about the house, his addiction to anal suppositories if one had a fever. Living with Thomas,

I could only see that he was, in advance of our modern era, a househusband and not the leader of resistance and political infiltration.

I don't remember him cleaning, perhaps someone came in to do that, but he cooked and shopped and tended to me. When first I arrived in Prague we lived in an older quarter and as we were moving soon, I was enrolled in a German-speaking school that was two trolley lines away. Bright and early, almost at dawn as schools started at 8A.M., he would get me up and travel on the two long trolley rides to get me to school. And then at the end of school at 1P.M. he came again to bring me home. He also prepared my "Gablefrühstück" (second breakfast or "elevens") and served us Mittagessen (the main meal of the day) and supper. He supervised my bath and insured that I did not drown in the tub. However, he was so piqued when I refused to leave the tub on time, because I was playing, that he refused to have anything further to do with this supervision. He was finicky and seemed obsessive-compulsive about household activities, orderliness, and the neatness of our home. In fact, my sister recalls once taking a book from his bookshelf and then returning it to the same place. Thomas knew the book had been moved because it stood out a quarter of a millimeter from the row of books. Apart from his household chores he spent hours in his room writing, or rather recreating, his opus "The History of Russia." The original manuscript had been confiscated by the Nazi German border guards upon his exit from Germany. He wrote on paper lined in squares, such as accountants used to use, in a small, very neat, readable hand.

To my mind his behavior was unmanly. I could not imagine why my mother picked such a man. I really didn't believe that theirs was a great passionate romance. She knew his history, of course, and might have admired him. What she said to me was that after being so subjugated by my father she was happy to be in control of her own life.

I, on the other hand, would lie in bed daydreaming of another apartment on the same floor in which lived my father with Elsa. Somehow the idea of this foursome comforted me.

It was only in the late 1990's that I was informed, by Jim Martin, who was writing a book *Wilhelm Reich and the Cold War*, about who Thomas really was. One could then understand what might have attracted my mother to him. After the fall of the Soviet Union KGB archives were opened and suddenly there is a flurry of research about a man called "Comrade Thomas." Martin mentions at least three German researchers writing about "Comrade Thomas." At the same time as Martin was writing his book, our family was contacted by a retired Oxford professor, Walter Kendall, who was also writing a book about Thomas. (I never found out whether that book was ever published.) There is still controversy to this day about Thomas's real name, origin, or his real date of birth. This has led to some fantastic speculations by one of the German researchers, Udo Vorholt, that he was originally a Polish anarchist who murdered the Russian governor by throwing a bomb. We reject this version of Thomas's life knowing how un-athletic he was, he could not even throw a ball. So, it is most unlikely that he ever threw a bomb. What is known is that he was part of the inner circle of the Bolsheviks. He then fled with Lenin's entourage to Zurich after the 1905 Russian revolution. Then together with Lenin traveled in 1917 to Russia, on the famous sealed train through wartime Germany, to help make the Bolshevik Revolution. According to Martin, Thomas was a protégée of Radek and Zinoviev, both early top-ranking Bolsheviks murdered by Stalin in the 1936 purges. Thomas was sent to Berlin in 1919 to head the newly formed Western Europe division of the Comintern. (This was the Moscow led international arm of the Communist Party, which oversaw the many local Communist Parties.) Thomas led this division from a shabby, small bookstore as a front for his real business. Thomas received millions of Reich Marks from Russia, which he had to launder and distribute to Communist Parties, especially to fund local revolutions, all of which failed. He led a low-profile, hidden life in Berlin while he spied on the German Communist Party for Russia, and at the same time transmitted the orders for the party's actions. He never attended party meetings and was only known by a few leaders of that party. Somehow, he ran afoul of the German super inflation of 1923 and lost much money, so that the Russians sent someone to investigate. It then turned out that his bookkeeping was very shoddy. He was even accused of absconding with money but was cleared of those allegations. He did return to Moscow for these charges but was protected by Radek and Zinoviev. He returned to his post in Germany but in 1926 he broke with Stalin and the Bolsheviks and joined an opposition Communist party in Berlin called SAP. Later, as a refugee in Prague, he joined New Beginning. It should be noted that he as well as my father and mother had lost all their radical ideology and connections by the time they came to the US.

Unemployed by his break with Russia, Thomas seems to have 'lived off' Ruth Österreich, (that at least is my speculation), a woman he was living with and by whom he fathered a child in 1923, also known as Ruth Österreich. Marriage, even with a child involved, was considered a bourgeois institution. He occupied himself by writing. He published two books, one under the name of Thomas and the other anonymously, about the Russian Revolution and about the civil war in Russia. He was in the process of writing a full history of Russia, which comprised several volumes. When the Nazis came to power, he had to flee Germany. He shipped his furniture and possessions to Prague but at the border his precious manuscript was confiscated. Thomas spent the rest of his life trying to rewrite it. Confusing to me, and contradictory, is the fact that he had a Russian passport under the name of Arnold Rubinstein, which had to be renewed every month at the Russian embassy. At the same time, he was hiding from Stalin's agents who were abroad killing the opposition. How could he both be in constant contact with the Russians for passport renewal, and also in hiding?

According to my sister, his not unrealistic fear of assassination by Stalin's agents, made him forever vigilant that no one had trespassed in his room or no suspicious strangers had inquired after him. He actually would place a hair on his desk to see if it had been moved. He was an expert at disguising and distorting his history in order to hide his true identity and had made up so many false biographies that it is hard to know what the truth about him is.

By 1933, when he came to Prague, he had assumed the name of Arnold Rubinstein. He had also joined the New Beginning, an organization which brought together all kinds of ex-German left-wingers, trying to work from within the system of existing democratic governments like in Britain, Czechoslovakia, and Norway to have some power and control in post Nazi planning. This group also helped with the anti-fascist resistance movements in Germany, mainly by constant currier service to keep other countries informed about what was happening in Germany. Smuggling people out was another activity they engaged in. It seems to be a little-known fact that there was a German, as well as an Austrian, anti-fascist resistance movement. Many prominent people were part of this organization, for instance Willy Brandt, later chancellor of the Federal Republic of Germany. According to Martin, Thomas was prominent in the New Beginning organization in Prague.

If Thomas was a leader of an important resistance movement, I had no knowledge of it. The only time I ever personally saw that he was involved in anything was one night, in Prague in 1938, when I saw him agitatedly and nervously pacing about. That was the night Edith Jacobson—a Berlin psychoanalyst, a member both of the Kinderseminar and the New Beginning movement—was being smuggled out of Germany. Emmy Minor traveled from Prague to Berlin with a second passport, owned by Mädi Olden, hidden in her clothes. I knew somehow that Thomas was the organizer of this rescue mission, later confirmed by a letter written by Jacobson, (see reference below) though there is no way he or Mother had talked to me about this. All, of course, was very hush-hush.

Edith, though Jewish, had remained in Germany after Hitler's rise to power and was active in New Beginning. She was arrested by the Gestapo and questioned, I believe about a patient, but refused to answer. She was sent to prison—please note not a concentration camp—as a political prisoner. In prison she developed severe thyroiditis and diabetes and was permitted by the authorities to go to a hospital. From there it was possible to organize an escape.

[for Edith Jacobson's story see May, U. and Mühlleitner, E .2005]

If Thomas was one of the organizers of the Czech branch of New Beginning, he was a most experienced conspirator, who could live in the same house with someone and give absolutely no hint of his activities. Personally, I am very surprised that he was still playing such an important role. He had no secret visitors, did not get phone calls, and did not seem to go on mysterious errands. So, did he do all this conspiratorial organizing while I was out of the house? On second reflection however, he was such an experienced conspirator that it is possible he could completely hide his activities from a child—a child who was in bed by eight in the evening.

What exactly my mother knew of Thomas' background and activities I don't know. But I assume it was enough to make her admire and respect him, thus she could tolerate what became his total dependence on her. As an adult I have come to value his cultural interests and prescience over world affairs. As a child, though I was negative in many ways, I did actually accept him as being part of the status quo. My sister, who joined us a year later, hated Thomas all her life and had terrible teenage struggles with him.

Coming to Prague and living in a family seems to have been marvelously effective for me. In general, I was, though still somehow alienated, a happy child there. Being separated from my torturing sister was curative; I stopped having anxiety and nighttime problems. Part of my improved mood was my mother's mood. She was no longer depressed, but active and vigorous and though she still paid no attention to household matters, she was a positive presence in the family.

By 1936 my mother had established a new life for herself in Prague. She was part of a very small, tightly knit, German speaking, psychoanalytic community. They studied together, socialized together since they were not an integral part of the Czech population, and analyzed each other. Yet they generated a psychoanalytic excitement, unusual in such a small group. They were led first by Frances Derie; when Mrs. Derie left for America, by Otto Fenichel; who, in the meantime, had quarreled with Wilhelm Reich and had left Norway for Prague. It is my impression that the group thought psychoanalysis had reached its perfectible zenith and their ideas were later codified by Fenichel in his 1944 book *The Psychoanalytic Theory of the Neuroses*. A recent interview with Lilo Gerö published in the newsletter of the International Psychoanalytic Association (IPA) describes this Prague psychoanalytic group. It was informal, not structured into classes as in Vienna and Berlin, with students freely mixing with the training analysts. Intellectual demands were high and challenging. And there was a fervor and excitement which knitted the group together. My mother blossomed in this atmosphere and shared this excitement. The group was still trying to tie psychoanalysis together with Marxist, but not communist thought. At this they failed and there is no record of their cogitations.

It was during her time in Prague that my mother started writing a few, highly respected psychoanalytic papers, still cited today. After her death, they were published as a collection called *Psychoanalytic Contributions*.

I remember some of the psychoanalytic colleagues from Prague. Most of them seem to have been left-wing refugees from Nazi Berlin, amongst them were Mädi Olden, Henry and Yela Loewenfeld, and Edward Kronold. Most important was Otto Fenichel. He was the man who had originally sent my mother to be analyzed by my father, and he had been a friend of both of them. But in Oslo he and Wilhelm came into severe conflict. Fenichel did not approve of the theoretical direction Reich was taking. My father started to distrust him and turn the Norwegian analysts against him. Undoubtedly the underlying tension which lead to the break was because Otto had not supported Wilhelm openly when Wilhelm was kicked out of the IPA in Lucerne. I am sure that my father turned on Otto with the same kind of rages he had expressed in Berlin. In turn Otto started writing in his *Rundbriefe* that Reich was "crazy."

I often visited and played with little Hanna Fenichel, and even more often with Andreas, the son of the Loewenfelds, who was my age.

In Prague, our daily life was organized around Mother's work schedule and, of course, my school schedule. Meals were promptly served the minute the last patient left and were eaten as in Berlin in the room which also served as my bedroom and playroom. This brought some conflicts around neatness. Thomas's neatness must be contrasted to my mother's. She slept on her office couch, as in Berlin, and every morning unmade her bed and certainly removed all evidence that her office was a bedroom, but she never otherwise concerned herself with the household. She never picked up my toys or clothes, nor asked me to pick them up, though she might give a general "clean up your room" order, without any helpful hints of how or why. Thomas, on the other hand, would show open disapproval. Apparently, I did not properly follow their guidelines on neatness for, what was after all, the "common room." Mother's solution to this dilemma was therapy.

At some time, I was informed that I was to start psychotherapy with Steff Bornstein. This was Berta Bornstein's sister, who lived and worked in the apartment house next to ours. To me these sisters looked identical, same body shape, face and hairdo. However, Steff's face was not marred by the birthmark that Berta bore. Also, these sisters were not anything alike in their methods of treatment or their personalities. With Steff I connected and had genuine conversations. When I asked her why I was being sent to therapy, as this had not been explained to me, she told me it was because I was so messy and because I was so rude to Thomas. So at first I worried that I was going to have to become "a good girl," but actually Steff never focused on these issues.

I have wondered later how it was possible that I was sent to therapy for a messy room, instead of my mother helping me or teaching me how to clean it up. Steff was an old-fashioned analyst, uninfluenced as far as I can see now, by ego psychology and very much into the symbolic expressions of the unconscious. Thus she informed me that the reason I was unable to eat the so-carefully-prepared slices of meat and pommes frites Thomas cooked for me, on the days that school had afternoon sessions, was because I thought of them as sliced up segments of Thomas' penis. I think I received this interpretation with skepticism because to me the meat was simply dry and unappetizing. But I do think her suggestion helped me integrate my knowledge of my general eating disorder and the fact that all the things that had disgusted me were parts of bodies or body secretions. She also continued my sexual "Aufklärung" (sexual education). I remember she told me the penis became as hard as "a nail" so that it could penetrate the vagina. This was an unfortunate choice of words, as I took the image literally. At one point she showed me her diaphragm to illustrate birth control. There was only one time when I was troubled, on my way to school, by a man opening his overcoat and "flashing" me with his penis. Steff carefully explained to me the castration anxiety that lay behind his motives. Nobody worried that I might be molested or attacked.

Steff was a genuine resource for me. To her I could confess my troubles with friends or the lack thereof, and I remember one occasion when she absolutely rescued me. But I will return to that later.

I have described my mother as being somewhat removed from me and the cares of the household while at the same time greatly involved in her psychoanalytic practice and scientific meetings. This is not completely accurate. She became very involved in seeing to it that I had fun in my life. I remember, for instance, that the night before my ninth birthday my door opened, and I heard a swishing noise. Then the door carefully close; I got up and turned on the light. There lay an area rug so my feet would not get cold as I arose from bed, and upon it were laid a whole bunch of toys and games. I am sure it was Mother who thought up and spent time planning this surprise. She also installed something between the jambs of the study doorway so that I could swing. Unfortunately, Mother chose rings instead of a swing, the kind of rings that gymnasts use that show how strong they are. Of course, I was unable to lift myself onto the rings, but she certainly had cared to do this.

Mother also arranged for many of my afternoons, since school mostly let out at 1 P.M. leaving me free, while she, after the "Mitagessen," had to return to work. Some of these attempts were failures, like having some maid take me to the park; I was too old for a promenade with a bored maid and wanted friends to play with. She then arranged some afternoons with Emmy Minor—one of the rescuers of Edith Jacobson—under whom years later, in New York, I worked as an assistant nursery schoolteacher; but her name inexplicably, had changed to Anna Zarabova. In Prague, Emmy ran an after-school program, as well as summer camps and winter ski camps. After school I went swimming with her at a pool. In the warm weather I had swimming lessons in a roped off area of the Moldau—now known as the Vlatava River. A male instructor walked on the bank holding me in a kind of a holster attached to something like a fishing rod, while I swam below him and learned a beautiful breaststroke. There had been some activities at Grete Fried's, but nothing like the intensity and frequency I experienced in Prague. I liked Emmy well enough, but I never felt about her the way I had felt about Nushi Plank in Vienna. Emmy was efficient and full of energy, but not the extraordinary warm nurturer that Nushi had been. It was my mood that had lifted. I was less needy and more satisfied with life.

By the next school year, I seem to have dropped out of Emmy's after-school program, but not her vacation camps. I was taking piano-accordion lessons. This was a fun instrument, of course not the full adult size, which I trundled for miles as I walked from our house to the park, down an embankment, over a bridge over the Moldau, and to the lessons somewhere on the other side of the river. In general, I seemed to have walked all over Prague. We lived on the "Kleine Seite" (small side), but I walked to the other side frequently, crossed the Charles Bridge, which was far from our house, went to an island in the middle of the river where I bought little pottery pieces for Christmas presents. I wandered in the Jewish Quarter, often passing the square in which stood the famous clock with the apostles.

Mother had arranged for me to meet a child my own age, who lived in the Jewish quarter, though at the time this was no longer a ghetto. Her name was Vera Franklin, and she became my best friend. We were very much alike. Every day that I was not occupied with some of the other activities I would walk the miles to her house. Her mother also worked, but Vera had a grandmother who took care of her.

For my ninth birthday, Mother gave me a new game called "Business" which we pronounced "Booziness." This was actually the American game "Monopoly." I still have the set with carved wooden figures of the devil, a monk, a housewife, and a Rabbi, as well as wooden money and houses. The street names were from Vienna, and because of this game I knew where I was in Vienna when I visited recently. I seem to have gone through a period of obsession with this game playing it frequently with Andreas Loewenfeld and some older boy, who I think had a crush on me. This was probably my first experience of the power of women over men.

There were some notable glitches in Mother's ability as a child raiser. The most notable one occurred in the summer of 1937. I had been sent to Emmy Minor's camp, some place in Czechoslovakia, and was then to join my mother in Grundlsee. Complicated arrangements had been made for my transport from camp to Austria. Some person from the camp was to take me back to Prague, where Vera's grandmother was to fetch me from the train and put me up overnight, together with Vera. The next day we would then take the train to Austria, I would be left off at Badausee, the major town near Grundlsee, and Vera and her grandmother would continue on the train. The glitch was that I became very ill in that camp and was laid up for over a week, but then was able to travel as had been planned. All went smoothly till I got off the train at Badausee. I got off, my trunk was removed, and the train left. There I was standing on the platform all alone, no grown- up in sight.

For a child of nine there is a very sinking feeling when left alone in a strange town on the railroad platform. There wasn't even a railroad official about. I had no idea what to do and hoped against hope that the people to pick me up, meaning my mother, were just late. How long I waited I have no idea. Just when I decided I had better walk into town and do something, I did not know quite what, when a horse drawn cart appeared. The cart was shaped like a flat-bed truck, and it was driven by a man wearing a black, French looking beret. He looked at me and said, "Aren't you Annie Reich's daughter?" He then introduced himself as René Spitz—the famous psychoanalyst and child researcher who had studied marasmus and hospitalism in neglected infants. He must have met me previously in Berlin or in Marienbad; how he now recognized me was a miracle. He had come to the station to pick up some freight. He immediately offered to drive me to Grundlsee, though he was staying in Altausee. It must have been quite a long round trip for him. My mother was duly surprised when I drove up, but was able to utter, "I thought you were too ill to travel." I am sure there was no telephone at Mädi's house, or at the camp, but how did she expect to retrieve me?

The other flaw in my life in Prague came with the arrival the following year of my sister, Eva, who had remained in Vienna to stay in analysis with Berta Bornstein. It may be remembered that in our family the children's room was always combined with the dining room. Around the table was a set of corner benches with backs and one chair. When my sister arrived, I was moved from my bed, a sort of day couch, and was to sleep, from now on, on the narrow bench by the table. My bed now could no longer be covered by a spread but had to be taken apart every day and remade at night. This sleeping arrangement was narrow and uncomfortable, and I did not feel up to making my own bed. My mother usually did this for me, but one night, I remember, my sister was to do it and she just flatly refused. I felt displaced from my kingdom. It is remarkable that when I think of my life in Prague, I always picture myself in the old bed, even though that was for only half of our time there.

Furthermore, my sister was in a foul mood. She was 13, had been semi-independent for a year, had probably spent another summer with my father, and above all, bore a terrible hatred for Thomas. She introduced a sour note into our household. Thomas grew more tense and rigid in response to her; Mother again looked on at their struggles from the sidelines.

Whether my sister tried her horrible teasing of me again, I don't remember. My memory of her in Prague is sparse. That is because, luckily for me, she soon found a radical group to belong to, called "Die Gruppe." Her school day was longer than mine; also encompassing afternoon classes, and then she would go and join her group. Thus, she was gone for most of the day. She would brag to me about her belonging to the group, managing to make me feel inferior, and then she would boast about her great love affair with George. I believe now that this was a sexual affair, but happily I knew nothing of that at the time. Helene Deutsch has written in her book *On the Psychology of Women* what an effect it has on the younger sister to learn that the older one is sexually active. This reaction I was spared till I was much older and then I did find it a great shock.

One other notable event that happened during my second year in Prague is that Thomas' daughter Ruth suddenly appeared and visited us regularly once a week. Where she had come from, whom she was living with, or any other facts about her were never told. Later I did learn that she was staying with her mother, but the latter was never mentioned during these visits. Ruth was a year older than my sister, thus 14 at the time. She was a poised young lady, in dark crepe dresses with proper embroidered peter-pan collars, who seemed much older than my sister. Her visits seemed to be with the children, since I don't remember that she would join Thomas in his study where he sat writing his Russian history. Undoubtedly, she shared a family meal with us.

When we emigrated to the USA in 1938, Ruth stayed behind with her mother. I always thought of this as an abandonment of a daughter. I do not know whether her mother did not wish her to go, or whether Thomas' own difficult visa and passport situation made it impossible for him to take her along. She was not legally his child, as he never married the mother. Her subsequent fate was traumatic. After the Nazi's overran Europe, her mother was arrested, perhaps in France, and later killed. Ruth at age 15 was left alone in France. She was raped and impregnated by German soldiers, but eventually rescued by nuns. Finally, she met a Belgian soldier who took her with him to Belgium and lived with her and the daughter she bore until he died of old age. However, he could not marry her, as he was Catholic and was already married. Apparently, Ruth, the daughter of two revolutionaries who disdained marriage, never overcame the shame of her unmarried state. After the war Mother and Thomas did help her financially and did offer to bring her daughter to the U.S., but this never happened. Eva and her daughter did visit her in 1973, and I had some Christmas card exchanges with her. But at some time she moved, and we never had her new address, and so lost track of her.

Despite of some glitches, most of my life in Prague was busy and very happy. On a recent trip I returned there and was amazed how much of the city remained the same. Little mosaics on the sidewalk or on roofs came back to me as forceful memories. The river was beautiful, though the peasant pottery market on the island was gone. Where I had roamed through the wonderful medieval little streets and castle above, and the square with the old clock all by myself, the city now was crowded with sightseers and pickpockets.

The Hrachine castle was still there, but the torture chambers that I had visited with my school on a field trip were gone. We had been shown the iron maiden into which victims were placed and when it was closed pierced with sharp knives, the well into which prisoners were dropped to starve, as others were chained above it to watch, a place where prisoners were smoked, and other devises and racks. It is odd that a school trip should be shown these wonders, but in a way that was a more authentic tour of how things had been in the past. For instance, the story of the clock maker, whose eyes were put out so he would not tell how to make the clock to another king, is the kind of tale that we now protect our children from. Just as I loved the

Grimm's Fairy tales full of torture and maiming as they were, I loved the view of the old torture chambers, though it scared me and horrified me, and stayed with me all my life.

School, in general, required quite an adjustment from me. It was my first public school, and I was not used to the regimentation, rote learning, and lack of individual expression and exploration. I still have an art folder from my third-grade class where we had to draw, in pen and ink, geometric shapes like triangles and squares, and then carefully fill them in with watercolor paint. What a difference from the free art of my Montessori school. We sat on benches with wooden desktops in front, and with inkwells wherein we dipped our pens. I think the fountain pen was just being invented and had not yet trickled down for the use of children. Girls sat on one side of the room and boys on the other. We were seated in rows by our height, the smaller ones in front. The girls mostly wore braids and only a couple of us had bobbed hair. For recess we circled the great, long hallway, two by two, without speaking. We did have gym once a week where we changed into big, dark blue bloomers. We wrote in Old Gothic German script, instead of the more modern Latin script. We had penmanship exercises. When I accidentally dropped my notebook into a dirty puddle, my teacher made me rewrite the whole book of work for the school year. As a result, I became a very sloppy writer and I have never regained the control for beautiful penmanship. Was this a case of revolt?

The teachers were kind. My third-grade teacher was a man who brought a gun to school to show us how it worked. He seems to have been interested in military affairs. My fourth-grade teacher was a woman who had the grace to express shock when a pupil who was leaving the school gave a "Heil Hitler" salute as she left.

The state religion was Catholic and once a week a priest came to teach the catechism. From this class about four of us were excused. I was an atheist; one child was enrolled in a Jewish religious class elsewhere and the other two were Lutherans. This public exhibition of difference did not sit too well with my classmates, who informed me that I would land up in hell because I was not a Catholic. However, instead of being cowed by this, I felt a pride in my difference. I have therefore wondered sometimes about the way we tend to protect children nowadays from ever feeling different, assuming always that it will make them feel inferior. On the other hand, I did not display my feeling of difference in a challenging way. I remember one little girl, my size and therefore sitting near me in class, took me into a bathroom stall one day to, in hushed tones, whisper something about the monthly period. She was in awe about this new knowledge, and I did not let on that I had access to lots of "Aufklärung." It does show the way most children at the time were raised about sexual matters, and how very unusual my family was. The school was friendly, and I don't remember children being vicious or teasing or ganging up on others, but I don't think I connected with anyone really. Just how impossible making friends might have been, was shown to me when one day some of the bigger girls, therefore sitting in the rear of the class, asked me to come home with them. We stood in the hallway of a house and then they all said "Heil Hitler" arms outstretched in the Nazi salute. I am ashamed to say that I joined them in this, somehow not able to stand up for myself.

There was going to be a big event in a stadium in which our school was to participate, and our teacher asked us if we had a play, or knew of a play, we could put on. I raised my hand and said I had such a play. I am not sure of why I did this. But the result was horrific. The teacher asked me to bring it in. Full of agony and guilt, I reported my dilemma to Steff. I had no idea of how to wriggle out of this. I am grateful to this day, for instead of analyzing why I would tell such a fearsome lie, Steff sat down and wrote a play. I remember it had something to do with a rabbit. The play was accepted and actually played at the event, my only disappointment being that I was not given a role to act in it.

When I told my mother and Thomas about the plan for this event, they frowned and hesitated, and seemed reluctant to let me go. They neither explained what it was about nor did they forbid my attendance. In retrospect I cannot understand why they permitted me to go, or why they did not say a word about it. They could not have worried about appearing "different," as I already was, because of the religious instruction. I think there was a reluctance to discuss serious matters with a child. This covered so many aspects of my life that they cannot all be mentioned here, but examples are the fate of my stepsister Ruth, or even her living situation in Prague, the fate of my Viennese grandfather, and plans for emigration.

In contrast to my time in Berlin where I knew all about the good guys and the bad guys, my mother and Thomas had not explained to me what was going on in Czechoslovakia or for that matter in Russia which was in the midst of the infamous Moscow trials. The difference between my parent's notions of how to bring up children was most pointed. My father felt that children were sensate little grownups who should participate in adult life. My mother felt children should be protected from all knowledge of the unpleasant facts of adult life. Besides this consideration I think my mother had become used to a habit of secrecy. All of Thomas' previous life, identity, and perhaps current activities were secret of course, but then so also were the nature and details of my mother's work. She could not explain what she was doing without violating the confidence of her patients.

Given the aura of secrecy in our house, it should be no surprise that no one explained the "Czech situation" to me, and of course I did not mention my participation in the shameful Nazi salute. After World War I, at the treaty of Versailles, Czechoslovakia had been gerrymandered together out of various left-over pieces of the Austro-Hungarian Empire. In a half-ring around Bohemia, abutting on Germany, was located a German speaking population, the Sudeten Germans, who were actively agitating to leave Czechoslovakia and be joined to Germany. It was because of this large

German speaking population that there was a parallel German-speaking public school system in Prague. Once a week we had compulsory Czech lesson. I could navigate very nicely about Prague with only German, needing just a smattering of Czech words for storekeepers and trolley drivers. However, even while I lived in Prague, there was a great surge of Czech nationalism, so that Czechs increasingly frowned on the German language. Czechoslovakia was a democracy that prided itself on its civil liberties and its government. Masaryk was revered, though, by the time I lived there, Benesh was the President. The German population, however, was predominantly Nazi. It is no wonder that so many children in my school had Nazi sympathies.

Nazi Germany was also pushing to annex the Sudetenland just as it was pushing to join with Austria, claiming a pan-Germanic interest in both places. This demand by Germany for unification was causing opposition within both nations by their government and at the same time rebellion by some of their inhabitants. England and France were involved because they were pledged to uphold the Versailles treaty and were supposed to defend Czechoslovakia. The infamous Munich pact in September of 1938, where Chamberlain handed over permission to Germany to annex the Sudentenland in order to sustain "Peace in our Time," was the denouement of this whole situation. So it is no wonder that Czech nationalism was running high, and the use of the German language met with frowns and resentment.

Hitler in the meantime organized a huge demonstration of school children in a Prague stadium to celebrate their Germanic heritage and to press for unification. Hitler had a real flair for dramatic public occasions. It is this demonstration that our school attended and for which our class, amongst many others, was to present a play—the play Steff Bornstein wrote. We went to a huge stadium filled with German school children and had multiple ceremonies and exhibitions both of sports and of dramas and singing. The atmosphere was festive and exiting. There were speeches, but I have no memory of them. I have no idea whether any of the children knew what this was about, certainly I did not know.

On March 11, 1938, in honor of my tenth birthday, my grandfather came from Vienna for a visit. We had a very nice time. It struck me as amazing that my grandfather should come to Prague to visit me. I was extremely pleased. Then the entire visit became a nightmare. Hitler chose that weekend to invade Austria for the "Anschluss" (uniting or combining) of Austria into Germany. My grandfather became agitated and wished to immediately return to Vienna and his wife Malva. My mother was adamant that he should stay in Prague and immediately get Malva out. In the end Grandfather returned to Vienna, which turned out, in my opinion, to be a huge mistake. The Germans did not immediately close the border so Malva could have come right out. Their subsequent fate, I only understood recently when I found a letter from Uncle Lutz.

My grandfather, it turned out, was the son of a half Jewish father, and therefore in Nazi parlance a "¼ Jew." This was enough for the Nazis to close his business down sometime in 1938 or 1939. Then Malva, who was not Jewish, became very frightened and apparently so nervous, that my uncle described her as "non-functional." In the meantime, some other elderly relative of Malva's moved in with them. Grandfather was caught by these three women, who dared not make a move. My uncle who was making his own plans to emigrate kept urging my grandfather to make a move but generalized "paralysis" seems to have settled over his household. Finally, the Nazi's came to look over their apartment to see if it should be confiscated. At this point Malva had a stroke and died. Only after this was my grandfather able to make plans and emigrate.

After the "Anschluss," Czechoslovakia, expecting a similar fate, mobilized troops at its frontier and prepared for war. Tension in the city was high, people walked about with strained faces. There were air raid drills, which in my child mind, were somehow compounded by the gray sky overhead, as if this grayness made the threat more real. I would look up at the sky to watch for airplanes surfacing over the gloom. It was early in the history of commercial air travel so one very seldom heard the drone of any plane. Once, before the crisis, a plane flew over while I was at school, and the entire class rushed to the window because airplanes were so rare and few. This occurred before the threat of war, but now aerial bombing of civilians had already been used in Spain two years before and Prague expected to be bombed. I felt an oppressive gloom had settled on my heart and over the city.

Black-out drills were ordered. Thomas had heard that blue blocked out light, so he obtained large sheets of transparent blue cellophane to cover our windows. The night of the drill, Ed Kronold was a guest for dinner. We sat in the dining room/children's room eating alcove when the air raid sirens went off and the blackout was to start. Of course, the blue cellophane did nothing to the light and soon the air raid warden was ringing our doorbell. We moved to the curtained off area of our hallway, where patients used to wait in privacy, but the light from there still shone out to the street through the curtain covered glass door of the dining room. The air raid warden came again. And this time we ate in total darkness. It was during that drill that Kronold accidentally put his hand in the salad bowl, and I laughed. He got angry not thinking it funny at all. Actually, writing about the whole fiasco I still think it was extraordinarily funny.

One day I returned from school and found a letter *from my father*, addressed to my mother, my sister, and myself. What a wonderful surprise. I had not heard from him since 1935 and thought I would never see him again. I know now that there were other letters, which had been confiscated by the adults with whom I lived. One from 1935, is quoted by Martin in *Wilhelm Reich and the Cold War*. So I know now there were some attempts by Father to stay in touch.

110

As the letter was addressed to me, I opened it. There I read that my father was against our emigration to America, he wished for the children to come to Norway instead. I was amazed. No one had mentioned emigration to me. America of all places! I associated it with gangsters, and wild Indians and perhaps cowboys. I had met a number of Americans in Vienna, people who were studying psychoanalysis, but this did not alter my wild impressions. The thought was totally alien for me. It did explain why recently a young woman had come to the house and started to teach me a few words of English. She gave me a most wondrous fairy tale called *Red Feather* which we read together. I own it still. The illustrations were divine, the story of changelings finally finding their right place, and I loved it. That we were going to emigrate was news to me.

When Mother came home, she forbade me to mention this plan to anyone. However, a few weeks later our teacher asked me in front of the whole class which school I would attend next year, as our school ended at fourth grade; Gymnasium or Realschule. So then I said in front of everyone that we were emigrating to America, and I would not be attending either school. The next day I was scolded at home for revealing the secret. It turns out that one of my classmate's mother was a patient of my mothers. It was precisely so that patients would not find out that I was not to tell.

Then preparations for the move began in earnest. I had to give up most of my toys again, keeping only my trusted teddy bear and the game of "Business," and then I was packed off to another summer camp with Emmy Minor while Mother packed and closed up everything and we were ready to leave.

Lore's parents getting serious, 1920 with Otto Fenichel & Berta Bornstein, and unknown man

My parents at a beach party, 1927

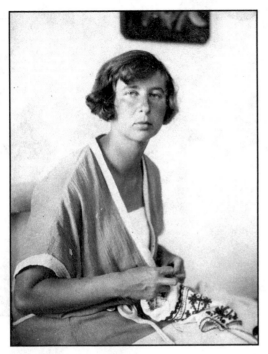

Mother, pregnant and depressed, 1928

Reich unhappy family, Lore as newborn, 1928

Lore and Eva, 1928

Eva, age 5 in baby carriage,
Lore 1-3/4 years old, walking, 1930

Lore, 1930

Lore, 1932

Wilhelm Reich visiting Communist
Children's Commune, 1931

Wilhelm and Eva in Davos, 1932

Wilhelm and Annie Separate, 1930

Wilhelm Reich, c. 1930

Eva & Lore in Annie's embroidered dresses, 1933

Lore with Teddy Bear, 1934

Lore with Madi Olden in Grundlesee, 1936

Lore and Eva at Marienbad convention, 1936

Happy Lore, Skiing 6 months later, 1936

Lore's class at Nazi rally, 1938

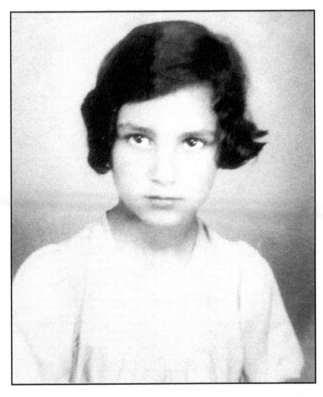

Lore's passport photo, age 10, 1938

Chapter 7
IMMIGRATION (1938)

EMIGRATION

Emigration to America is a very strange experience, both alienating, and humiliating. Why this should be so, when one has already resided in several other countries, is not immediately clear. Living in Berlin or Prague, we still felt as a family, that we were who we were. In Prague, surrounded by Czech speakers, we did not feel in the least inferior or unusual. Everything else about the country, besides the language, was very much central European. Trolleys were the same, the goods in stores were the same, the types of clothes we wore were the same, the method of going shopping was the same. It is true that before the Anschluss the Austrians drove on the left as opposed to Germans or Czechoslovakia, but these seemed minor adjustments. Austria was still there; we returned to it and Grundlsee every year, and the Austrian Alps were still available for skiing. We had the same vacation schedule, holidays and festivals. The people we knew in Vienna, like the Fenichels or Mädi Olden were still there in Berlin and then in Prague. Emigrating to another continent was a different matter.

Our experience with the Americans started out with a series of petty humiliations. To get our visas we needed a physical. At the consulate we, my mother, sister and I were told to strip to the waist. So there we were in our underpants, my mother and sister without bras, breasts dangling. Then a tall, good-looking, utterly bored, white male American doctor walked in. Treating us like so much chattel, he examined us by rolling up our eyelids looking for trachoma—trachoma of all things in the middle of Europe! It meant that it made no difference who we were or whence we came, middle class, upper class, or the huddled masses, we were all inferior because we were not Americans. There were other indignities, minor and major. We could not get a visa till my mother could prove she owed no money. It was discovered that in her haste to leave Nazi Germany she had not paid her phone bill. Somehow having to pay what was owed to those Nazis was infuriating.

One could not get a visa unless one had an affidavit from someone in America stating that one would not become a charge of the state. The affidavit giver guaranteed the sum of, I think, $2,000 per person in case the immigrant became ill or unemployed. After my mother died, as I was going through her papers, I came across many, many painful pleading letters from acquaintances, some rather far removed, seeking affidavits so they could leave Nazi Germany, and later wartime Europe. Not everyone could get a visa even if they met the above conditions. There was a quota system for each country, only so many persons per year could enter. Here we were lucky. As Austrians we fit into the Austrian, not Czech, quota, and by this time the Germans had closed the Austrian border, so we did not have much Austrian competition. Thomas was another matter. I am not quite sure what nationality his passport professed, and certainly he also had obtained the affidavit and his credit record, but the Americans were suspicious of him in some way. Considering who he really was, this was actually very perceptive of them. At that time, in order to enter the U.S., one had to declare that one wasn't, and had never been a Communist. As both Thomas and Mother had long broken with those people, this did not constitute a real case of lying. Nevertheless, a visa was denied to him. Then something happened which was so quaint, it could never happen now. Mary O'Neal Hawkins, the American who had been studying child analysis in Vienna, marched into the consul's office and said, " How dare you not give a visa to my friend Arnold Rubinstein (Thomas), I will write to my senator about this right away." I know this would never work in these hardened times, but America was young and naïve in certain ways and impressed by connections, and so Thomas eventually obtained his visa, though he had to travel many months later.

Indignities were not only handed out by the Americans; the Czechs had their own role to play. One could not leave the country with any substantial sum of money; difficult if one is emigrating and not coming back. So my mother was forced to hide money in various places in our luggage. I remember one place inside the hole in spools of thread, another hiding place was in the little toy briefcase I had been given as a goodbye present and that I joyfully clutched. Since one could not go by train via Germany, we had to fly, which as has been noted, was a wonderful new adventure. We arrived at the airport, Mädi and Thomas seeing us off. However, there was some problem, and Mother was stopped concerning an issue over money. Thomas had to be paged to present documents she had forgotten. Then they decided to search us. Mädi took hold of my little briefcase and said, "I'll hold that while you are being searched." I resisted, but somehow her stern demeanor made me give in. The woman to search me watched all this calmly and then took me to a little room. There she stripped me, looking even into my underpants, to both my prepubescent and her embarrassment. I have never forgotten the indignity of this search; when I later found out the money was in the briefcase, I marveled at the stupidity. Flying itself turned out not to be such a joy either. The plane was little and rocked a great deal, I was forced to use the airsick bag so courteously provided. The Austrians also contributed to the indignity by revoking our citizenship, thus making us stateless.

We stopped off in Paris, which was a pleasant interlude. It had been arranged that I would stay with my best friend Vera, whose mother in the meantime had married a Frenchman. Mother attended the congress of the International Psychoanalytic Association of 1938 and for once left me in the right place. Where my sister stayed, I do not know. Paris was amazing; women wore bright red nail polish and bright red lipstick, rouge, powder and high heels with silk, not lisle, stockings. No place where I had lived before had women donned makeup or worn heels. Men wore berets and everyone seemed to carry about long sticks of bread sticking out of their briefcases or shopping bags. Vera and I had a glorious time including playing "hockey" on a little machine in a bar near her house. Apparently, we overstayed our time and were roundly scolded by her new stepfather, another ill-tempered, ill humored, European man. We hung our heads embarrassed by his display of temper. What else we did I am not sure, but I did see the Eiffel Tower and Versailles.

The trip to America was like a fairy tale interlude. We trained to Boulogne on the west coast of France and then a tender took us out to our ship, the New Amsterdam, part of the Holland America Line. As we crossed the harbor, I kept looking at every boat asking, "Is this the ship?" Then I saw it! It was absolutely huge, beyond imagination, and resplendently white and clean. It had multiple decks reaching to the sky above the tender, and unimaginable turrets and smokestacks.

The first shock was ascending the gangplank ladder and being told, "Watch your step!" in English. Why should English have been a surprise when French, Czech, Swedish, Norwegian had never fazed me? But here were the first English words I heard spoken; my English lessons long forgotten. I remember those words but don't know if I understood them or guessed at them at the time. Apart from seasickness while crossing the English Channel, I spent the most idyllic ten days of my life. The New Amsterdam was a luxury liner with swimming pools, game rooms, toys, and lots of playmates. How I regretted when the trip was over. The only bad experience was when I saw the New York skyline from far off and shouted,

"Look trees!", only to be told by a somewhat older boy, "There are *no* trees in America." This completely dashed me, and I had to run to my mother who reassured me that indeed there were trees in America. Of course, they were both right in some ways.

ARRIVAL IN NEW YORK (1938)

The pleasant interlude ended with our arrival in New York, and the indignities continued. The immigration officer interviewing us on the ship had that same cold, bored expression as the consulate doctor. It was not a welcoming feeling and besides it made Mother nervous. On the dock we were met by our Berlin friend, Sandor Rado, who had issued our affidavits. He drove us by taxi to the upper east side of Manhattan where an apartment had been lent to us. It was August or late July. People were on vacation. I remember the large gloomy looking, unadorned apartment houses looming over us, so much taller than the six-floor limit in Europe.

The apartment was terribly hot; this was in the middle of a New York heat wave. There was so much soot and pollution in New York at that time that the windows had openings like small slits in them but could not be raised. The apartment had no fans, not that we were familiar with such a device, and air conditioning had not been invented. We were stifling, could not breathe, and could not sleep. We had never experienced such heat before. As is normal in central Europe in August, we had arrived in woolen clothes and desperately needed thinner things.

Our immigration had been arranged by a committee run by the American Psychoanalytic Association under the direction of Lawrence Kubie, whom we had known in Vienna. He set out to rescue as many Central European analysts as he could, and actually he did a wonderful job. For instance, the apartment lent to us had been obtained through the committee. Rado let us off and had gone back to Connecticut where he was vacationing. Mother had no idea how to obtain summer clothes. She called the person in the office of the committee who said, "Why you just take the subway down to Macy's and there you can buy clothes." We were not used to 'ready-mades,' we did not know where the subway was, how to use it, or how much to pay for it. My mother enlisted the aid of her closest friends, the Loewenfelds who had arrived a few weeks before us. Together they ventured into the unknown subway system to buy suitable clothes and sought suitable permanent lodging. Both families felt bewildered and estranged. So despite the really wonderful help the committee had given, we were dumped on our own in a strange city, luckily not in a strange language. In a few weeks the Loewenfelds ended up in a furnished apartment in a brownstone, and my mother in a furnished residential hotel, close to each other, on the upper west side of New York. Mother had taken eight years of English in school and was well versed in it. In fact, as soon as she was able to get a patient, she was able to analyze in English.

I missed the Macy's adventure, because the day after we arrived the Rado's invited me to stay with them in the summer vacation home in Stamford Connecticut.

The Psychoanalytic Rescue Committee did a very good job arranging for stranded Central European analysts to come here, obtaining affidavits, and helping with transportation. I have not heard of any analysts who, if they desired and it was before the war, did not succeed in emigrating to the United States, thanks to the committee's efforts. What to do with all these refugee analysts once they got here was another matter. The local American analysts were not too pleased with such a great influx of competition. It was in the middle of the great depression and patients who wished to undergo this new and unknown treatment were in short supply. Kubie had expected the new arrivals to disperse across America. Here he was defeated, as the refugees preferred to congregate amongst other people they knew.

Nevertheless, my mother —after having disposed of me to the Rados and my sister to a camp where she got a job at age 14 as an assistant counselor—traveled to Cleveland to be interviewed by Douglas Bond for a job at Case Western Reserve. Dr. Bond was not eager to have her there, saying that they had enough analysts. My mother felt rather despairing and remembered sitting on a Lake Erie dock dangling her bare feet and having no idea what to do. Much later, Annie Katan went to Cleveland and was well received. After this, Mother tried to see if she could join Fenichel in Los Angeles. Again, although the committee had been overall helpful in getting the analysts to America, there was no one to advise her on how to go about traveling to Los Angeles. Therefore, Mother went to Thomas Cook, the travel agency well known in Europe, but probably top-of-the line in America. They told her it would cost $300 per person to travel to Los Angeles, an enormous sum which she could not afford. So that is how we stayed in New York. Adjustment to America was painful and difficult even for this elite group of refugees, though they had professional connections, a desirable career, and contrary to previous immigrants, spoke fluent English.

There were other, well-known analysts whose arrival in America was totally different. These were not *refugees* but invited guests with prearranged jobs, mostly at universities. These analysts were wined and dined, honored, listened to with rapt attention, their office hours filled even before they arrived. Such people as Helene Deutsch, Horney, Rado, and Franz Alexander had a totally different experience from us —experiences that did not rob them of their self-esteem and sense of self identity. In fact, they were idolized and blossomed in the attention lavished on them. However, this experience did not translate necessarily to their spouses. Felix Deutsch for instance, an internist, who came with his wife Helene, was not welcomed and had a terrible time reestablishing himself.

Analysts who came as refugees were definitely not wined and dined. Few American analysts welcomed them or ever socialized with them. Exceptions were those American analysts who had themselves traveled to Vienna or Berlin to be trained and knew the refugees personally. Thus, the refugee analysts huddled together and braced each other for the rigors of adjustment to this new country. At first my mother clung to the Loewenfelds, who also came from Prague and previously from Berlin. Later more friends arrived in New York: Edith Jacobson, Mädi Olden, and Berta Bornstein (one of the few lay analysts to be accepted by the New York Psychoanalytic Institute). These women were part of my mother's very intimate circle. As immigration continued, many other analysts arrived from Europe including the Isakowers, the Krises, the Hartmans, and the Loewensteins. It is my belief, though I have no proof of this, that the initial snubbing and lack of welcome by the American members of the New York Psychoanalytic Institute contributed to the refugees not integrating properly into that institute, instead forming a self-contained clique. Of course, the refugees also felt snobbish toward the American analysts, thinking that only *they*, the refugees, were the true bearers of the Freudian torch. It is no surprise then that as the number of refugees increased, they eventually took over the leadership of the New York Psychoanalytic Institute, to the chagrin of their original American colleagues.

Another indignity that the refugee analysts had to undergo was to obtain a license to practice medicine. Actually, an analyst could practice without a license by not being a *medical* doctor. Whether the elite, invited analysts, therefore escaped the need for a license is not known to me. But because the American Psychoanalytic Association (APsaA) had legalistic membership requirements that only physicians could be members, the ordinary medically trained refugees had to take this exam— lay analysts with rare exceptions were excluded from membership in the societies and institutes run by the APsaA. The medical analysts first had to pass an English exam, and then these medical analysts, who in general had not practiced medicine and never had had an internship, needed to take a state licensing exam. Fenichel for example was required by the state of California to take an internship, which he did in his mid-forties. In those days—and probably illegally even now—interns were on duty all day and every other night. This is hard for people in their twenties, but for a man in his mid-forties it was too much, and Fenichel died of a stroke, I believe, before he could obtain his license. My mother studied mightily for these exams, ironically flunked the psychiatric section, and had to repeat it. It is not surprising that she failed this subject, as she had never had a residency in a mental hospital and had gone straight from medical school into a psychoanalytic practice. In the meantime, she was able to develop a small practice, earn a somewhat meager living and in a few years repay the loan that had enabled us to come here.

Contrary to the fears of the American analysts however, the most amazing thing was, that psychoanalysis became more popular with the arrival of these refugee analysts, and the patient pool expanded. By the time the war ended, there were great shortages of couch time, but this eventual outcome in leadership and acceptance of psychoanalysis was not foreseeable in the summer and early fall of 1938.

While Mother was trying to put a life together, Emmy Rado came and whisked me off to Stamford Connecticut where the Rados had a weekend and summer second home. In those days, Stamford could be considered countryside while nowadays it is a much built- up urban environment. The Rados belonged to a beach club on Long Island Sound. Their house was large, with painted white siding, surrounded by huge pine trees and a lawn. They had two servants and more than one car. From this description one can understand that Rado, who had come in 1933 as an invited guest of Columbia University, had established for himself a very comfortable, upper middle class, American lifestyle. The family had a son about a year younger than I and an older son of about 19, who might have been the product of an earlier marriage. Emmy was a very pretty, pleasant and gentle woman who was extremely kind to me. She made me feel comfortable and welcome. The first morning I came downstairs in completely unsuitable clothes, and she hastily bought me two pairs of shorts and two striped tee shirts. How I treasured those gifts! She took me along shopping to the A&P and I marveled at seeing a supermarket, although this supermarket was a small shabby affair compared to what we have today.

The Rado sons were less welcoming. The older one seemed surly. He had a car with a rumble seat which he reluctantly let us use one day, but was worried that we would get caught in the rain and ruin its leather seats, which of course, is exactly what happened. The younger son might have resented the intrusion of a *girl* and though he was not rude, he did not really interact with me. Sandor Rado was a man who was a little like my father. I remember he had terrible temper outbursts, which frightened me badly and subdued the mood in the household. Even though the beach club was wonderful and Emmy a really great person, I was not totally comfortable in that household. They did speak German so that at least was not a problem.

All went along smoothly till my sister arrived for a weekend visit. Eva has told me in recent years that she resented my living in the lap of luxury while she *had to work*. I knew she was still or again in a terrible mood. She had left behind in Prague her boyfriend and the "group" she belonged to. She had been happy with these people in Prague and had not wished to leave. Now again, as in Vienna three years before, she let this mood out on me. She proceeded to get the boys to gang up on me as she had done at Grete Fried's and subjected me to terrible teasing. I must have experienced a warning of a recurrence of the terrible anxiety neuroses I had suffered from in Vienna, I became very depressed. Suddenly, to my ten-year-old psyche, the strange country, the new adjustments required of me, the necessity of my mother not keeping me with her were too much. I wrote my mother a letter threatening suicide if she did not remove me from there. My poor mother, beset by her attempts to settle and earn a living, suddenly had to contend with this crisis. It is the only time in my whole life that I dared turn to my mother for help and actually expressed what I was feeling. She responded immediately, but not quite in the manner that I had hoped.

I was taken from the Rados and bundled off to a camp in the Poconos. This was a Jewish camp for children, girls and boys in separate camps, while at the same time their families could stay at the main house, which was a hotel, and eat in the communal dining room with the campers. Mother found this for me because Yela Loewenfeld had become the camp doctor for that summer. I was received kindly by the camp, which outfitted me in left-over and discarded uniforms. I had never been in a camp with uniforms before. Most strange of all was that, besides Yela, no one spoke German. It is true that I had had English lessons in Prague, but I don't think anything stuck, so now I was in a strange camp, though a kind one, where I was surrounded by another language of which I did not speak a word.

There are all kinds of theories about how humans learn language, and it is generally believed that babies imbibe the language while adults have to learn grammar and vocabulary in a formal way. Thrown into this situation I had to ingest words and phrases somehow without processing them through my conscious mind and learn the language the way a baby does. The other campers were helpful, spoke slowly, and I caught on sufficiently to survive.

Certain scenes stick out which make me realize that I must have picked up quite a few words. We are standing in line, a girl behind me starts crying, and I understand she is seeing spots in front of her eyes. Another memory is that we have a swimming competition, and my job is to do the breaststroke. As one may remember, I had learned this by being dangled on a sort of fishing line in the Moldau and my form was perfect. I hear one of the girls on the other team complain that it is not a fair competition because I am European and therefore know how to do the breaststroke better. So I must

133

have guessed or understood quite a bit of the language in a very short time. Nevertheless, it is a very eerie feeling to be thrown into another language, and to be struck dumb and uncomprehending.

Other adjustments were also needed quickly. I had been to many camps, but never this type of American camp. They wore uniforms, there was a schedule of activities and we changed from one to the other when a whistle blew. In Europe the day was not organized so tightly, though one might go on a scheduled excursion. Generally, I think we just "hung out." The new activities were strange, like archery and badminton and baseball, which I had never even heard of, as well as something called arts and crafts, where we braided leather key chains—very different from the embroidery lessons I had had in school. The strangest thing of all was the "color war" which occupied the last week of the camp. During that time, one wore the buff or the green uniform depending on which bunk one belonged to and every activity was a competition between the buffs and the greens. I can't remember whether I was a buff or a green, but I do remember that it was a great strain to be in competition all day for a week. It included how neatly we made our beds as well as excellence in sports. My contribution was the breaststroke.

When I returned from camp with a bundle of uniforms tied with string, as I had no suitcase, I did not mention anything about camp, or my "freak out" at the Rados. Nor was anything asked about it. I suppose it was just assumed that I had pulled myself together.

Camp had had a calming effect on me, being so totally removed from anything I had ever known before. From now on I endured our travails in varying states of denial, sometimes stoicism, and sometimes a withdrawal into a miasma of daydreams.

Mother had moved into the Hotel Franconia on West 72nd street. We had two rooms: a living room with a kitchenette alcove and a bedroom with bathroom behind it. Thomas arrived some months later. Eva and I shared the living room at night, while our elders had the bedroom. Mother had apparently started a small practice. She would see patients in the living room, and we would be huddled in the bedroom, having to be absolutely still so as not to disturb her or the patient. This was like being in jail; I had nothing to do, apparently nothing to read, could not play the radio. I remember lying on the bed in utter boredom and paralysis. I learned to empty my mind completely and to stay in a vacuum. I think there are some followers of eastern religions who would have envied me this capacity. What Thomas or Eva were doing, I don't remember. Luckily my mother's practice was not yet very big.

We cooked in the tiny kitchenette, on hotplates. Often at night my sister and I again, as we had in early Vienna, ate porridge, farina with small chocolate shavings sugar and milk. We must have been short of money because Thomas would order one quart and one pint of milk every two days, and on the second day we were always short of milk. Did I dare think at the time that we should order two quarts? I don't know, but I have thought this ever since. In the mornings I was amazed to get cold cereal; we never had seen this in Europe. It does seem we ate a lot of one or another type of cereal. The boxes themselves were astounding, full of cartoons, puzzles, and ads. On the back of one of the cereal boxes was an ad; for ten cents sent with a box top to Planters Peanuts one could receive foreign stamps, or some other trinket. With great excitement I sent a dime, the box top and my name and address. Every day I anxiously awaited the mail, but my promised order never came. This may seem like a major disappointment, but instead it taught me a lesson of great value. I became resistant to all ads and offers, cynical and suspicious. I am sure this has saved me a lot of money and disappointments over the years.

It was also in the Hotel Franconia that we children were introduced to household chores. My sister and I were required to alternate washing dishes, as well as doing the family wash. This we did in the bathtub, bending over, and scrunching our backs; it was awkward and at the same time strenuous.

As has been said, my mother had begun to work, and so certain tasks fell to the children. For instance, I was told I needed a haircut. I had arrived in this country with the bobbed, short hair that most children we knew wore, and was ashamed and horrified to see that here it was a fashion for girls to wear their hair long, not in braids, but hanging about their face. So I was pleased my hair was growing. I was given money and told to go to the barber—that is the men's barber—down the next street and get my hair cut. I think most ten-year-olds would be taken by a parent to have their hair cut, but I dutifully went alone. Of course, they cut it much too short for my taste and I was upset and hurt.

I realize now that my mother was as bewildered as I about all the new adjustments required of her, and had no room left over for the niceties of various hair styles. For her, I think the whole experience might have been a repetition of her own trauma during World War I. The experience of immigration, having to adjust to a new culture, make new friends and make a living to support two daughters and Thomas was probably a repetition of the having to *do it all on one's own* experience in her youth. Furthermore, she had already had other upheavals, moving to Berlin and Prague, reestablishing herself each time, as well as a messy divorce. So one should understand that she was tense, anxious, worried, and preoccupied. But the fact that the hair cut has stayed in my memory all these years, when in the scheme of things, it was so minor, reflects the fact that I badly wanted my mother to be more attentive to my needs and me.

There were other problems encountered in New York that were different from our lives in Europe. It may be recalled that I had traveled on my own all over Vienna at age six, and certainly had roamed all over Prague by myself. Now at age ten it was expected by me and my family that I would be able to go places by myself. In many ways New York was much safer than it is now. I remember as a young teenager traveling on the subway at 2 A.M. without any fear. However, there were obstacles, never encountered before. First there were, what can only be termed, "dirty" men. Men accosted me on the street and tried to touch me, or to get too close. I remember backing away from one man, totally embarrassed, unable to just turn and run. Later I learned to make absolutely cutting and rude remarks. In the beginning this was so horrifying that I could not mention it at home. The other obstacle was roving gangs of little black boys, in Central Park. perhaps ten years old, coming down from Harlem, who accosted and threatened one. These incidents were totally different than the later ones caused by tense race relations. These children meant no harm, just having "sport," but it was scary. In fact, I had no understanding of race at all, having never dealt with black people. I did not understand that these boys were picking on white people; I thought they were picking on girls, and that in turn must have startled these little boys.

It was time to enroll in school. Early one morning Mother accompanied me to the local public school located somewhere on or near Amsterdam Avenue, I have forgotten exactly where, or the school's number. When we got to the school, which was a very large, very old, brown building, Mother found to her dismay that there was a long line of parents and children at the principal's office. Mother had no time; she had an appointment with a patient and had to get back. We wandered disconsolately down the hall, and a teacher seated at her desk inside her classroom asked us what we were looking for. Mother said the fifth grade, and the teacher said, "I'll take her"

and Mother gratefully deposited me and left. The teacher, I believe was called Mrs. Katz, and was quite nice.

The school was formal; we sat at desks and during intervals had to put our hands in front of us and put our heads down. To speak one had to raise one's hand, but that I had already learned to do in Prague. In the morning on arrival there were separate entrances for boys and girls, which was strange too, but perhaps that prevented fighting and teasing.

In this school I was again confronted by my lack of English. I hardly could talk and understood little, and therefore I don't think I interacted with the other children. We studied explorers, I heard names like De Soto and Balboa, but I could not get interested in this history. Was it badly taught or was I just bored? I don't know. The previous year I had studied all about Bohemian history, which in the face of things is less interesting than the exploration of America. So I must have appeared rather dimwitted, but when we took a surprise written math test, I shone like a bright star, as of course I had learned much arithmetic in Prague. I remember the teacher's eyes lighting up as she discovered the little genius behind the stupid facade.

To help my English along, Mother gave me Huckleberry Finn to read, but it was overwhelming with all kinds of dialogue in dialect. Then she tried Mary Poppins. A light went on. I devoured that book with pure joy, and possibly my recollection is faulty, but I believe that after reading that book, I *knew* English. And I believe that since I used the baby method to learn the language—that is skipping over my conscious mind directly into new synapses in my brain's language center, I thought in English from the beginning and did not have to translate first from the German. I even dreamed in English. On the other hand, when I spoke in, or read German, I thought in that language. However, my husband claims that when he first married me, I would mumble in my sleep in German.

Having gotten no further than the American explorers in our studies of colonial history, I was suddenly moved from my public school to an elite, progressive private school called Walden—probably after Thoreau's pond. This was because Berta Bornstein had recently arrived in New York, had become the psychoanalytic child consultant to the school, and was able to wrangle scholarships for my sister and me. Here, instead of America, we studied ancient Egypt. This consisted, as far as I can remember, of building an Egyptian village out of papier-mâché. What I came away with was knowledge of how to make the papier-mâché. We also learned arithmetic entirely on our own through workbooks. I think I rapidly worked my way from the fifth to the eighth grade in these books, and I have forgotten almost all of what I learned. Certainly today, the handling of fractions remains a bit vague in my mind. Spelling was taught to us by writing long imaginative stories, poems, or essays and having the teacher mark up the papers in red pencil where there were errors. As English spelling is beyond the imagination of a child who grew up in the German language, my papers were crawling with red marks. These papers I carefully filed and never looked at the corrections. This lack of drill has left me virtually crippled in later life as far as spelling is concerned. However, my creativity was enhanced.

Walden also had many very good aspects. I learned wonderful arts and crafts, for instance making jewelry and metal bowls. In art I painted an oil of my mother in the nude. The art teacher solemnly told me that her abdomen was too yellow. I did not know the word "abdomen," and thought perhaps he was referring to her yellow pubic hair. I do believe that this portrait shows I was willing to adapt in two directions: the conventional restricted, proper mode of ordinary society, or the free progressive expression of my early upbringing, where sex and bodies was in the open and *anything goes*. At Walden we called our teachers by their first names, something that I had been raised to do with my parents (though in this memoir, I refer to Annie as Mother and Willi as Father.) One day Mrs. Katz, from the old school, appeared to learn about Walden, she recognized me, and I believe that I behaved in a sassy manner to her—though I had liked her —she represented the repressive instead of the progressive to me.

At some point, perhaps a year later, our container arrived bearing all our furniture and we moved to an apartment of six rooms, on 96th street near Central Park West. This became our permanent home for almost 25 years. It was a tall apartment building and we moved to the 16th floor. It had doormen, elevator men, and two wings, a fancy lobby and an awning that went to the street, so one would not get wet in the rain as one got into a taxi. To outward appearances we settled into New York and seemed to begin to live a "normal" life. At least my mother must have settled in, she had enough income to meet the rent—which because of the depression was rather low—and to feel that she could reestablish a home. We even acquired a maid, who I believe worked for $8/week. She was called Mamie, to me a very strange name. Thomas again did the cooking, and we children washed the dishes. There were washing machines in the basement which Mamie used, so Eva and I stopped doing the laundry in the bathtub.

Chapter 8
ATTEMPTS AT ADJUSTING

Having ensconced ourselves in a permanent residence, with Mother in the process of establishing a practice and the children placed in a school, we seemed to have arrived at a suitable adjustment to living in America. However, in reality, the aftermath of the dislocation took many years to heal. Of all of us, Mother had made the most fortuitous accommodation to her new surroundings. She was enveloped by a number of very close female friends, all of whom settled on 96th Street, within our building or across the street. The Loewenfelds were right around the corner, and a number of other friends lived within walking distance. The New York Psychoanalytic Institute and Society soon resembled a reconstituted Viennese Psychoanalytic Society admixed with members from Berlin and Prague. Despite the Depression, psychoanalysis began to flourish. Fairly soon after we moved to our apartment Mother seems, despite persistent worries about finances, to have established a full, though low-fee, psychoanalytic practice. Thus, she was able to maintain her basic identity, that of a psychoanalyst.

Not everything was smooth sailing for her; there was the matter of licensing, there were struggles within the psychoanalytic community, and there were general cultural adjustments to be made. I remember Mother sitting in her bedroom/office studying for her licensing exam. How difficult this must have been for her. She had never practiced medicine, had an internship, or worked at anything besides psychoanalysis. She never even did psychotherapy; all her patients lay on the couch and came five-days-a week. Perhaps some came four-times a week, but somehow, I doubt it. Since licensing was not necessary to practice psychoanalysis, she was lucky in being able to practice while the arrangements for these examinations were prolonged over more than a year. She had no experience with psychiatry, neurology or mental retardation. I admired her ability to study and to concentrate; I also never sensed resentment against the unnecessary requirement, imposed by the American Psychoanalytic Association that only medical doctors could be members.

The European psychoanalysts came here with the desire to continue the agenda set by Anna and Sigmund Freud, of preserving *"true psychoanalysis."* Historically Freud had adhered to this agenda over many splits and upheavals within the psychoanalytic movement. (Bergman, M. 1997). Now these desires, or one should say anxieties, took on new meaning. The wish to preserve the '*true psychoanalysis*' had had severe blows in the past five years. First there were the negotiations and compromises with the Nazis to keep psychoanalysis alive in Germany. Then Anna Freud came to England in 1938 and found that the British were embracing her rival Melanie Klein. Finally, Freud had always thought that the Americans would *dilute* psychoanalysis, clean up its sexuality and deny the Oedipus complex; the refugee analysts felt they needed to ward off this dilution. They ignored that they themselves were forever changing or advancing psychoanalysis, even themselves veering from sexuality and the Oedipus complex, that is diminishing their importance, and so were not open to ideas held by others, especially Americans. The psychoanalysis that evolved in New York was basically different from the one Fenichel had preached in Prague. Fenichel adhered to the structural theory and conflicts about guilt, especially from the oedipal period. The New York analysts led by Hartman, Kris and Loewenstein added the concepts of conflicts between libido and aggression, neutralization of aggressive energy

142

by libidinal energy, and the use of this neutralized energy to form ego functions—which were adaptive, and creative, and often autonomous from the instincts. They were also trying to expand psychoanalysis into a general psychology that could be used to explain all mental phenomena.

Not all the New York analysts were quite comfortable with these more abstract theories. I remember Berta Bornstein complaining to my mother that one did not need this whole new theory of aggression. Berta basically stuck to the more classic structural theory. Faced with the terrible aggression that was building in the world, these analysts could not deny the importance of aggression. Indeed, I agree with this, as my future patients suffered often more with aggressive affects than sexual desires. These analysts also stressed adaptation. Considering what they had personally gone through before they arrived here, one can understand that adaptation became for them a very important ego function. The forerunners of the ideas of adaptation were seen in Anna Freud's work with children where she stressed adaptation and education in behavior and ego functions. In fact, the New York Psychoanalytic Institute resembled an extension of Anna Freud's Hempstead Clinic in London.

Anna Freud had a lot to do with the developing dissension within the New York Psychoanalytic Institute during which time a series of analysts were ejected or squeezed out, Horney, Thompson, and Rado amongst them. Once these splits had occurred the ejected analysts were persona-non-grata and were extruded not only from the organization, the journals, and the meetings, but also from social contacts. This must have been awkward for my mother who was indebted to Rado for his help with our immigration and the fact that she knew him well from Berlin. From my vantage point, I only saw that Rado had completely disappeared, was never mentioned, did not exist.

I am not sure that Horney had ever been a friend of Mother's. Horney's "crimes" had started around 1926, when she dared question Freud's concept of penis envy, and came up with a much more interesting set of theories of female psychosexual development. For these ideas she was literally hounded out with witticisms and humor. I remember Bert Lewin, years later, while giving a talk in Pittsburgh, incomprehensibly bursting into raucous laughter while describing that Horney once in Berlin had discussed a dream where a field of asparagus was being cut down and had denied that they represented penises. Horney's reaction to this criticism was to start questioning many of the psychoanalytic precepts. She developed a theory of neurosis based on "today" and not the past. Clara Thompson was much influenced by Ferenczi, who at that time was in disrepute, by stressing interpersonal relations in therapy. So both of these women had to be extruded—though in fact they themselves walked out of the organization—so they would not "corrupt" the candidates studying at the institute. Rado's crime was that he formed his own institute at Columbia University, which threatened political control rather than theory. Later he also started to deviate from "true" psychoanalysis.

In my view, Mother went along with all these rejections, and stuck strictly to the sense of orthodoxy that ensued. It was obviously dangerous to disagree with Anna Freud and if one wanted to further develop theory one had to couch it in terms that led back to Freud's writings. Melanie Klein was "bad" and "wrong" because she thought "an infant had a superego." Erik Erikson was vague and confused, those American analysts who lived in Chicago were into "dependency needs" and Mother asked, "What is that?" She actually sneered at the idea. Dependency needs were not part of the libido theory. I find this ironic because in my own upbringing she never recognized this same need in me.

It is my opinion that Mother was so rigid in these opinions because she had to make sure that she was an integral part of the New York psychoanalytic scene. She had left Vienna under a cloud, having defied Anna Freud. She had been married to the rebel Wilhelm Reich who dared question Freud on masochism and eventually developed theories about

144

muscular armor. Anna Freud, her analyst, had been pressuring her to leave her marriage and my mother had defied her by rejoining my father in Berlin. I think, she felt insecure and afraid that she herself might be suspect or put out on the fringes. Indeed, in many ways she was on the fringes, always politely treated and socially acceptable, but never part of the inner core. The inner core was a much more formal group, who, I am sure, had proper houses with proper dining rooms and bedrooms, proper parties, and were properly married. The inner core was deeply involved with Anna Freud, considered friends by her, while Mother always had a formal association with Anna and had to prove her loyalty for ever and ever. One could observe the tension and formality Mother exhibited around the Hartmans, Kris's, and especially Anna Freud, compared to her relaxed attitudes around Edith Jacobson, or Mädi Olden. However, I believe that her adherence to classical psychoanalytic orthodoxy was genuine and heartfelt. So, it can be understood, that even though Mother did not have to adjust to the American psychoanalytic scene, this belonging was fraught with tensions predating immigration. She had avoided these conflicts by moving to Prague instead of returning to Vienna, but they now had caught up with her.

Adjusting to American customs, cultural attitudes and mores was a struggle for Mother. She did immediately get legally married to Thomas, as their casual arrangement was not acceptable in this country in the 1930's. Over time she became more formal in her appearance—actually wore some lipstick—and home decor. However, she remained a cultural snob, feeling that European culture was vastly superior to American. She disdained Hollywood, bestsellers, comic books, jazz, and the blues. She had no comprehension of dances like the Lindy. She frequented foreign films, classical music concerts, and read good literature. She developed, over time,

145

enough flexibility to appreciate the Broadway stage and the musicals that developed in New York after World War II. She appreciated modern art and was very taken with Picasso. However, at the beginning of our stay here, we children heard nothing but put downs of what America had to offer and great anxiety that our taste would be corrupted by the popular culture around us. Luckily for her it was possible to get European cakes and cookies at the bakery across the street.

It was inevitable that mother's adherence to European cultural values would clash with my budding identification with America. We first went head-to-head over comic books. I discovered them and was enthralled. Mother would have fits of anxiety if she discovered me reading one. She was sure my tastes in both art and literature would be forever corrupted. And eventually one might suppose she was proven right, as I developed much appreciation for the more sophisticated versions of American pop-culture. She started me off reading, at much too young an age, the great literature of Europe. But I ended up admiring books like "Rebecca" by Daphne Du Maurie. To her this was trash because it was a best seller. In anticipation of Andy Warhol, I had a memorable discussion with her at about age 11 while walking toward Broadway on a very rare shopping trip. I pointed to a large billboard with the face of a man and asked, "So why is this not as good as a Rembrandt?" Agitatedly she fumbled for words but could formulate no proper discussion on aesthetics.

Her biggest adjustment problem was never resolved; it was to recreate the outdoor life she had led in Vienna in her youth. Vienna is surrounded by the Wienerwald, and she used to walk there on any Sunday that she was in town. Walking had been the main way she socialized with her friends. In summer one could also go swimming at little lakes or little beaches along the Donau (Danube). There were difficulties already in Prague to keep up this habit because Prague is surrounded by flat ugly countryside. In New York it felt impossible to her. I remember a painful Sunday excursion with a friend called Tät, and the Loewenfelds, soon after we arrived here. We took a Greyhound bus out of town, perhaps fifty miles, then hiked to a reservoir, through thick woods, and then went swimming where I am sure swimming was forbidden. On the way back the bus did not stop for us, and we had to ask for a ride at a gas station. What stuck in my mind was the desperation with which we tried to recreate the familiar activity. After this, over the years, Mother found little patches of natural spaces, often packed between highways, where one could take a walk. Eventually she discovered beautiful places one could travel to on vacation: The White Mountains, Bar Harbor, and finally the West; over time her complaints against America faded.

In general Mother exuded to us children anxiety, tension, worry, and a great sense of her total responsibility. She also had a terrific work ethic, which she tried to pass on to us, and an extremely regulated life. She started work every morning at 7A.M, broke for a two-hour break for lunch, then worked till 7P.M, at which time Thomas would have the meal ready on the table. All this took a toll and by 1942 she was diagnosed with severe hypertension. Whether this was due purely to stress or partly to kidney problems in her youth, I don't know. There was no treatment available at the time and instead she underwent horrendous diets of absolutely no salt; at one time eating just rice as it was thought that the Japanese were healthier because of their rice intake. Eventually this hypertension led to a series of strokes and disabilities.

In contrast to my mother, who all in all adjusted fairly well to America, Thomas was diminished and demolished by the immigration. For one thing he could not learn English. Here was a man who spoke several Slavic languages, French and German, but simply could not grasp English. Perhaps at approximately 56 years of age, he was too old. Perhaps the will to adjust had gone out of him. Whatever importance he had had in the past was not known or appreciated here, and there were only a few people around who had known him before. Thomas was reduced to cooking for the household, and endlessly rewriting his Russian history.

Stalin's power was at its height and there were several political murders committed overseas, the most notable was the murder of Leon Trotsky in Mexico in 1939. This was important to Thomas because it meant the Communists were pursuing their enemies even outside Russia. Thomas felt pressure, I believe, to remain obscure and avoid a similar fate. One day he saw a psychoanalyst, who lived on the other side from us across the apartment house lobby, in the company of a GPU (later KGB) agent whom Thomas knew. Afraid of having been recognized, Thomas hastily withdrew back into the elevator, badly shaken. This incident shows how deeply entrenched the Stalinist Communist party was in America before the war; so that ordinary people like psychoanalysts were still associated with it. This is despite the infamous 1936 Moscow trials, that kangaroo court where Stalin got rid of his worst rivals, the subsequent purges of millions of Russians, and the Stalin-Hitler non-aggression pact. Thomas felt himself in danger and he might very well have been in danger, but these fears made him more anxious in general and thus seem to have contributed to his increasing obsessions about the house. It must not have helped that he had no more role to play in life and felt totally dependent on my mother. He had a few friends in New York, left over from Prague, and greatly enjoyed them, but I don't think he was part of my mother's psychoanalytic world.

The children had a very difficult time adjusting. The problem was how to remain "ourselves" and at the same time fit into our peer group. Mother expected us to be "well adjusted" and that meant fitting into the peer group. At the same time of course, we also needed friends and acceptance. America was in the midst of the Depression, but amongst the people we met there was an ambiance of smart-aleck jocularity, wisecrack repartee, and an unwillingness to show any deep emotions. Added to this was a New York type of sophistication and nonchalance best illustrated by the *New Yorker* magazine of that time. Into this atmosphere came two refugee girls who had anxiously seen Hitler advance into Czechoslovakia and then start a European war. We felt we had narrowly escaped Hitler, always a step away from his invasions and we did not feel safe yet. We were much too serious for the youth of New York. We did not understand the kidding that was ubiquitous. Either we did not laugh when we should, or we tried to join in and were too aggressive. We could not grasp the nuances or idiom of the culture. We could not understand why young people were so totally uninterested in politics and in the impending war.

Furthermore, we were serious about money, and future careers. The idea that one should be a housewife was anathema to my mother. We expected to have careers and we never thought a man should support us. So, at a time when women were supposed to grow up to be mothers and housewives, and the fondest dream of all men was to earn enough so their wife would not be forced to work, we were swimming against the stream. Now perhaps the stream has caught up with us, but at the time "liberation" was alien and not approved of. Even as children we expected that we should earn money as the burden of supporting us was, we felt, too hard on our mother. We had lived enough years on an economic edge fraught with anxiety and had not yet come to foresee that our life in America would turn out to be financially so much more lucrative. These attitudes made us much too serious company for our American peers. It must be remembered that we had settled on the Upper West Side of Manhattan and went to a private school. This area of New York was divided between masses of poor people and the relatively financially secure, who lived in the large apartment houses. The two groups

149

never mixed. Perhaps in households more affected by the Depression and poverty other children also held our attitude about money.

Perhaps because of her early communist training, my sister could not accept our financial well-being when it finally developed. As an adult she lived as if she had taken a vow of poverty. Any excess money, that she accumulated, she would give away to "good" causes thereby always living on a perilous edge. At the same time she would express angry, envious comments about "Yuppies," who had wealth and comfort.

Since the 30's and 40's the relationship between the sexes has also undergone an enormous change. At that time popularity was all important, girls had to date as many boys as possible. If a boy called for a Saturday night date after a Wednesday she had to refuse, pretending she already had a date, because if one was dateless, one was "not popular." On top of that, boys were out to get as far as they could go sexually with a girl and then add it as notches of conquest to their belts; however, girls were not supposed to allow the boy anything. If a couple did get sexually active, they were not supposed to go "all the way," because the girl had to save her reputation. Boys would brag to each other on how far they got. Girls would be known as cheap and too easy if they were doing more than necking. Necking was above the waist; petting was below the waist and could ruin a girl's reputation. Virginity in women was highly prized. Magazines such as *True Confession* and *Red Book* were full of stories of girls who gave in once to sex and ruined their life forever with a pregnancy. Boys on the other hand were not supposed to be inexperienced. This was called the double standard. In Europe there was no "dating." Boys and girls hung out in groups, and when they were serious, they paired off, and in advanced circles became sexually active. In America dating was a very tense activity, as one had to be entertaining and light. Girls had to be very interested in the boys' hobbies and interests but have no interests or hobbies of their own. Girls were not to be smart. I remember one boy derisively calling me a "brain" when I was in college. As one was supposed to date widely the couple really did not know each other well. The idea of "going steady" was a post-war phenomenon not yet invented. When a couple finally did get serious it was practically an engagement.

To two girls raised in a radical European family, whose father was the chief proponent of "sexual freedom" for adolescents, these American customs were completely incomprehensible. My sister, who I suspect had already been sexually active in Europe, utterly refused to go along with these mores. Perhaps that is why she had to continue her analysis with Berta Bornstein, when the latter arrived here. I was never told what that was about, but I do know that Berta would insist that one should not latch on to a boy or be so intense.

I, on the other hand, started to grow up in utter confusion. I arrived here at age ten, too young for dating, and with only a very vague romantic interest in boys. I found the combination of taboo and rules of permission unsettling and confounding. In fifth grade I was introduced to the game "spin the bottle," which actually shocked me with its daring and promiscuity, but also offended with its requirement one kiss a boy one did not like. Later, the artificiality of dating seemed necessary but not really enjoyable. One often would go out with a boy only once and then never see him again. Was this because I was flawed in some way, or because it was all part of the sampling of popularity? The boys would pay for everything, though they were not working yet, and then it was required one repay them with a kiss at the door. The messages on sexuality were ambivalent but biased against any real involvement. I finally settled on an internal double standard, a split between my family values and my outward conformity.

Trying to "fit in" to the prevailing fifth grade culture, I wished to copy the activities of the other children. The girls all had scrapbooks of movie stars which they showed proudly, sharing romantic fantasies with each other. So

I also made a scrapbook, but I failed to understand the fundamentals of the star system and the fan system. I had not seen movies, knew nothing of stars except for Shirley Temple and Charley Chaplin, and so missed the underlying motive for the scrapbook. I randomly cut out photos from magazines and pasted them in my own scrapbook. The other children looked at me as if I were nuts.

I was better at catching on to the game of jacks, a game gone from our culture today, which we played with great concentration. It consisted of bouncing a little ball while picking up little metal double star shaped jacks, first singly then doubly then triply etc. Great skill was required. Coming from a school in Prague where we never had occasion to play in school, or socially interact, I found this aspect of my new life enjoyable and enticing.

What I had a hard time adjusting to was the use of makeup on relatively young girls. There was no makeup worn in Central Europe at that time—despite Sally Bowles in *Cabaret*. If it was worn in clubs or at night, I never saw it. Besides this, my mother had belonged to the naturalist movement of the Wandervögel who would have disapproved because it was artificial and not necessary. Now I saw 12 and 13-year-olds not only wearing lipstick, but also a gooey mess called pancake makeup. This was smeared on the face, then powder and rouge were applied, as well as mascara. I did not know what to think of this. I did not find it very pretty and nothing would induce me to gook up my face with stuff that would not let my pores breath. I never applied this kind of cover to my natural skin, and I don't think I needed it. Like my mother I did grow up to use lipstick, though at that time this was bright red and looked funny on my face. I did envy what girls could do with their hair, and never was able to learn how to do it, but I never envied the makeup. In my freshman year at high school the other girls were so shocked at my bare face that they tried to teach me the fundamentals. I thought them strange, and they thought me strange. There were even some models in my senior class, they walked around in perfect makeup, looking much older

152

than the rest of us, but to me they seemed as if they had dried out dust for skin. On the other hand, they exuded a poise I could not emulate. I believe they were very nice people, but one could not get to know them because of their maturity and grace.

There were also graver difficulties in adjustment. If the children I knew had no interest in politics, the coming war, or Hitler, there were too many grown-ups one met, who were Communists and "fellow-travelers." In Europe, I had only met people who were disillusioned with the Communists, hated Stalin and distrusted Soviet propaganda. Now suddenly New York was full of idealist, ignorant grown-ups who worshipped the Soviet system, believed it had the best health care in the world and could do no wrong. For years, even past the war into the middle fifties, these people followed the Communist party line, having no idea it was dictated by Moscow, marched in May Day Parades and thought of themselves as "good people." They saw no contradiction between their own income, often from capitalist sources, and their dedication for the "cause." They went through the party line changes of "popular front," "socialist realism," Stalin Hitler pact, and "open up the second front" with unquestioning enthusiasm. The Moscow trials of 1936, the ensuing persecution of millions of Russians as capitalist agents, who had to be placed in gulags or executed, the murder of Trotsky, the forced collectivizations, with their ensuing famines, the expansion of Russia into Poland, the Baltic states, the invasion of Finland, and the neighboring Asian states, and the forcible movement of whole ethnic populations had no effect in damping enthusiasm. These aberrations, if they were admitted to, were simply thought to be "growing pains" in a new social experiment. Their adherence to "the cause" helped people form social bonds not seen again till the student movement of the 60's. Currently, remembrance of this idealization of the Soviet Union has been completely forgotten, replaced by the horrors and strains created by the excesses of the Joseph McCarthy witch hunts of the 50's. Now people believe that "you saw a Communist under every bed" and deny how large a following there was, at least in New York. Of course, these people were not spies as they were out in the open. Instead they did put enormous pressure on public opinion, the arts, and the media.

I first met this enthusiasm for all things Soviet when as a fifth grader, new from Europe, fearful of Hitler's expansion. I was confronted by my Communist fifth grade teacher. The party line at that time was opposed to American armament for war. This was related to the "popular front" period of the Communist party and the party line was for peace and against armament. My teacher was opposed to armament, and I was desperately hoping for American intervention. There I was, a ten-year-old child arguing with my teacher. I was shocked because by this time I thought no sane person would underestimate Hitler's intentions of expanding into all of Europe and possibly the world, nor that they would not comprehend what was going on in Russia.

As an adolescent, I began studying modern dance in the Martha Graham mode. It was tremendously enjoyable. After a while, a group of us were asked to give performances in places like union halls. I spent much time in classes, rehearsals and performances. One day in 1941, my dance teacher invited us to a mass meeting at Madison Square Garden. The whole arena was filled with people, a huge crowd. There was a great atmosphere of belonging and togetherness. Speeches were made, people were wildly enthusiastic. I had just turned 13 and was probably not too aware of what the evening meant. After such a late meeting I was hung over at school the next day. When I explained to my teacher that I had been to a meeting, she exclaimed "little girls should be in bed on a school night." On later reconstruction this was the time Hitler invaded the Soviet Union, thereby undoing the Stalin-Hitler non-aggression pact. The Communist Party had to change its "line." From now on its followers were to be pro-war, pro-armament, pro-draft, and to support the Soviet Union in its time of stress. After this meeting one of my fellow dancers came to class and explained to us that we were being

154

used; that we had been performing in front of Communist party meetings without this ever being made clear to us. The Modern School of Dance was a Communist front organization. Putting this together with the mass meeting I had attended, I had to agree, and a whole number of us quit the troupe; unfortunately, also giving up a most enjoyable activity.

The greatest shock, making adjustment difficult, had to do with ethnicity and religion. The American ideal at that time was the "melting pot," in which all immigrants would be slowly mixed into the culture and become Americans. In reality it was a country full of ethnic and religious awareness and prejudice. Not only was there Jim Crow, hatred of Poles, Italians, and Irish, but also many clubs, hotels, resorts, and possibly apartments houses had restricted against Jews. As a result of this prejudice, these immigrant groups held on to their identity and pride in who they were. Wherever we went the first question asked of us was our identity. Were we Jewish? Were we German? We had no idea that Jewish meant an ethnic identity, we thought it was a religion. Nor did we know how to respond to being called German. For us this was anathema, for by this time German meant "Nazi." We were *Austrians*, not Germans and had a different cultural ethos and history. The pressure on us to conform and belong to one of the identity groups was insistent and intrusive. Actually, we did belong to such a group, but since it was minuscule, it was not known and therefore not recognized as legitimate. Over the years I have met many other people who belong to our group. They were mostly Viennese, but also other Europeans; they are non-believers, uninterested in the ethnic identity of people, but culturally and intellectually sophisticated, modern in their sexual attitudes, gender attitudes, and probably in their own way frightful snobs. The greatest trouble my sister and I encountered was because we celebrated Christmas and Easter, true in its original pagan form, but still perceived by others as Christian holidays. We had never heard of Hanukah or Passover. This made

155

us anti-Semites in the eyes of our questioners. Many years later, I remember one woman physician, we thought of as a friend, who, when she found out we had a Christmas tree accused me of having murdered her grandmother. What could we, refugees from the Nazis, say to a statement like that? Even much later a Catholic Priest at an agency where I was employed as a supervisor of therapists, accused me of being "just like Hitler" when I opined that a woman whose life was seriously endangered by a pregnancy should have a therapeutic abortion. I had all I could do to prevent myself from pointing out that my family had done more to fight Hitler than his beloved church.

No one talks of "the melting pot" anymore, and maybe it was an impossible ideal, but I think my sister and I adhered to this ideal. Not that we would become amalgamated and identical, but that we were all Americans and had a common culture even if we also had different backgrounds and beliefs.

I have tried to portray that it took my sister and me some years to fit into American culture. We did this eventually by reconstituting ourselves into recognizable personas.

Chapter 9

FATHER ARRIVES (1939)

My father arrived in New York in the fall of 1939, on the last boat to leave Norway before the war started. He had been granted a special visa for teaching at the New School for Social Research. I had not seen him, really, since 1934; the summer I visited him in Denmark which ended in the disastrous expulsion from the IPA in Lucerne, where he had become so angry and frightening. It is true that he appeared in the summer of 1935 to return my sister, but I don't think he interacted with me at all. After that at the request of Berta Bornstein he had no contact with my sister or me because it was "interfering with Eva's analysis." In general, he had been obliterated, was not mentioned, and did not exist. At the same time that he did not exist, we were made to understand that he was "crazy" and therefore deserved not to exist. Many years later, reading the *Fenichel Rundbriefe*, I realized that in 1935 there was a general preoccupation amongst his former left-wing psychoanalytic colleagues, to disassociate themselves from Reich and calling him crazy was very important to aid this endeavor. My mother had very strong motives to convince herself, and us, that he was crazy. She had been enthralled and abused by him and had finally been able to separate herself by denigrating him and feeling contempt. At the same time, she was terribly afraid that he would unduly influence us girls, and she fought valiantly to protect us. Her methods were to let us know he was crazy and at the same time to obliterate him, never mentioning him, and I am now

157

sure, censoring the mail and presents that were sent us. How one can both call someone crazy and at the same time never mention him is a puzzle to me as I write this. However, this was accomplished, for me he was a blank, a space, a non-existence.

So here in New York, in the middle of the painful adjustment to our immigration there appeared this crazy, non-existent stranger, who was determined to pick up his relationship with us where it had been left off. Psychoanalysts talk of splitting and that is the only way I can explain my relationship with him. I compartmentalized our relationship as it developed in the next couple of years, keeping it separate from the view of him that he was persona non-grata, not to be trusted and unpredictable in his temper. This compartmentalization was necessary because the real man had a lot to offer. He seems to have had more money than my mother. There was none of the aura of poverty, financial anxiety and uncertainty that hovered about my mother's house. He rented and later bought a house in Queens. (Recently when reading James Martin *Wilhelm Reich and the Cold War*, I understood that some admiring students at the New School bought the house for him.) The only person I had ever known to own a house in a city was my uncle Lutz, but I don't think he moved into it while I lived in Vienna. In cities people lived in dark apartment houses without yards. And here my father lived in a house, but I don't think it had much of a yard or that gardening was done. Furthermore, he bought a car, a convertible, very sporty and exciting. He was much more fun than my mother, who was hedged in with anxiety and worry. He would invite a friend and me and drive us to Jones Beach, or take us to the World's Fair. He believed in having fun; he ate in restaurants; he played tennis; he even went dancing in clubs. Immigration seems not to have left him with the bewilderment and tension we had at home. Reading his diaries, one realizes this was not completely true, but what is true is that he could forget these things and enjoy himself. It took my mother years to gain or regain a sense of fun.

I remember sitting in the convertible, the breeze ruffling my hair, as we sped to Jones Beach—a beautiful long sandy beach, reachable only by car. Very little traffic was on the road to bother us privileged few who could afford to ride to this public paradise; the sun shining, my father in a good mood, my friend impressed. I don't remember that we went swimming or sat on the beach. Maybe this was not beach weather and that is why it was so empty and beautiful. I remember endless days at the World's Fair. In fact, I did not realize that this was a temporary institution. I took it for granted as a New York entertainment. I went there often, not only with my father. I remember the GM pavilion, where one sat in moving seats and passed an amazing panorama of superhighways with clover-leaf ramps. These were predicted for the future, nothing like it existed. And I remember a demonstration of television. One was televised in one room and then went into the next and saw oneself on the screen. I don't think I had any idea what it was I was watching, probably comparing it to some sort of instant film. Because of the war, actual television was not commercially developed till the late 1940s. My father took us to the amusement park section of the fair, where there were rides. This was expensive and I never thought of going there when on my own. He did not go on the rides himself. I realize now that he was acting in the same way as most divorced fathers, who have visiting rights with their children, that is, needing to entertain them. Just as most children, I saw my mother concerned about life and work and poverty while he seemed to have not a care in the world.

But there were reminders to be careful with this relationship and not to get too involved. There were several heated arguments with Mother on the telephone, exasperating her, probably frightening her, and tending to let us understand that we were transgressing in these visits. It reminded us that the man was unpredictable, could become irate, insistent, and difficult. They fought about my piano lessons. I have no idea what the contention was about. Certainly not money, for he never paid for us, and Mother never asked. Perhaps he wanted a more prestigious teacher. I do know that the end of my piano lessons came when I agreed to let him send me to a well-known violinist called Kolish to continue my studies. Kolish had lost a part of a finger in an accident, and I think was giving lessons because he could not play professionally, but I am sure all his students were real musicians. It was typical of my father to imagine that if you were studying the piano, you were studying professionally, just as if you wrote a composition for school or a short story, you were aiming at being a great writer. Kolish was probably a patient of my fathers, or so I imagine now. This relationship between my teacher and my father led to a great deal of tension in Kolish, lending itself to an atmosphere which I could not grasp; a mix of resentment for having to teach me, curiosity about me, and probably fear that my father would not approve of the results. At the same time, I found the tension unbearable and vaguely sexual. It might just have been the intimacy with a strange man. But certainly Kolish expected me to sit with him and play duets while sight-reading. This was way beyond my abilities, as I had just practiced pieces till I knew them by heart. I was so embarrassed I gave up the piano altogether.

Soon we were introduced to a woman my father was living with, called Ilse Ollendorff. He later married Ilse and begot a brother for us. My brother and Ilse are still part of my family long after both my father and mother have died. What was strange to me about Ilse is that she ran a household, cooked, and acted in general like an ordinary wife. My mother never went near the kitchen. When we lived with my father in Berlin, the family rarely ate together, but here was my father eating supper with us at the kitchen table, cabbage, pork chops and mashed potatoes. To me this not only seemed strange but somehow belittling, almost lower class; so firmly had I established the idea that our lifestyle in Berlin had been normal. Perhaps it was the act of eating in the kitchen instead of in the dining room that seemed so déclassé to me. (Although in my mother's house we still ate in the combined dining room/children's bedroom, and I never thought about that!) I am sure the dining room of my father's house had been co-opted for workspace. In Denmark we had eaten on a vine-shaded patio, and that seemed all right. My silent scorn was a sign that all was not great between my father and me; he was on trial and being judged. He also tried valiantly to include us and interest us in his ongoing experiments. He showed us photographs of one-celled organisms, tumors in mice, and the fact that a gold leaf would sway under some electronic impulse. All these things were meant to prove something, but he never explained what it was he was working on. We were to be impressed, to ask questions and get involved, and perhaps my sister did these things. I just stared uncomprehendingly, but with skepticism. The stricture I came with and labored under was that his work was crazy and nonsense. People who have read his work or know of it, realize he was developing ideas of the generation of life under certain conditions, working on a cure for cancer, and beginning to have ideas about energy, later called orgone energy, that could be measured. He asked me to look at the sky and then I would see shimmering translucent circles swarming about. To him this was orgone energy; to my mother these were red blood corpuscles floating by. I could not develop a genuine interest in the things he showed me, and being a very perceptive man, I am sure he knew it. Our relationship therefore stayed superficial and did not deepen.

There were subtle tensions between us that eventually led to a break. For instance, he urged us to ask him anything we wanted to know about sex. So I asked him if he had ever been to a prostitute. This produced a storm of rage in him, reminiscent of my early childhood, where asking him questions had had the same result. He did not explain what enraged him so. I know now that sex was sacred for him, it was not to be profaned with a prostitute, but I had no idea then. What I got out of this conversation was that he was unpredictable and that I had to be cautious. All this emphasis on sex made him somehow dangerous. Also, it may be remembered that in Denmark he forced us to have a nude picture taken. The humiliation of that incident was not forgotten. He went on a campaign to have us sleep over. Apparently, a room had been prepared for us. I adamantly refused. How could I explain to him that he made me uncomfortable?

My refusal to stay overnight at his house had dire consequences. Father was very sensitive and worried that he was being accused of being a child-molester by my mother and that she was conveying this to her children. He felt misunderstood and hounded in general over his sexual theories and research. In Denmark there had been a vicious newspaper campaign against him as a "sex maniac" and he had been expelled from the country. In Norway he had been under similar pressures. Whether he already, at that time, believed that my mother was behind all this persecution, I don't know. It was his intensity and insistence about the overnight stay that was too much for a thirteen-year-old girl, and his sensitivity made it impossible for him to understand.

The upshot of my refusal was an absolutely horrendous fight with my mother on the telephone, to which I unfortunately listened on the extension. My mother, much put out, finally laid out a number of complaints at him, including that he had been her psychoanalyst and then he had taken her to bed. He responded with a sarcastic remark implying that she had enjoyed it. This was too much for little ears. I hung up, terribly embarrassed that grown-ups could so openly talk about their sex life. Of course, my mother heard the click as I hung up. Not understanding what I had taken away from the conversation, she, as an analyst, worried terribly about the future transference implications about hearing that he had bedded her after being her analyst. Sure enough, when a few years later she referred me to an analyst, she mentioned to him that I had heard this conversation. Actually, that is not what I had focused on; it was his remark that she enjoyed it.

Mother never said a word to me about listening in on her phone conversation. Not confronting issues was so much her style; but this made my father's insistence and intrusiveness so much worse for me. I was not used to speaking openly about embarrassing topics. I was caught fundamentally between two styles of being. My mother, always cautious, avoided confrontations and expressions of feelings, my father demanded that one look him straight in the eye and open up one's deepest feelings and thoughts. Somehow, I missed the nuance of this with him. Unable to ever express my deepest feelings to him, I yet managed, when I did open up with a statement or a question, to "put my foot in my mouth."

My father was unaware how his very nature, as well as his theories and technique of therapy, lent themselves to misinterpretation. He had been influenced by the German nudist movement, nudity was normal, the body part of nature. He was also convinced that sexuality should not be suppressed by authoritarian society and that children and adolescents should enjoy their bodies, masturbate freely, and in adolescence enjoy intercourse. In fact, suppression of sexuality was thought to lead to character armor and pathology. But his nature was authoritarian, and he tended to impose himself on people. I think he wanted to force them to exhibit their sexuality to him and to surrender themselves to his authority. If one reads *Character Analysis,* one already gets the impression that he was able to pressure his patients into *admitting* their negative thoughts and I think by this admission to submit themselves to positive feelings for him. Later when he invented anti-armor body techniques, he would make patients be able to burp in front of him and pass gas; I am sure also to experience orgasm in front of him. His rationale was to release tension in the muscles created by inhibitions. But other people sometimes experienced his methods as making them expose themselves, ostensibly to overcome shame, but perhaps unconsciously to make them feel shame. If he had such desires he hid them under strong theoretical rationales. But I don't think he was ever prurient or salacious. He always was deadly serious about the theoretical necessities for his behavior.

The effect on me was to absolutely wish not to give in to him. He wanted absolute honesty, I was evasive, he wished confession, and I was secretive. I think I understood that giving him anything would lead to further demands and a kind of taking over. I felt he wanted to shame me and force me into some kind of submission. I can say in retrospect having watched my sister, and seen how her life evolved, that my observations were correct. My stubborn resistance saved me—my identity and my integrity—but at a price; as we all know defense mechanisms that were helpful in childhood often become misapplied in later life.

The great fight with my mother about my refusal to sleep over was the end of his trying to be charming and entertaining. He started pressuring me, threateningly or so it seemed to me, and repeating and insisting that I sleep at his house. Finally, I got the impression that he was threatening my mother. In a valiant effort at defending her, I felt I had to threaten him back. I said that my mother had powerful friends who would defend her. He started cross-questioning me tightly about who these friends were. His insistence was overwhelming. "The Psychoanalysts," I stammered. "Who, who" he asked. Finally, I mentioned Lawrence Kubie, the only name I could think of. This remark of mine led to a cause célèbre, which he spread to all his followers and friends. By misfortune, shortly after our forced and pressured conversation, my father was arrested and sent to Ellis Island. Now he proclaimed to all who knew him that he had proof that the psychoanalysts were behind this arrest. Nobody seems to have believed me in later years when I tried to explain how this misunderstanding had come about. Even in 2000, when Jim Martin was writing his book "Wilhelm Reich and the Cold War," I had a hard time convincing him that there was no conspiracy, that I had made up "the psychoanalysts" and "Lawrence Kubie" to defend my mother.

My father always believed that he was arrested, accused of being a German spy," and it was mentioned, ironically, that Hitler's *Mein Kampf* had been found in his bookcase. The FBI seemed unconvinced that an educated person would own this book in order to inform himself of the enemy's plans. Apparently, also, in his police file there was a notation that he had given a sweet-sixteen party for my sister at which one of the guests had drunk a whole bottle of scotch and passed out. The police had to be called and subsequently in his police file it was noted that there had been a "Negro" youth at the party. My father made these ironic remarks about the FBI afterwards, when he had been cleared and released. At the time there was nothing ironic about the arrest and certainly it was not a time for gallows humor. There was every danger that he would be deported, though to where is not clear. Back to Norway, now under German rule, would have been a death sentence, nor could he go back to Austria without the same result. In fact, just like his ex-wife and daughters, he was stateless at the time. When, while living in Norway, he had tried to renew his German passport a couple of years earlier (Austria was now under German rule) the German Consulate insisted that his middle name be changed to Isaac, Isaac the Jew. But my father adamantly refused this name change. (Rackelman found the correspondence between Reich and the consulate in the now defunct East German STASI files and sent them to me.) I do not know whether he just traveled without a passport, as we had done, or whether he won his battle. It was a brave and principled thing to do. At any rate at the time of the Ellis Island arrest, my father had no home to be deported to. His anxiety must have been enormous, and I believe he broke out in his generalized urticarial rash, as he had done after other incidents of extreme tension.

Of this anxiety, I of course knew nothing. He did not mention it later. Instead, we heard loud and bitter complaints that my sister and I had not visited him on Ellis Island. I had no idea how one went to Ellis Island; I would have needed help from someone older and wiser. However, my mother did not wish us to go. This was because Thomas, my stepfather, with his false passport, did not wish us to call attention to ourselves with the authorities by appearing on the visitors list and perhaps be investigated. He was probably right since no FBI file seems to have existed for him till

1966, eleven years after his death. Thomas knew how to keep a low profile, something my father was incapable of. Not only my father was embittered that we did not come to see him, but 50 years later Ilse, then the future wife, complained to me that "Willi was arrested" and "no one called or came to see me." She was also an immigrant to this country, newly arrived, and she probably knew very few people. To my mind at the time, though later I had second thoughts, my father's recriminations were an example of how my father did not distinguish between children and grown-ups and expected things from us that we were not capable of effecting.

As already stated, my mother truly had nothing to do with this arrest, nor had "the psychoanalysts." It was only in 2001 that I received Reich's FBI files from a researcher who had asked for them under the Freedom of Information Act. Here I now learned that my father had been on Ellis Island only 6 weeks in 1942, and that he was not arrested because he was suspected of being a German spy, though it was during the war. He was arrested because there was another man by the name of Reich, who taught at a Communist school on 12th Street in the Village, while my father taught almost next door at the New School. Someone, an informer, mixed up the two Reichs and denounced my father to the FBI. It must be remembered that on entering this country at that time, one had to declare that one was not a Communist. My father had been ejected by the KPD in 1934, and by this time was a virulent anti-communist. The FBI carefully noted this mix up of two men with the same last name in their files and released him as soon as they could. Of these facts we knew nothing till now. It was assumed that my father's laboratory in his basement, his equipment which might have brought thoughts about secret radio communications, his experiments, his many visitors, were all suspected of espionage activity. The FBI files have revealed, that though the FBI was on a different quest, his neighbors were suspicious of Reich. I remember one entry of a complaint made by an unknown person—in these files the accusers are always blacked out—that my father must be up to no good because "he paid his rent on time." This type of picayune complaint running all through the FBI files, portrays an atmosphere of distrust and hostility which surrounded my father at this time. I am sure it never occurred to him to mingle with his neighbors and to put them at ease. In Central Europe where we grew up, one never mingled with people to whom one had not been properly introduced; that is, unless they were idealized peasants of Grundlsee, or proletarian factory workers in a socialist or communist setting. My mother lived in an apartment house in New York City for twenty-five years and never spoke to a neighbor in all that time. My father might have been oblivious to his neighbors prying eyes and questions of the strange goings on in the house next door.

The arrest finally and completely destroyed the carefree atmosphere my father had cultivated in our presence. I think it broke through his defenses against a sense of imminent danger. There must have been a pattern of denial, confrontation with reality, and breakthrough of anxiety for him. In Berlin he obviously had been very anxious after Hitler came to power, as noisily as he had fought him previously. In Denmark he was so relaxed, that he enjoyed a carefree summer, but under an assumed name, even though the Danish government had thrown him out, and he was there illegally. In Lucerne, when the IPA kicked him out, he was very anxious and angry. Then apparently, he relaxed again. Jim Martin writes in his book *Wilhelm Reich and the Cold War* that in 1935, Reich smuggled himself back into Nazi Germany to help his then companion Elsa (not Ilse) to have an abortion. I seriously question whether this event ever took place; what an act of bravado to sneak back into the country, which you had previously left on foot because you were about to be arrested. Apparently, there was a newspaper campaign against him while he lived in Norway, but he seems to have felt immune from persecution and was relaxed. He risked not having a passport, without experiencing anxiety while my mother would have fallen apart with anxiety over losing her passport. He seems to have denied that Norway was in danger from Hitler, despite the fact that Hitler's European expansion plans were clearly described in *Mein Kampf.* For this reason, a pure denial that there was any threat of war or invasion, he tried to interfere with his children's emigration. When he came to New York on the last boat to leave Norway before the war he betrayed none of the anxiety of "wow I just made it!" which might have been expected. But the Ellis Island arrest broke through all this denial, I think, and showed him how close he was to danger.

A corollary to the fluctuations between denial and anxiety can, I think, be found in my father's work preoccupations. As he was shuttled about from country to country, and in constant danger, as he was kicked out of both the IPA and the Communists, my father compensated by creating more and more grandiose work. In Denmark he was experimenting with human sexuality way ahead of Masters and Johnson (who never gave him credit) and working on his Vegetotherapy against character armoring. In Norway he continued this work, but here he began to postulate the relationship between character rigidity and cancer. As the outside pressures mounted in Norway, I think he began thinking of the spontaneous creation of cancer cells and then the cure of cancer. At this point he was deviating from his base of knowledge and his educational background. The group he formed in Norway, and who really admired him a lot, were left behind when, under further emigration pressure, he started working on energy concepts, externalizing the original libido energy of Freud into a cosmic energy called orgone energy. I think this was his way of handling overwhelming anxiety about annihilation. He also feared annihilation by being forgotten and insignificant.

After his arrest, he stopped entertaining me or driving my friends and me about. At this point Ilse stepped in, probably in an effort to rescue the relationship, but perhaps also out of a wish to have us think of her as a stepmother. She started the kind of activities that my mother was too busy to undertake, and which my mother found culturally unacceptable. My mother took me to the movie *Gone with the Wind* so reluctantly that it was my lasting impression that the movie was a piece of trash that she suffered to endure. But I liked the movie, and when it was replayed after years of absence, I still liked it, when it was on television. I realized that it never was trash, it was a classic in the making. My mother thought all best sellers and book-of-the-month club selections had to be trash. Ilse on the other hand, with great patience, took me to all kinds of movies including *Lady Hamilton*—which was a piece of trash—and stood in line for hours at Rockefeller Center to see it. She took me to roller skating rinks, sitting on benches while I skated about. She took me to concerts at Town Hall, and indulged me in choosing clothes, which were my choice, no matter how tacky. All this I accepted willingly, but I don't think I had any intentions of giving her the honor of considering her a stepmother. Nor was this wish of hers ever verbalized to me.

As my father's anxiety rose after his arrest, there was a growing tension and anger between us. He would insist on "truthfulness" and "look me in the eye." I was comfortable with a superficial fun filled relationship, but not with this intrusiveness. Finally he asked me whether I believed he was crazy. This is an unfortunate point where a lie would have been appropriate, but instead I told the truth. I did not actually think him crazy; I had been told he was crazy and was under obligation to my mother to believe it. But not thinking him crazy was a non-verbal state, "crazy" was the party line. So, I said "yes." As usual when he encouraged truth, he became enraged. He was screaming at me in full voice, and then he told me to get out of his life and out of his house and that he never wanted to see me again. This was the first of a number of open breaks. The original break had occurred in 1934, that had been sub-rosa, but now I was cast adrift. I was 14 years old, and very frightened, guilty and regretful over my provoking him, but I was proud. Certainly, I was not going to plead with him or apologize to him. And I am not even sure he wanted this. I was kicked out of his life in the middle of a busy commercial street in Forest Hills, Queens, and I went home on the subway. My sister who has played a very ambivalent role in my relationship with my father, sometimes separating us deliberately or doing it by unconsciously motivated destructive behavior, could also be the conciliator. This time she was the comforter, she went home with me on the subway, and helped me as I was blindly sobbing.

For my fiftieth birthday my sister with good intentions gave me copies of my father's old European correspondence with my mother. She said to me this was to "show how much he loved and cared about me." I know she honestly meant well, but her unconscious sibling rivalry won out. Of the 50 or so pages she handed me, only 3 mentioned me at all. The others were a record of my father's struggle with my mother over his oldest child, Eva. Where he mentions me, it is to complain that I am developing a "masochistic character." Now my father had written an article on masochistic character, in effect saying it was not developed because of self-destructive urges due to the "death instinct" that Freud was postulating at the time, but because of an expression of skin eroticism and a wish *to be loved* and stroked. The masochist presented his buttocks to be hit, in reality in order to be loved. It is not to be thought that my father sympathized with this need to be loved and stroked. On the contrary, he had contempt for it. So here I was a child of six, already separated from both my parents for over a year and living in a group home now for about eight months, who was developing this horrible whiney personality because she wanted to be loved. I was not aggressive or had temper tantrums and was not difficult like my sister; I was whiney and unhappy. It seems to me that during that idyllic summer in Denmark with my father I was happier and at peace, but he discovered that I needed to be loved, that I was developing a masochistic character and therefore, I assume, should be dismissed. For as already mentioned, the next summer when I refused to visit him, at age seven and at my mother's implicit demand, I

170

was not fought over and when he returned my sister, he ignored me. What had happened within me, now at age 14, however, was a rebellion against the whiney, clinging kid. I had given up my masochism and my compliance and I had fought him off at all points. Now I did not know he had labeled me masochistic, but I had sensed his contempt. So, with this long history already behind us, we were stuck in our foreordained roles. Now, he was demanding love, respect, and compliance and I was refusing.

An emissary from my father, or so I think now, was a patient of his. One day, our apartment house phone rang and a stranger, a man, grown up but not frighteningly so, requested that I meet him downstairs. He said he was a patient of my father's and he understood that my father and I were not getting along, that I did not believe in my father's discoveries and thought him crazy. This perfect stranger wanted to talk to me about all of this. So we went for a walk in Central Park. I had no conscious idea at the time why I would agree to this meeting, but of course, I was suffering from the separation. The walk was very uncomfortable. I was defensive and gave the impression that my father's work was nonsense. I actually knew nothing about it and could have just pleaded ignorance. Instead I felt confronted. But I was also disapproving; I knew that mingling with the family of one's psychoanalyst was strictly *verboten*. At home we had to make sure we never bumped into a patient in the hallway or elevator, nor make noise while patients were passing outside our door. So I knew something was very wrong in this visit. How did this patient know anything about me or about my relationship to my father? There was only one way, my father had complained about me. Of course, I was also keenly aware of the photographs of my baby-age, enlarged, foreshortened genitalia hanging for all to see in my father's hallway. It was probably this latter thought that made me so very defensive and non-conciliatory. I must have known the man would report back to my father what he had heard, but I acted as if this conversation was just between the two of us. I have always been under the impression that the patient was "acting out" in his analysis. But now I think my father ordered him to come. My father often gave people assignments, and this must have been the patient's. Perhaps the patient also had been defensive and resistive. (I am only speculating.)

Ilse also played a conciliator role. During this interval in my relationship to my father she continued to stay in contact, inviting me to movies and concerts and other activities outside his home. Did he know she was doing this? Or possibly had he ordered this? Probably, but I did not understand that. Ilse would not have risked her relationship to him by seeing me secretly. I don't think I actually thought about it. I must have sealed off the memory of the connection with her during my separation, because up to writing these memoirs it never occurred to me that Ilse continued to have contact; and that implied my father was not ready to completely cast me off. She was desperately trying to conceive a child, she was 33 years old, and certainly needed her relationship with him. After some kind of operation, she did conceive. I remember her dragging her mighty belly to Town Hall where we listened, together with all the other Germanic refugees, to the classical music of Bach, Beethoven, and Mozart. In the intermission she would have to rush to the ladies room and then barely make it back by the time intermission was over. One concert stands out. I had gone roller-skating earlier in the day and had met a sailor (it was during the war) and then excused myself because, as I told him, I had to go to a concert. This was of course an incongruity, as people who attended Town Hall did not roller-skate and people who skated did not go to concerts. I met Ilse and we listened to the old music. At intermission we went outside the hall for some fresh air. Ilse suddenly mentioned to me that a sailor wanted to talk to me. There he was from the skating rink asking if we could meet after the concert. Now this shows how kind and easygoing Ilse was. My mother would have frowned and been embarrassed. And I would have been equally embarrassed. With Ilse I felt comfortably accepted and normal in wanting to date.

After my father kicked me out at age 14, it was my sister who, three, or so, years later, arranged a reconciliation; and it was my sister who managed to break us up again a few months after that. I will return to this story later.

Chapter 10
ADAPTING TO WORLD WAR II

GRANDFATHER AND THE WAR

The war that had been threatening since the spring of 1938 finally broke out in Europe in September of 1939. We had been expecting this war for a year, had practiced for it in Czechoslovakia, before we left, with air raid and black out drills, so the actual onset felt like just a continuation of the feelings about the dark shadow over Europe. For most Americans the war was a very distant event, and many did not wish to get involved. However, my family was very anxious about Grandfather and sixteen-year-old Ruth, Thomas' daughter from a previous marriage. (For Ruth's story see pp. 103–104 in chapter 6 "Life in Prague with Mother and Thomas")

An extensive triangular correspondence between my mother, her brother Lutz, and my grandfather, Alfred, typewritten and carbon copied by Lutz and Alfred and handwritten by Mother, who never could type, has been carefully preserved by my mother. This means that I know what the men wrote, but not what Mother wrote, save for one letter written 10 years later by which time she had a secretary. These letters detail the struggle my uncle Lutz had to get my grandfather to leave Vienna, before the Germans outlawed travel. Alfred had already suffered under the Nazis. He was ¼ Jewish and had been removed from his business and his apartment was being examined for confiscation. Only after Alfred's wife, Malva, died

175

could my grandfather mobilize himself to leave. By this time the only way England, overrun by refugees but short on domestic help, would accept him was as a servant. So this seventy-two- or three-year-old solidly bourgeois businessman and proper Victorian gentleman, who had been married twice to excellent "Hausfrauen" and probably had never washed a dish or made a bed in his whole life, adapted to his new status. He handled this situation both with an excellent wry humor and with practicality. He got married for a third time and hired himself and his wife out as a couple. His witty letters describe him drying the dishes while his wife washed, and otherwise sitting on a stool in the kitchen while she cooked and did everything else.

The woman my grandfather chose to marry presented huge complications for my mother. Her name was Ottilie; we called her Otti. She had already been in our family as the wife and then widow of my father's brother Robert. She had been my mother's detested sister-in-law. There was a long and unpleasant history between them which is too lengthy to recount here. Now, thirteen years later, Mother suddenly acquired her as a stepmother.

Now that the war had broken out, my uncle urgently wanted my grandfather to move to either America or Australia. But this plan was terribly complicated. German U-boats were sinking as much shipping as they could in the Atlantic, making overseas travel extremely dangerous. Reportedly, over 400 ships were sunk during the first year of the war. At the same time, neither the US nor Australia wanted to admit any more refugees. The letters contain detailed descriptions of visits to consulates to obtain visas and trips to shipping companies to try and obtain berths. Visas would expire while a place on a ship was awaited, and berths would have to be abandoned because visas had expired. In the end it was not till 1942 that my grandfather and Otti could leave for the United States.

In the meantime, the Germans started the heavy blitz bombing of London and my grandfather found refuge working in a small village, which complicated the whole process of visa applications and berth seeking, as travel to London was required for these endeavors. Uncle Lutz, who had been the carefree, daredevil bachelor while he lived in Vienna, now wrote as the overanxious, worried son; while my grandfather, always so sensible and upright, was now writing with witticisms and humor, rendering his letters full of charm.

Then suddenly one day when the US was already at war, and the Atlantic Ocean shipping subject to U-boat attacks, we received a call from a sailor with a frightful cockney accent telling us our grandfather had arrived in New York. Transatlantic shipping was by convoy of a number of merchant ships, escorted by destroyers and was top secret, so that the Germans would not know when the ships were sailing. My grandfather arrived suddenly, unexpectedly, and without any preparation for accommodation. He was accompanied by his new wife, Otti. It was a misty unpleasant New York night, my mother taking me in tow, had to rush down in a taxi to a pier and retrieve my grandfather and Otti. My sister Eva seems not to have been at home at the time. Instead of moving us children about, even if we had to sleep on the floor, Mother with the new arrivals wandered about New York in the taxi looking for open hotel space. It was wartime, hotels were occupied, so it took quite a while to find a place. To me this has always appeared like a bizarre welcome, rather an "unwelcome." In my memory Mother had very little to do with these grandparents. I know I was delegated to keep in contact, visiting them often, but I have no recollection of them dining in our home. I can't vouch for this of course, but this is how I think of it. Whether mother's inhospitality had to do with her prior relationship to Otti or was part of her general state of abstraction and business, I have never been able to determine. A year or so after his arrival, as grandfather, suffering from arterial sclerosis, started being difficult and wandering about at night in his neighborhood in his nightgown, it was Otti who took total care of him. Yet I know that Annie dearly loved her father.

I have so compartmentalized the above events that I never connected them with what was happening with my father. I know my grandfather arrived when I was thirteen years old, and he died 1942. I was fourteen when he died, so his death was close to the time my father kicked me out of his life. But I remember these events as totally isolated and unrelated.

WAR IN THE UNITED STATES

A background, heavy feeling of anxiety hung over me as Hitler bulldozed his armies over Europe, conquering country after country, leaving England finally to face him alone. There was no television, but many newsreels portrayed the stunning rescue of the British soldiers from the beaches of Dunkirk, using every private boat afloat in England. These pictures turned what was really a terrible defeat into a great heroic victory, elevating the mood for all. The Soviet Union's treacherous pact with Hitler, while at the same time they invaded Finland made us angry. Anger, it turned out, was a way to alleviate anxiety. And because the Americans around me were so oblivious of the danger, and not at all affected by anxiety, I was able to push my feelings into a recess in my mind and let my life move on.

Compared to Europe and Asia, America escaped unscathed from World War II. But in more subtle ways the war had a deep impact on American ways of life, its mores, its beliefs. People realized, perhaps for the first time, that resources were not unlimited, that America was not isolated from danger and might be bombed in the future, that U-boats invaded our waters, that we could be torpedoed and that spies could land unseen. But also the relationship between the sexes changed. The war spelled the end to the dating system that had plagued the youth, with its phony repartee, double standard, cult of virginity, and the demand for empty "popularity" instead of meaningful connection.

The actual start of the American war was a total, unexpected shock. Our group was returning from a hike to the Palisades Park, crossing the George Washington Bridge over the mile-wide Hudson River, when a motorist slowed down and shouted that we were at war. It was December 7th, 1941. Someone turned on a portable radio and we listened how Pearl Harbor had been sneakily attacked. It was a wintry gray misty day and I remember that the gloom around me combined with a very heavy feeling in my chest. I had had similar feelings when Czechoslovakia had mobilized for war. I thought life would be forever changed, that from now on I would have to be grown up, and also brave. Walking home across the George Washington Bridge, I felt trepidation that we would be bombed, we seemed so exposed. In my memory I always combine this event with a year later, when we again went to the Palisades Park. One of the boys accidentally dropped a briefcase and it fell under the bridge where it was still spanning over land. He clambered down to retrieve it. But then a soldier who was guarding the bridge threatened to shoot him if he did not get away from there.

The start of the war filled us all with patriotic fervor. The next day I went to the Red Cross and took home materials for knitting a Navy sweater. It unfortunately took me years to finish it and then it was only large enough for a child. I had knit it much too densely. At school assemblies we pledged allegiance to the flag with intense fervor and a feeling of melting oneself into the crowd. We were stirred into a group cohesive war support. I believe the whole country was united into this same ardor of patriotism. As teenagers we were too young for any real contribution to the war effort, and we envied the older girls who could go to the USO and entertain the troops by dancing with them. But we did collect quarters to buy war bonds. Unfortunately, when I had finally filled in the card with enough quarters to make $25 the money disappeared. I have always suspected my sister of that theft. We collected scrap metal, made balls out of "silver foil," flattened cans and donated anything we could. The beautiful wrought iron railings around our subway station disappeared, turned into scrap, and probably many other ornaments about the city ended with the same fate. Gradually shortages occurred, rationing started. I remember on one of our hikes being stuck in the mud and when I was able to get out, one of my shoes had sunk into the mire. What an upset there was about this at home! Shoes were rationed; it was no joke to lose one. Meat, sugar and butter were rationed. Eggs at times were in short supply and certain ersatz items appeared in stores: powdered eggs, powdered milk. Thomas suffered horribly when coffee disappeared or became scarce. He must have drunk several strong cups a day. His way of making coffee was to boil water and drop the coffee into it, then let it rise up in a boil three times. This was the Turkish way of brewing it and I think it was very strong. I am sure the shortage gave him genuine headaches as I have experienced this and seen it in others when they were withdrawing from coffee. At the time I don't think I had much sympathy for his suffering. Skirts went up several inches, so that one's knees showed, and they were cut straight to save material. Early in 1941 Annie had bought her first car, a Plymouth, and some brave soul had taught her how to drive. Now with the war gasoline was rationed. She carefully saved all her coupons and amassed enough so that the next summer she could go on her vacation as usual.

The war news was so bad for several years, especially in the Pacific arena, that I could not bear to hear it, and tuned it out. So probably I am the only person who lived through that war who is not sure what happened at Midway or at Guam. Also, news was leaking out about the mass transportation of Jews to concentration camps, but we did not hear of the gas chambers till after the war. Our spirits remained high, no one doubted that eventually we would win.

In the summer of 1943 New York State organized the Farm Labor Victory Corps because there was a shortage of farm laborers to pick crops. They asked high school students to come to the Hudson Valley and other places to help with the harvest. They organized hostels for these students and arranged with the farmers where they were needed. At the same time the Ethical Culture Society organized a work camp for the same purpose. Unfortunately, this work camp charged large fees, so my farm earnings did not even come close to covering the cost. We were sent to farms near Highland, New York. We worked next to migrant farm laborers. I remember picking currants, and also raspberries, for four cents a quart box. One can imagine how much money these farm laborers were living on. No wonder that anyone who could, would prefer working in war industry. The farm laborers of course did not pick clean. We would pick all the raspberries that were ripe from a bush, they would pick only from the top in order to fill more boxes. Nevertheless, the wages were pitiful. These migrant laborers were probably from Central America, perhaps Mexico. They kept to themselves and would not or could not speak to us. The fields were full of sprayed insecticide. While working in the tomato fields, our arms were covered with a thick green dust of arsenic all the way above our elbows. Our clothes too were covered with the dust. We laughed about this. But now we are of course environmentally conscious and can be horrified at what farm workers were exposed to. Consumers also would be unaware of their danger as the dust was not visible on the tomatoes. I learned to grade tomato size. We picked them green and were allowed to eat any ripe ones. I think of that summer as a true experience on how other parts of our society live. At the end we got an emblem we could sew on our blazers that said, "N. Y. State Farm Labor Victory Corps." I wore this proudly.

Our war lasted four years. Eventually it had a profound effect on my social life and turned my life in an unexpected direction. More will be written about this in the next few chapters.

Chapter 11

ADOLESCENCE

HOME LIFE

My mother was very abstracted and therefore unrelated to my everyday life. She was very busy, having to work long hours, probably at low fees, both to support us and to pay back the debt that our immigration entailed. She had to fight for her place amongst the analysts, and demand that she be made a training analyst. Probably in conjunction with this she had to write important scientific papers. She was not reluctant to write these papers, but the children felt left alone in an "empty house." Mother practiced in part of the apartment, Thomas lived in his study which was also the living room, and we children lived in the dining room, kitchen and maid's room, a tiny chamber off the back hall and kitchen with its own tiny bathroom and mini bathtub. We all ate supper together and then Thomas and Annie would disappear into their own chambers. Nothing was said to us about what she was doing. We knew that Thomas was writing on his endless Russian history, which was never published. But Annie was also writing, after a full day's work, so she was home but completely unavailable mentally. Writing involves an internal dialogue and thinking, which goes on long before a pen is put to paper; and psychoanalyzing patients can lead to a similar unconscious abstraction. I remember Jim McLaughlin, a training analyst in Pittsburgh, once describing how after a full day of analyzing he would retreat to his woodworking shed, where, while doing some kind of carpentry, he could silently decompress from his day's activity. It appeared to me that Mother was absent, the house empty and that we lived alone in the children's quarters. Later I thought that my mother wrote her papers "off my teen-age back." As a result I did not read them till years later, even though people would come to praise them and quote them.

When Annie was not writing, she was attending committee meetings. Endless meetings were necessary to run the volunteer organized New York Psychoanalytic Institute.

It seems to me now, however, that her involvement with the New York Psychoanalytic Institute failed to create the excitement in Annie that she had experienced in the small group in Prague. I always thought that, apart from teaching, she thought of all her activities in New York as duty, onerous tasks that had to be performed. Nor did the Prague group need any committee work; it had no real structure, no paperwork and no bureaucracy. Of course, the structure of an organization like a free-standing psychoanalytic institute has become vastly more complicated in today's climate with its need for extensive documentation for insurance companies, government agencies, funding agencies, and protection against possible lawsuits. But in the U.S., even in the early 40's, much more documentation and structure were required for student progression than had ever existed in Prague. All this paperwork and documentation probably took the joy and sense of adventure out of the psychoanalytic movement. As a result of this lack of excitement, I did not envy my mother's involvement, as I had envied and yearned in Prague. On the other hand, the New York Psychoanalytic Institute considered itself the center of the psychoanalytic universe. They looked down in disdain at other institutes located in New York and thought of the rest of the country as "beyond the pale." When I left New York in 1964, my advisor, Robert Bak, told me there was no psychoanalysis "west of the Hudson." So, though they did not engender the sense of excitement in Mother that she had shown in

184

Prague, they did ooze a sense of world-shaking importance, being in the forefront of Ego Psychology. It is very strange to think of this now, as the old Ego Psychology with its false preoccupation with *mental* energies has fallen into disuse, but Mother's paper on "Self Esteem Regulation" is still very much cited and admired.

Annie was also ill. It was not mentioned in the family. I found out about it the hard way. Thomas had always made me breakfast, so that I took this service for granted. But sometime when I was around age 13 or 14, he suddenly stopped. He probably felt, quite justifiably, that I was old enough to make my own. However, as nothing was said, I did not understand why he stopped and watched in dismay and envy as every morning he made, with a loving expression on his face, fancy open-faced sandwiches of cheese or ham, and brought them to my mother who was reclining in bed. Later she was put on an absolutely no salt diet consisting mainly of rice. I did not understand her laziness and his sudden indulgence. I did not make my own breakfast but went angrily off to school and later suffered excruciating hunger pangs— usually in the school library, where I had a job sorting newspaper clippings. I welcomed the pangs as a badge of honor and as the sign of my resistance. The hunger would disappear, but apparently it led to my gobbling food after school, which was not good for my figure. Only years later, did I learn that Mother had tried to obtain Life insurance and had found out she was suffering from severe hypertension. Why a simple explanation could not be offered to the children, I don't know. But as psychoanalysts were supposed to be anonymous to their patients, I think part of the secrecy was so word would not leak out that Mother was ill.

Our house was filled with life by the maid, with the odd and unfamiliar name of Mamie, and by my sister. The impending war hit me personally, when our maid, Mamie, disappeared from our life, probably hired away at better pay in war work. This caused home to be empty many an afternoon, when I returned from school. My sister was attending Brooklyn College

185

with very long subway rides each way and so gone most afternoons, my mother was closeted with patients and Thomas was ensconced in his study writing away at his Russian history. I felt inordinately lonely, somewhat like a latchkey kid. It is no surprise that I hung out a lot with my girlfriends and went to their houses as often as possible.

When Mamie left us, Thomas made Eva and me do the cooking. He was such a fussy gourmet cook that he did not trust us to do it right. So he left detailed written instructions what we were to do. Dinner was promptly at seven, as soon as mother's last patient left; we had to learn to get all the dishes made at the same time. His instructions were: "at 6:05 you turn on heat and fill (a specific) pot with water. Turn flame to high. At 6:07 add potatoes. At 6:30 turn oven on, etc. etc." We followed these instructions to the letter and produced the perfect dinners. After dinner we did the dishes. But neither of us ever learned to cook from him. One time, during the war when metal pots were scarce, I let the water boil out of the bottom of the double boiler till the flame made a hole in the pot. I never heard the end of Thomas' complaints. "How could you have been so careless?"

I believe it was this atmosphere that led my sister to leave home and move in with a college friend. I was left all alone in the back quarters of the apartment. Mother had decided that I was too messy for the common area where we ate, and I slept. After my sister vacated her room, I was moved to the tiny maid's room with the tiny bathtub and toilet, further isolated from the rest of the household.

I needed to "move on." This meant adjusting to the various currents in my new life in America and preserving an internal sense of wholeness. Caught between the intrusive demanding intensity of my father, and later his total rejection, and the vacuum of my mother's abstracted relationship to me, at the same time that each demanded, though subtly, that I be loyal to only one and not the other, I apparently developed the ability to block them

186

both out of my consciousness during my everyday existence and instead immersed myself in seeking peer groups.

SCHOOL AND PEER GROUPS

The best decision I made at the time was to leave Walden School with its total high school enrolment of perhaps sixty and change to a large all-girls public high school called Julia Richman. Here I was very happy and made a number of very close female friends. No one seems to have heard of the school. It was located near Second Avenue on East 66th Street, very close to the famous Hunter High School, that everyone seems to have heard of. My school was comprised of seven thousand girls—an amazing place. It was fully integrated black and white, rich and poor, but all females. There were up-staircases and down-staircases. Everyone was terribly polite to each other and called strange students, "Miss." No one was hustled on the stairs. There was no racial tension; but there was no racial mixing either. A black girl who was in my original class, before I went to the honors program, lived one block from me on 97th Street. 96th Street was white and affluent; 97th Street was made up of old brownstone tenements and was mostly black and Puerto Rican. We knew each other at school, but at the bus stop we were in different worlds. She would be accompanied to the stop by her boyfriend, perhaps pimp, who looked considerably older and mean, and we would not even acknowledge each other. I am sure, she was sexually active, and I was thinking of myself as very innocent. I understand that in later years Julia Richman High School went coed and that it became a dangerous place where students carried knives and were afraid to use the bathroom. But when I went there it was full of rules and discipline, which no one dared to break. The school had academic college bound tracks, commercial tracks, and a cooperative school where students shared a job, alternating with each other one week at work and one week at school. It also had a little unit called "The Country School," an honors program for three hundred girls, which I believe was equal if not superior to Hunter High School. After my first semester I was admitted to the honors program. I must have done poorly on the entrance exam and so had to prove myself first. I got an excellent education there in the social sciences. They had an experimental English program that combined literature with the history and social context of the era. Math was perhaps not as advanced as nowadays and trigonometry and calculus were not taught. Physics and chemistry were taught by one of the male teachers. I had a civics course and an economics course that have been the basis for my knowledge to this day.

A school of seven thousand young adolescent girls is something hard to believe. We had a few male teachers who had been there for years and felt comfortable, but I remember one young and new male teacher who caused riots similar to the ones played out in front of the Paramount Theater when Frank Sinatra appeared there. Screeching, screaming girls mobbed the glass window outside his classroom door. I think he lasted a week. With my European side, the cultural snob in me looked down my nose at these hysterical girls. Did I envy their ability to be so free and childish?

I entered Julia Richman in September of 1941; I was thirteen years old. I was serious. I read literature, not comic books. There was no television of course, instead, I read a lot. At age 13, I read about five Dostoyevsky novels and wrote a school book report about them. My mother also gave me Gorky and Gogol to read and *Tyl Ulenspiegel* by DeCosta in a beautifully woodcut illustrated volume. (I recently sold it at the scandalous price of $10 to a secondhand book dealer.) I think I was much too young for all these books, and regret that I did not read them later. However, I tried rereading *War and Peace* a few years ago, but did not enjoy it as much as a when I was a teenager. Annie had a real fear we would become uncultured; she felt it was time for us to read seriously, and above all to stay away from best sellers and comic books.

Outside of school I participated in as many activities as I could find, cultural, artistic, do-good social service as well as a full social life with girlfriends and much dating. All this frenetic activity did not seem to satisfy my need for belonging. My ideal was to belong to a group. I have no idea what Eva's "Gruppe" had been, I believe it may have been radical, but she seemed to have felt so enveloped and close to it and so all-absorbed, that whatever it was, it had become an ideal for me. Also, my parents in belonging to the psychoanalyst group, the Wandervögel, and to Marxism had seemed to have been so happy and complete in their youth, that I wanted the same. And then in high school I finally found it. Better stated, I "pseudo" found it. Through a girl in the school who was a German refugee, and I believe a Quaker, or some other religious denomination, I was introduced into a group of other refugees. I think there were twelve of us, six boys and six girls. I have no idea where they came from or what language they had spoken originally; we all spoke English to each other; nor did I know what social class they were, or even if they were college bound. Apart from the girl, Hanna, who originally introduced me, I don't think I ever went to any of their homes or met their parents. I don't even know what their politics were. Some of the boys were working as diamond cutters, but whether they also went to school I don't remember. I was the youngest of the group, perhaps by two years. We had none of the commitment to a "movement" that had made my sister's and parent's groups so exciting and the associations they found there so profound. My mother's associations lasted a lifetime. My sister's greatest hurt and complaint about coming to America was that she was separated from her group. My group's cohesiveness consisted only of an outdoor life, similar to the one that my mother sought in America and could not find. Perhaps, once a week we went to a park, this could have been far away, we walked miles, used public transportation. I don't think we played games, perhaps we threw a ball, but usually we just walked and, of course, talked. We did this winter and summer in all weather. I remember trips on the Staten Island Ferry and then walking a few miles to a park located there, and trips to Van Cortland Park and to the Palisades Park on the west side of the Hudson River. To get there we walked across the George Washington Bridge, which I don't believe one can do anymore. And the park itself, I think, is just land for a superhighway these days. Through Hanna's religious connections, we also knew of a weekend farm we could go to, and there were camping trips to Bear Mountain State Park, again walking miles to get anywhere. We had a feeling of a group! I have no idea if I had anything in common with them in other ways. There was some pairing off of the sexes, but as far as I know the group was chaste, there was no necking, no kissing. In that sense it was very much like the youth groups in Europe. In fact, I remember in Bear Mountain where we had camped overnight by trespassing on a Boy Scout camp, we were kicked out by the State Police, who certainly looked askance at a coed camping group. In this group I was first paired off with Alex, who then announced to me that he was "breaking off" and passed me on to Henry with whom I stayed till he was drafted, about a year later. The chasteness of the group of course ended at some point, but not within the group. I do know that very late in our encounters the boys had had some kind of sexual experience, which they were keeping a secret from us girls. The boys believed in the chastity of women so they "honored" us by not making any advances. I think the girls believed in chastity also. It was a very different atmosphere than I encountered with American dates—with the obligatory goodnight kiss, and the struggles to politely push off bodily advances which the boys wanted, but if they succeeded would lead to scornful feelings about the girl.

I have been struck how in writing these memoirs of my adolescence, I have been stressing my innocence and chastity. I was the daughter of Wilhelm

Reich, who almost compulsively demanded sexual freedom and sexual activities by adolescents, who was revered in many circles as a founder of the "sexual revolution," and was the author of two books on sexuality, *The Sexual Revolution* and *The Function of the Orgasm*. These books which had recently been published in English—though I never dared ask anyone what the word 'orgasm' meant—were making a splash among intellectual circles, at least in New York, at that time. Counter-balance to this were my own experiences with my father, both in childhood and in the 1940's; his demand that I ask him anything about sex, his open question of whether my mother was preventing me from sleeping over at his house because she was afraid he would molest me, this question asked of me in a candle lit romantic restaurant, and I think, my unconscious knowledge that he wanted to deeply discuss my own sex life, but was afraid I would clam up and so he desisted. Besides this was his overwhelming angry, intrusive, demanding personality which I was determined not to give in to. Many years later, I heard from various sources how uncomfortable adolescents were either with him or with Reichian therapists, who intruded vigorously into the youth's privacy about sex.

Added to these experiences with my real father, was an unfortunate experience with a camp director, who was of similar age as my father. This happened the summer I turned thirteen. My mother, who, because she worked had to find a place for me each summer, found a camp meant for teenagers. It was a wonderful camp with challenging activities, sailing, and riding and several camping trips lasting for many days, walking the Appalachian Trail and many other activities. It was run by a couple, teachers from one of the other independent progressive schools, and seemed ideal. However, the camp director was a sexual "predator" who loved to ask all the girls when they would "have their periods" so he could "plan" his camping trips. Then away from his wife on these trips, he would induce skinny-dipping, actually tearing off the towel one girl had wrapped about her, and other "sexy" activities. One night he took me away from the others, which seemed in my innocence, like a great honor conferred on me, like an overnight sleep-over date; but then he tried to have intercourse with me. Fortunately, he did not succeed. But it had a horrible effect on me. And then, the next day, he started treating me shabbily, was maliciously hostile, so that on top of the seduction there was a total rejection. I think the whole episode demolished me. The attempted intercourse and the rejection were both equally traumatic. Nowadays we call such an incident "sex abuse" and so it was; but in those days we did not have that concept or the language with which to express it. I was left to blame myself for my stupidity.

After this I seem to have split my mind into two pieces. Somewhere in my consciousness was the awareness of my father's belief that youth had to have a free sexual life; on the other hand, I treasured innocence and chastity. I felt no conflict about the split in my mind. My mother also contributed to the difficulty. She never interfered in my sister's very early sex life. I think she was torn between her real emotions of worry for her girls and the ideology of her youth.

The European group was perfect for me. It supplied companionship and boys that one could know much better than on a "date" and yet because of their ideas about sex and chastity for girls, were strictly "hands off" just when I needed it. At the same time, I did not trust men, so I formed no deep attachments to these boys. When Alex decided to drop me and told me so with a heavy heart, I had no reaction, hardly cared, and was just as happy to be passed on to Henry. It is not that I disliked these boys. I just wasn't going to get myself involved enough to get hurt again. Considering that I went to an all-girls school, this belonging to a coed group made life much more normal than it would have been otherwise.

LOSS OF THE GROUP

But in the fall when I was 15 things changed. The life I had created for myself with such difficulty came to an end. The boys in our European group were turning 18 and were drafted. The girls were not able to keep this group going and so it fell apart. Suddenly I was without my group. Henry and I became "engaged," when a year later he returned on furlough, and we wrote to each other daily, while he was in the army and overseas. But in actuality we were seriously drifting apart. We never really exchanged too many ideas and I think we basically had very different attitudes toward life. When he came back, we mutually realized our lack of interest. Unfortunately for him he died a few years later from lymphosarcoma.

At age fifteen as my world came apart again, my wonderful defense system broke down, and I became horribly depressed. My peer group had been drafted, my father had kicked me out, my mother was "absent," my grandfather had died, and I lost the daily contact with my best girlfriends by being unceremoniously promoted out of my home room at school; then the final straw was that my sister, who had given life to our backstairs existence, moved out of the house. I felt truly alone and abandoned. I had no idea I was depressed, but I lost all joy and all energy. Thomas and Annie seem not to have recognized my state. Thomas was contemptuous because I simply stopped picking up my clothes or my possessions. Annie became hurt and expressed it, so unusual for her, because I had "forgotten *her* birthday." This latter episode still puzzles me; was she so totally self-absorbed? Could she not know what was happening to me?

I cannot recall how long this mood lasted, but at some point, I recovered and started looking for a new peer group

Chapter 12

NEW GROUPS

It seems to me, while writing this, that my life consisted of repeated new beginnings. At age 15, having painfully established my peer group after the dislocation of immigration, I was forced again to find a new sense of belonging. The men in my group had been drafted, and the women could not hold the group together. So I was left without the stability and sense of continuity that the group had given me. I think that the dislocation in America caused by the war and the separation of friends and family has not been abundantly written about.

It was pure luck that through a casual friend at school I was introduced to a brand-new group of girls and boys, who, being only 15 and 16, were not about to be drafted. This was the youth group of the Socialist Workers Party (SWP). How I met them or went to the first meeting I can't remember. But here was the ideal group for me. They evoked in me the memory of my parents' excitement in belonging to the Communists, their sense of group, of a movement, of belonging. That this was the wrong time in history, that there were no great movements going on at the moment, only occurred to me later. I was in the generation in between—the next real "movement" occurred in the 60's. This particular youth group was very small and very friendly and had wonderful boys in it. I really don't remember much of the political context, or how much we studied a platform or discussed Marxism. I just remember feeling at home. The advantage of this group was also that they were not Communist, i.e., Stalinists, but Trotskyists (most people called them Trotskyites), and thus they were not associated with the corruption of the Soviet Union.

The Socialist Workers Party had recently undergone a split into the Cannonites and the Shachtmanites. I have no idea what that was about, having come after the split. In general, the split involved the separation of the intellectuals and middleclass members from the working-class type members who were generally anti-intellectual and basically against college education. The Cannonites retained the name SWP and were the more "proletarian" group. After the split, the youth group remained with the SWP and I am just lucky it was actually made up of middleclass adolescents, who studied and liked school. Before the split six members of the joint party had been arrested and convicted under the Smith Act, which outlawed advocacy of violent overthrow of the government. This act was later declared unconstitutional, but these six members had already served a couple of years in the penitentiary. In my imagination it was these convictions which led to the split; however, there is not way to confirm this now.

The Shachtmanites actually had some very talented people as members. One was a famous writer, another started Cinema 16, the beginning of the art movie scene. I am sure that had I become a Shachtmanite I would have been amongst my own kind, but as a Cannonite, apart from the youth group, I was in alien territory. Yet for a time it was an interesting territory as I was able to meet people from walks of life I never would have mingled with. What struck me was the very different morality, especially about sex that was held by the working class. They did not seem to have the cult of virginity nor the habit of making belt notches for conquests; they did not look down on women who had sex. In general they were much more fatalistic, but at the same time, so much more practical. I am sure most of them had had a very hard time during the recent "great depression." Most of them were nice people. However, they were uneducated and really opposed to college and especially professional ambitions. The other strange thing about them was that they drank hard liquor, not wine or liqueurs, and for some reason, also not beer.

I do remember one "party line" because I disagreed with it. The Cannonites were opposed to the war. How could I with my background ever think that way! But I don't believe the youth group was too concerned with this matter. The SWP held to the position, also assumed in World War I, that the working class had nothing to gain in this war and was just being exploited for imperialist goals. This might have been true in World War I, but it did not quite fit the present picture.

What my family thought of this new group affiliation I do not know, as they did not comment. They could not have been too pleased, as we had not yet attained citizenship and Thomas always felt in danger that he would be deported. A few years later, Thomas did mention, with some disdain, that Trotsky could never lead a party. Trotsky had been murdered, in Mexico by Stalinist agents, just a few years prior, in 1939, a fact that both my stepfather and the party clearly remembered for different reasons: For the party it took the life out of their cause, for Thomas it presented an example of the danger he lived with.

I don't remember how much I had to do with the general party membership before I went off to college. Probably most of my contacts came later. I just enjoyed the youth group.

The group consisted mostly of boys, which was perfect for me while attending my all-girls high school. Some of these boys I have some knowledge of in later years. One became a reverend in an Indian religion, and another became a professor of astronomy at a prestigious university. At that time, before the age of space travel, this was a really "far out," strange interest. Most of the group quietly faded out of the party as they grew up. I remember only one, who in Russia could have become a party apparatchik, with a facial expression later seen on Putin, the new Russian premier, before President Bush put a smile on his face: humorless, intense, totally dedicated to the party ideal and capable of killing his grandmother if she were considered counter-revolutionary.

I don't remember what our meetings were about or our other activities. Supposedly we studied Marxism, discussed the Soviet Union as a "degenerated workers state," and tried to recruit other youth. Our main activity seems to have been to fight the ubiquitous and large Stalinist Communist youth movements. I remember one of their large meetings which Zog and I infiltrated where we were to pass out leaflets. I suddenly "got a headache" and left. Zog stayed, was beaten up and lost a tooth. I was also sent to infiltrate a huge "Negro" youth organization somewhere in the bowels of Brooklyn. Having taken the wrong subway, I walked through miles of the all-Black Bedford-Stuyvesant area of Brooklyn. The strap of my sandal broke, so I had it fixed by a shoemaker before I trudged on. When I got to the meeting it turned out to be in a huge auditorium where several thousand Black youths had gathered for what seemed to be a musical performance. The crowd was utterly enthusiastic and enchanted. I was the only white person there. And I can't imagine, how I was supposed to recruit from this joyous crowd who could not have cared less about Marxism or workers states. Basically, the best skill I acquired during this period was how to create leaflets in an age before Xerox. First one cut a stencil, a large, waxed sheet, and then one put this stencil on an inked mimeograph machine and cranked a handle turning out leaflets.

At the same time that I joined the youth group and was surrounded by boys, I also acclimatized myself to my promotion to a new class and new girls in school. I had been promoted from sophomore to senior because of extra NY State Regents credit. I did keep up with my two close friends but could no longer see them every day. Instead, I met up with seven radical girls in my new class and we formed a new clique. We were radicals, but each of a different political persuasion. That did not matter in the slightest. I don't remember what they all adhered to. One was a Communist, one a left-wing Zionist, who belonged to Hashomir Chatzair. and I was a Trotskyite. The other four were something else. The contradiction between our "ecumenism" and the factionalism of the SWP did not seem to bother me. I remember one act of vandalism we committed. There was scenery for an upcoming play left on stage in the auditorium, a tree of evil with apples for all kinds of sins. We secretly added Capitalism, Imperialism, and Fascism. What the play givers thought of this we, unfortunately, never found out.

The Zionist in our group, named Helen—later changed to the Hebrew Chaya—invited us to a New Jersey Kibbutz training farm for a weekend of helping with the corn harvest. This was in the fall of 1943, long before the British divided Palestine. But this Kibbutz movement was actively preparing for settling as soon as the war was over. The group living on the farm was older than my friend's Zionist high school age group, and they lived a Kibbutz life, learning how to be farmers. Our little clique from the Julia Richman High School was just a small group amongst many other high school youths, who had come to help with the harvest that weekend. What struck me most was the enormous enthusiasm and fervent belief in their cause that these "kibbutzniks" exhibited. My own group of Trotskyites was really a defeated and fading phenomenon, but these Zionists felt themselves to be part of a great future. The weekend consisted of very hard work, as it turned out that the corn that comes to the market has only the inner husks; there is an outer very strong husk that the farmer peels away. All one's strength was needed to achieve this and if we had not worn work gloves our fingers would have been shredded to bits.

The weekend was also strange in another way. Boys and girls all shared a huge dormitory; this involved dressing and undressing inside one's sleeping bag or not caring who saw what. The other kids seem to have taken this situation for granted, or perhaps they slept in their clothes. I did not know

199

at the time that the left-wing Kibbutzim raised their boys and girls together in children's huts in segregation from their parents. As these children grew up, they seem to have developed natural incest taboos and did not date each other. A similar observation has been made in those colleges that created co-ed dorms in the 1970's. One can speculate that this lack of sexual interest is a natural repression to defend against incest. In general, this weekend made a huge impression on me, but I was not interested personally in becoming a Zionist.

Supported by these close social groups I had a very enjoyable senior year in high school and look back on this period with pleasure. Unfortunately, after graduation, my high school group scattered, and we all lost track of each other. Ours was not the type of school that had reunions. It was the SWP youth group that provided continuity.

My family scoffed at bourgeois institutions and rites like graduation and marriage ceremonies. We did not attend my sister's graduation ceremonies for high school or college. Thus I did not attend my high school graduation. In fact, it never occurred to me, that I should go, or that my family should take pride in my achievement and celebrate. Not attending turned out to be a public mistake, as I had received an award in Biology and my name was called out several times. It was my friend's mother who had to tell me that I received an award and to ask, "where were you?" The first graduation ceremony I ever attended was when I finished medical school.

I had spent the long summer break (Oberlin started in October) joining the working class by working in factories in New York City. The Socialist Workers Party, with true Marxist ideology, required this. The belief was: "Only the working class can make a revolution." No matter that the intelligentsia, which usually forms the nucleus of revolutionary movements, have been universally recruited from the rebellious scions of the educated upper middle class. Just as the year before, when I had a small brush with the life of farm laborers, I now entered into a new and alien world. I am really very glad that I had that experience. However, in order to work in these factories, I had to hide my true middle-class identity. New York at that time was full of lofts housing small factories. So I had simply walked up Columbus Avenue from my home on 96th street and asked at one of these lofts whether they had any jobs. No ID, or social security number, or experience was required. In war time these small sweat shops were probably only too glad to get labor at minimum wage when others were leaving for war work. I was placed at a machine that manually attached closure snaps to wallets. There I sat all day pulling down a lever. Never in my life had I known such stultifying boredom. At one point I must have been falling asleep because suddenly the owner came behind me and yelled "sit up straight." I was startled and obeyed. The all-white workers in the place were long time employees and terribly loyal to this shop. There was no union, but they seemed very content. I don't think I got close to anyone or talked to them. I was supposed to mingle with them and enthuse them about Marxism, but there seemed no way to approach them. I think I must have puzzled them as well. For one day at the lunch break a woman insisted on walking all the way home with me, so that she saw me go into the apartment house with a doorman and an awning My cover blown, I fled and never returned.

I started hunting for other jobs to further my proletarian career and I remember applying at a factory where they handed me a contract, which stated that I would not mind placing "makeup on my face," consisting of substances that they were developing. Frightened, I fled. Finally, I landed a job in an eyeglass frame factory, where I hammered small nails into the hinges of the frame. This factory, also at minimum wage, had many white workers, male and female all older than me; they were of the generation that had lived through the great depression and were hanging on to their secure jobs. There were two young very dark-skinned Puerto Rican women of approximately my age, with whom I started to share the half hour lunch break. They taught me the Spanish word for the female genital, and asked me, leering, whether I had a boyfriend.

The factory manager was a woman, which was very unusual. She disapproved of my association with these dark-skinned girls, so I was moved out of the factory into the office area where I was taught how to package boxes for shipping. To this day, I know how to apply tape to the edges of a box and make proper corners with the tape. The whole outer office was excited about the factory manager's upcoming blind date. Nothing else was talked about for several weeks; what she should wear, how her hair would look, all was of intense interest. The day of the date approached, and there was mounting tension. The next day the manager was subdued and looked depressed, and the topic was hastily dropped. It was time by then to leave for college and thus ended for the time being my proletarian career.

In between these proletarian infiltrations—it should be quite clear by now that I was an abject failure as a socialist organizer amongst the downtrodden—I was to sojourn with my mother on her vacation in the White Mountains. At some point in her life Mother started taking two-month vacations. However, I don't think she had reached the economic security to do this yet. My sister and I were expected to join her for at least two weeks. Because my old boyfriend Henry was coming home on furlough just before being shipped overseas, my mother agreed to let me stay on in the city if I stayed at the home of a friend of hers. So, supposedly supervised, I spent a week with Henry. Our lives had drastically diverged, and I think I realized that we had little in common. I am sure I hid all my Trotskyite activities from him, and he told me nothing of army life or basic training. Nevertheless, I thought it my patriotic duty to have sex with him. Henry however refused, stating that once a girl had sex, she would want it over and over again. He was protecting my virtue. Instead, we became engaged. Because of train schedules, I had to stay in New York an extra night on the day he left. I hung out with some boys from the youth group, who had rented a room for the summer. It was an adventure for them to live away from their parents. It got late, so I slept over at this room. But the bed bugs were so bad that in the middle of the night I fled back to my mother's friend's house. The contrast between my two lives could not have been underlined more effectively.

The mesh of contradictions in my life were further exemplified when Henry's parents paid my family an unannounced visit in the White Mountains. As has already been stated, my imitation Wandervögel, European youth group never invited each other to their homes, or talked about family. In the three years I knew Henry, I had not only never met his parents, but had no conception about his home. But now that we were engaged, I suppose, his parents decided to rectify this situation. So there suddenly appeared a handsome, beautifully coiffed woman, bejeweled with pearls, and for the rural setting, rather formally attired. This was Henry's mother accompanied by the father. Thomas and Annie received these parents with an embarrassed, uneasy restraint, making for a very uncomfortable afternoon. I had seen this behavior in my mother before; a sort of social discomfort and unease not easily reconcilable with a successful professional woman, recently made a training analyst. Nor did Annie show the slightest intention of continuing this acquaintance. Did she believe in this engagement? Probably not. But it was also an act of terrible snobbism toward people, who though successful in their own sphere, were not of the intellectual elite.

My mother had rented a cottage near Randolph NH, which was attached to a hotel, where one could eat meals as part of the month's rental. Across the valley road were the grandiose peaks of the Presidential Range. I believe Mt. Madison was nearest to us, followed by Mt. Adams and then Mt. Washington. This was the closest Mother had come to recreating her life in Austria with its national sport of mountain hiking. And in this range, we climbed, and day hiked. There were a series of huts on top of these mountains maintained by the Appalachian Mountain Club, so that one did not have to lug heavy knapsacks and gear up the mountains. It was a beautiful landscape, and our activities were enjoyable. Years later I was shocked to learn that so many people use these huts now that one has to make reservations a year in advance and then may not succeed in getting in.

Amidst this wonderful scenery, I learned another painful lesson about American life. There was a local mountain club that had many teen-agers and arranged group hikes. None of these adolescents would talk to me or my sister or the child of another refugee family whom we knew. We would go on these group hikes and be totally ignored and snubbed. At the end of the summer my mother got a letter from the owner of the cottage stating that in future they would prefer to "rent to people of our own faith." We had stumbled into a community that was "restricted," meaning forbidden to Jews. Being refugees, of course, we had immediately signaled a religious affiliation. I had not heard about such attitudes, or rules. It contrasted radically with the concept of "the melting pot" and pointed cogently to how pettily and far these WASP New Englanders had strayed from the ideals of their founding fathers.

RECONCILIATION WITH FATHER

One day, during our sojourn in the White Mountains my sister said. "We have been offered a ride to Rangeley (Maine), would you like to go and visit our father?" I experienced a peculiar vibrating excitement. My sister wanted me!!! But I also felt a twinge of guilt, knowing that my mother would not be pleased to have us visit our father during her vacation, time set aside to be with her children. Did my sister arrange this to show defiance? I thought so, but of course said nothing. In fact, I secretly enjoyed the thought. But I did not consciously think of this as a reconciliation with my father, instead I pretended to myself that it was a "normal" event, as if nothing had happened for the past few years.

Rangeley was just a few hours away by car. We hitched a ride with some acquaintances who were driving there. We were dropped off in the middle of town, where we intended to phone our father to pick us up. But when we got to the town, there was my father, totally surprised to see either of us—I hoped happy to see us—but looking bewildered by our sudden arrival. My sister obviously had not apprised him of our coming. Both of us acted as if my arrival was nothing out of the ordinary, as if the past few years had never happened.

Father summered in a small cabin on Lake Mooselucmaguntic, a large wild lake, at that time not yet surrounded by vacation cottages. Ilse had recently given birth to my brother Peter, an event that obscurely threatened my future place in the family. And here we spent a peaceful afternoon and night as a family, as if there had never been a huge problem about my refusal to sleep at their house.

The next afternoon the Loewenfelds, old friends from the Kinder Seminar in Berlin, dropped by as they were passing through the region. This was a great surprise as the Loewenfelds surely thought of my father as "crazy" and at the same time my father thought all psychoanalysts were persecuting him and were behind his arrest and holding time at Ellis Island. He did not act as if he was having a joyous reunion, but he was courteous and civil. Father had just bought a large tract of land, on the outskirts of Rangeley, overlooking Dodge Pond. He was planning to create a large complex, which later became Organon. Here he later lived, taught and did experiments. But at this time, it was just a beautiful hill overlooking a lake. My father seemed calm, generally happy, and excited over the prospects of building his new estate. He wanted me to join in his joy and to admire his landscape. I acted nonchalant. I would not give him the pleasure of sharing his enthusiasm. The Loewenfelds gave me outraged looks, making me embarrassed about my behavior, but unable to change it. We were back into old patterns. He was not at ease with me. The silent intervention of the Loewenfelds must have changed something in my attitude. Awkwardly my father and I, the next day, came to an understanding that I was part of his family. No apologies were offered by either side, no explanations, we just acted as if we would erase the past. He agreed to pay for part of my college tuition, and actually did do this for one term. I felt vaguely guilty, as if I were betraying my mother.

In September I returned to New York to temporarily resume my proletarian career.

Chapter 13

OBERLIN (1944–1945)

I was ready for college at age 16 because of the several skips in grades. My sister, because of similar promotions, was ready to graduate from college the same year. She had attended one of the numerous free colleges of New York City and then had switched to Barnard in her last two years. For some reason it was assumed that I would go away for college. We had been living in this country for only six years and I had no idea where I wanted to go or what it meant. My mother knew about Radcliffe College, the women's college part of Harvard, as she had psychoanalyst friends in Boston. My sister suggested Antioch and Oberlin, which were more unusual. I applied to Radcliffe and Oberlin. Mother arranged, through what she called "pull," for me to have an interview with a dean at Radcliffe. However, she gave me absolutely no information or instructions on how to prepare for such an interview. I don't know whether she assumed I knew how to conduct myself, or whether she herself did not know what one did during such an interview.

So at age sixteen I arrived at midnight at the Copley Square railroad station and dragged my suitcase across to the Copley Plaza Hotel. What they thought of this teenager arriving alone at such a late hour I have no idea. They did not raise an eyebrow and duly registered me for a room. But something in their posture made me realize that this was a rather bizarre occurrence. My mother's friend Grete Biebring, a Viennese psychoanalyst, called me the next morning at the hotel just as there was a knock at the door—I was having my clothes pressed. When I told her I had to open the door she got very angry and said she was in a hurry. This was a woman I had known as a small child and somehow, I expected her to treat me in the friendly manner of an old family friend, so I was quite shocked. She informed me that I was to meet a graduate student she knew who would take me to the dean. But again, I had no idea what my interview was to be about, and after our little contretemps I did not feel I could ask.

The graduate student Grete Biebring connected me with was studying psychology. I met her in her house, which she shared with a number of other women. The walls were painted several shades of coral pink, which she explained was the color of the womb. I was amused by this symbolic preoccupation. I don't remember her name; she was very nice and took me to the appointment with the dean, introduced me and sat in on the interview, which was just to be a "get to know you" interview. This means it was not an official admissions interview. I of course knew nothing about such matters. All I remember from the interview is that I was completely tongue-tied and could not say a word, and the dean acted like a psychoanalyst. She just sat there, did not ask me any questions, and waited to hear what I would produce. I had never been so embarrassed in my life. The graduate student was probably equally embarrassed. So, it will come as no surprise that I only made the waiting list to Radcliffe and not the admissions list. Nor did I know, and probably my family did not know either, that people on the waiting list can call the admissions office, call repeatedly, ask them what the chances are etc. In fact, make a noise. My high school college counselor was disappointed, but I don't believe many students from Julia Richman High School ever went to Radcliffe.

The consequence of this miserable debacle is that I enrolled in Oberlin, for whose admission I wrote a wonderful essay about my chaotic life in Europe. Oberlin was very liberal, wanted a broad selection of students and was, I think, eager to have me. But the more important consequence for my future life was that I avoided an entanglement with the Boston Psychoanalytic community which was, I believe, extremely orthodox, and I avoided the Harvard-Radcliffe ambiance of intellectual snobbery. Of course, I also missed out on something. In later years, I realized, it does not always matter where one went to school to get on in life.

My family had no idea how to pack or prepare for college. I remember that the college gave some instructions, told us to bring a lamp and a bedspread for instance, and reminded us that we "dress up for dinner." I arrived with three skirts and three sweaters and some galoshes boots, I think for men, the type one buckles over one's shoes. As there was a lot of snow later, these came in handy, even if not very fashionable. It was October of 1944 and World War II was very much in progress. Even though we had invaded France and were nearing Germany, the news was not always good. The Battle of the Bulge reversed our progress starting in December.

I went by myself by train from New York to Elmyra, Ohio. It was a long overnight train ride. Because of the war the trains were very crowded and packed with service men and women. I was lucky to find a coach seat and tried to sleep. After we left the station, the lights were turned off in the car so we all could sleep. Suddenly a hand came on to my shoulder from behind. I shouted, "get your hands off me!" The lights came on immediately. A WAVE (Women's auxiliary Navy) came over and removed a sleeping and exhausted sailor's hands from me. I realized he had not been aware of what he was doing.

Arriving in Oberlin was a terrible shock. I had never in my life seen a countryside whose topography was absolutely flat. The town was a flat square surrounded by miles and miles of flat plowed fields, and straight roads that crossed at right angles. There probably are places like this where Europe meets Asia, but I had never even conceived of this flatness. And these long vistas of empty sky meeting earth probably also produced flat people. Because of the war, many of the dormitories were occupied by Navy and Marine college programs, causing a shortage of dormitory space for the regular students, so I was placed with nine others in a private home across the street from the MAY dormitory; a huge building of seemingly black fieldstone, looking positively medieval—a building that has been demolished, and it is no longer present in modern Oberlin. We were housed in the home of a Mrs. Dunbar who lived there with her husband and two daughters. And these were some of the flat people I was thinking about. Even though the daughters were our age, they never communicated with us college students living in their home. Oberlin was a college town; it had no other industry and did not even serve as the market town for the surrounding huge farms. And the town had a huge "town versus gown" problem. The local inhabitants in so far as they did not work for the college, never mingled with the college crowd. The narrowness of Mrs. Dunbar was later born out. Thoughtfully, I had been placed in a room with another woman refugee. She was German Jewish and had come to study piano. Mrs. Dunbar overheard us talking German to each other and reported us as German spies.

Oberlin College has a current reputation of being very "arty" and super-radical. But this is not the Oberlin I attended. Oberlin was the first co-ed college in the United States. As a result, it had some very strict rules of behavior for women. Freshmen were to be in our dormitories by 8:30 p.m. and "lights out" was at 10 p.m.—upper class women did not have a lights-out time. We could get permission to stay out till 10 p.m. about four times a term and had permission for a 2 a.m. deadline if we were going to the opera in Cleveland. Male students had none of these rules. We could entertain men downstairs in the living room, but not in our rooms. When I was approached later by two Socialists, who wished to recruit me and I interviewed them with *the door closed* to the living room, I was severely reprimanded for entertaining men with a closed door!

Women were allowed to smoke, but only in their rooms, never in public. Men had no rules. At some point the upper-class women petitioned the college to change some of these rules, but it was the freshmen women who resisted change, claiming they needed rules, having just left the protection of their parents.

Oberlin, a college of 3000, was divided between the liberal arts program, the music school, and a Theological graduate seminary. This latter school is no longer there. Though the college prided itself on its diversity of students, who included some blind students—a very revolutionary idea at the time—and several Nisei Americans at a time we were at war with Japan, "Negro" students, a rarity in college at the time, and some of us refugees, a pervasive atmosphere of pious Christianity prevailed. My dorm mates were absolutely horrified that I was an atheist and belonged to no religion. Every Sunday, for weeks, one of them invited me to attend their various churches, Methodist, Congregationalist, Presbyterian. They kept saying, "How can you have morals without religion?" My roommate, three years older than I, was wise enough to never proclaim her ideas about religion. I am sure, though ethnically Jewish, she also had no religious affiliation or belief. Our small dorm was a very mixed bunch. I remember there were two debutantes from Boston who wished to do something different for a while, that is not to go to the expected schools; some Midwesterners who were totally new to me in interests and style, but always "very nice" and polite; a Jewish girl aspiring to be an actress, who had promised her Broadway producer uncle she would get an education prior to her acting career, an orphan who was fostered by a Mormon family; an extremely flirtatious girl, perhaps also from the Midwest who wore makeup and fluffy angora sweaters, and us, two refugee girls. Living with us was also a junior who was our resident advisor, a Nisei woman called Yoshi. For such a disparate bunch we got along quite well and looked after each other.

Because the college believed in mixing students, we did not all belong to the same dining hall so that we could not go and eat as a cohort. I for instance, was assigned to eat at MAY. This meant entering the dining room each night, finding my cloth napkin, encased in its ring, inside its cubbyhole, and then finding a seat at one of the white tablecloth-covered round tables for eight. Except for one noisy coed group, there were no "usual" seats, and we did indeed mingle with different people every night. This was a bit of a strain but did achieve the purpose the college had intended. I once mistakenly sat down at the table that was "reserved" and found a very frosty atmosphere around me. Each night a student had to say a blessing. One night it was my turn, in desperation I looked at the wall and found a cross-stitched sampler whose message I piously intoned. This ruse was a complete success. The dining hall was served by waiters, students earning a little toward their room and board. Eventually I became a table setter, and thus escaped the strain of the MAY dining hall. I was assigned to French house, a small and interesting place. I also learned how to set an absolutely proper table, water glass at the point of the knife, spoon outside the knife, blade turned toward the plate and so forth.

In Oberlin, a place so far removed from the coast, we felt the war more keenly than we had in New York. As all the men college age were drafted, the only male students at the college were either theology students, or 4F classified. If there were also conscientious objectors, I did not know about them. I do believe though that the objectors had to either serve society in some capacity or were in prison. So there was quite a shortage of men on campus. Nevertheless, the college held to the traditions of formal proms. Here I had to wear an evening gown and high-heeled shoes. Luckily these items had been on the suggested list the college had sent to us at home. The Navy and Marine Students did not attend, were perhaps not invited. The Prom was a very boring affair.

The young men of the Navy and Marines did not share our dining halls or dormitories and I don't remember them in my classes. They were enrolled in an intense, accelerated college program in addition to all kinds of military drills, but I think were allowed to take our college courses as electives if they had time. But gradually, as one saw them traversing the Commons, we got to know a few of them. Doris, our flirtatious house mate, managed to meet quite a few. I remember watching in awe one day, when she accosted one handsome sailor by throwing a snowball at him and getting his attention.

The worst way the war affected us was in what we were served to eat. Meat gradually disappeared from our menus, followed by butter and coffee. In protest our little annex dorm one day went out to eat in a restaurant, where our two debutantes distinguished themselves by ordering *steak!* —a dish the rest of us could not afford. This does illustrate that there was meat available in restaurants. Our military units in the meantime were served lavish meals. One of the sailors once handed me a boxed lunch he had retrieved from his mess. It was full of the most delicious meats, butter, and deserts. I wondered at the time, whether the college was taking our food in order to feed these men, or did the government send shipments for them. One positive effect of the war was a new emphasis on physical fitness. Our gym class followed the calisthenics routine of the Navy WAVES, as a result I became toned and firm and had a wonderful body feeling.

Here, on this midwestern campus, surrounded by conservative traditionalism, I was required yet again to change my identity. But this time I could not do it.

So in Oberlin, surrounded by staid propriety and sobriety—Oberlin was "dry"—I decided to keep my socialist identity and asked Yoshi where the socialist club met. She was startled, but then got me in touch with some upper-class men, and together we formed a socialist club. This was very exciting and meant that I got to know a lot of new people on campus. We met once a week and talked, and we felt virtuous. It is very hard for me from this distance of time to remember what it was we discussed or even believed in. I know we went to a meeting in Cleveland, where the oft-repeated Socialist candidate for president, Norman Thomas, spoke. I remember asking him if he were for or against the war and was startled that he could not answer this question. I am sure that we were all for the war, but we just did not discuss this. The Socialist Workers Party was opposed to the war, but I kept my connection to them secret. At another time we went to a Socialist Youth convention in Detroit. After this, both Shachmanite Trotskyites and Socialists came to campus to recruit me, but of course I was already committed.

At Thanksgiving I decided it was too expensive—thirty dollars—to take the train home. So I got in touch with the Socialist Workers Party in Akron and went for a visit, and later they connected me with a small group in Cleveland. These people all were the true "working class," unionized and proud, very different from the people I had worked with in the sweatshops of New York. They had a practicality about them and a calmness in the face of difficulty and disaster that was truly admirable. At some point I spent many a weekend with them, and my 2 a.m. stay out late pass also came in handy. It is remarkable how little time any of us spent discussing Marxism or other political topics.

But they did make me understand why one can be hurt by a strike and still support the strikers.

I was truly happy that first term at Oberlin and went home at Christmas in a great mood.

It is even now hard to write about what happened that Christmas. I have already spent days avoiding continuing this narrative, but as I got past these events eventually, I think I am able to continue, after all, it was all a very long time ago.

Yoshi, who lived in a New York suburb, and I traveled on the overnight train together, and arrived at Grand Central Station sometimes in the forenoon. When we arrived, I joyfully went to a phone booth to call my father and make arrangements for a visit. My stepmother, Ilse, answered the phone and in a very flat voice told me: "I am sorry your father doesn't want to see you." I remember fingering the flowers embossed in the metal wall of the phone booth, somewhat smiling and actively suppressing my affect. Suppressing the memory of this event took a little longer, but I know that by the time of my return to Oberlin I had no conscious knowledge that this conversation had taken place.

I must have arrived at my mother's house, with Yoshi in tow, in a subdued mood. Yoshi was to eat lunch with us and travel on to her destination. Thomas and Annie were excited to see me, but graceless in their unwelcoming attitude to Yoshi. Did they feel she was an interloper in the family reunion? Luncheon was conducted in a very strained manner. Despite their excitement at seeing me I experienced a sense of lack of welcome. And then with a shock I saw that Mother had sold my piano and was in the process of converting this combination dining and my room into her own room. I had effectively been removed from home barely three months after I left. It must have been with this recognition that I stopped conceptualizing that I had a family. I simply eradicated the idea that I belonged anywhere. It was not an act of defiance or rebellion. I just had a blank in the space where a family is usually affixed. I continued to go through the motion of belonging attending required events, but I felt no connection to the people involved.

Eventually, I must have mentioned that my father refused to see me, and it was then that Eva owned up to the fact that I had written such a charming letter about Oberlin that she had taken it to show to Willi. The beginning sentences of the letter stated that I would come home for Christmas, and if Annie did not have the $30 for my fare, I could "get it from Reich." My father only got as far as that in the letter, and he blew up. He was absolutely enraged. To this day, I don't know whether he felt financially exploited, or resented being called "Reich." I did form my own opinion about how come this letter was shown to him. My sister, after all, must have seen these

215

beginning sentences. I am convinced that she had done it deliberately, even if unconsciously, because she wanted her father to herself. She regretted that she had made peace between us that past summer and had reverted to her destructive mode. I have never voiced this opinion and I am sure some people would find it shocking. However, I had experienced so many episodes of her envy, jealousy and deliberate meanness. And in subsequent years, after she "went over to Reich," she certainly acted secretive about him and possessive, and always when mentioning him to me at all, referred to him as "*my* father."

I returned to Oberlin without consciousness of what had occurred. Repression is written about, but to actually experience it, is almost bizarre. Memory does not disappear: if someone reminded me of it, I would surely have recognized its validity. But by myself, though I was reacting acutely to what had transpired, I had no knowledge, no thought, no connection. At Oberlin I intensified my outreach to others, the socialists, my housemates, and the Cleveland SWP, but I was more restless, more driven, and less happy in an obscure way. I tried to solve my problems with a necking session with one of the men in the socialist club—it was no more than a hug and some chaste kissing. His name was Tom, and in later years, I wondered amusedly, whether I was suddenly attracted to a Tom (read Thomas my stepfather) as a reaction to the rejection by my father.

This light dalliance led to a drastic occurrence, which probably doomed my stay in Oberlin. Another man in the socialist club, a Nisei called Kenji Okuda, a great friend of Tom's, took a terrible exception to this flirtation. He grabbed hold of me and stuck his tongue forcibly down my throat, and then in a stern, righteous and accusing manner, told me I was oversexed. Only years later, did I realize, it is the cultural habit of the Japanese to use shaming as their way to discipline. This accusation must have reached into the depth of my unconscious, where was hidden the struggle between my upbringing with its incestuous dangers and its promulgation of sexual

216

freedom, with the contrasting surrounding culture and its cult of virginity. I tried to defend myself to Kenji, but basically, he accomplished his purpose. After this, I felt alienated and ashamed with the members of the socialist club, and uncomfortable and undesirable. It did not help that one of the male members called me "a brain." Today, I would take that as a compliment, but it was not meant that way. I did manage to meet other people at Oberlin, but the joy had gone out of my stay.

At the same time my classes began to annoy me. During my first term at Oberlin, I had been turned on and excited by some of my classes especially world history, where I learned about ancient empires I had never heard of before, and also the history of the expansion of the Arabs, and the partially successful conquest of Europe by the Ottoman Turks. In the first term only English had been difficult, as with my checkered school career I had never learned grammar or spelling. But this second term in Oberlin, I seem to have lost heart. My English professor annoyed me when she criticized my choosing Eeyore from Winnie the Pooh in an assignment, where we were to describe a character. The professor claimed that Eeyore was not a person, but I felt she had defined the term, 'character' incorrectly because certainly Milne was describing a character type. At that moment, I was so alienated from people that I could think of nobody to write about. And it fitted my mood, it was describing the whining and complaining that I had suffered from years ago at Grete Fried's in Vienna, when I had also been alienated and separated from my family. Inwardly I must have felt just like Eeyore.

When the professor required précis of essays by Ruskin and Emerson. She undid me. I could not concentrate on these essays, and ever since feel I could not write a précis. In the meantime, after my great enthusiasm for world history, my classics course was a tremendous failure, as another narrow-minded professor spent his time talking of army maneuvers in the Peloponnesian Wars and Roman Phalanx formation.

217

With my mother and father, I acted out the feeling of "no family." I stopped writing to my mother, and I did not answer an inquiry from a publisher whether they could include my picture in a book written by my father. I recognize only now, as I am writing this, that this was a subtle approach by my father toward reconciliation. According to his diaries he wrote me a letter in February which, though scolding and critical, seems to have been an attempt to establish communications. I have no memory of this letter. Was it ever sent? But it does not seem alien to me that I might simply have ignored it. I really never understood until now that my father was capable of grand explosions wherein he expelled people, but that he somehow did not mean it, and that the victim was supposed to try to crawl back, repentant for whatever sin had been committed. To me such a response would have been precisely the kind of behavior that he abhorred as representing a "Masochistic Character."

My mother must have had a sixth sense about my alienation. After all her abstraction and seeming lack of interest, she suddenly wanted me badly. At first there was one of these peremptory summonses that I was to go on a ski trip with my sister and her in March. As people with children know, Spring Break is a difficult time to organize a family vacation, as every school has a different schedule. Mother decided that my sister's medical school was more important than my college and scheduled this ski trip during my sister's vacation, but at a time when I was already in classes. I was not too pleased therefore with this invitation. But this kind of summons had a force behind it that one did not dare refuse. It also entailed an attempted seduction, as skiing had been my favorite occupation as a child, and this was to be our first ski trip in America. This pattern of planning amusing or interesting entertainment, one that I could not possibly afford on my own, became Mother's standard technique of keeping me involved with her. I had blanked out my sense and knowledge of family, but I dutifully complied with this trip. It entailed getting permission from all of my professors for

218

a week's absence. It was my classics professor who refused. But as Oberlin allowed three "cuts" per term, I was able to go anyway.

I do love skiing and I enjoyed the ski school classes where I learned more sophisticated techniques than I needed as a child. Also, there were lifts, a wonderful new way for me, taking away the painful climbs up the mountain. And during the day I was happy. I have no memory how I interacted with my mother and sister. However, one night there was a dance, which we attended. I remember dancing and being asked on a date with a man, which I refused. But after that, I got horribly depressed, without any understanding of why. My mother and sister were puzzled, but I could tell them nothing. I know now that I suddenly felt I was alone.

My depression lasted on my return to Oberlin. I remember sitting weeping on the back stairs; Yoshi being worried deciding that it was because I had no date for the final prom. So reluctantly I went to this prom with an arranged date, but I knew that this was not the problem. I began to feel alienated from all the people I knew and hanging out more intensely with my 'new family,' the SWP. Mother sent me letters I did not answer, then she sent telegrams which I also did not answer. She became more and more frantic, but I felt nothing about her or her worry. Family was finished for me; Oberlin was finished for me, and when my roommate decided not to return next year, I decided I would also not come back.

Eva, Annie, and Lore at World's Fair, 1939

Grandfather Alfred Pink, late 1930s

Julie (Julius) Rubin, 1948

Lore and Julie, Mid 1950s

Lore and Julie, c. 1960

Annie Looking Professional, c. 1950s

Thomas, 1950

Chapter 14

RETURN TO NEW YORK
(from 1945 on)

RETURNING HOME

Returning home to one's family after being at college for a year is never easy. One is neither a grown-up independent individual, nor is one the child one was. So neither the parent nor the child knows quite how to deal with each other. When I returned from Oberlin, Annie and Thomas felt a constraint and a sense that they should not interfere or express opinions about how I lived. Rules about attending dinner at a precise time, getting up in the morning, or vague instructions about when to come home, seemed no longer to apply. They probably still hoped for this but did not know if they should mention it. It did not help that my mother had converted my former bedroom cum dining room and general hang-out room with a piano, into her own bedroom/eating-nook. I was relegated to the tiny maid's room, with its tiny bathroom. I am not sure they understood that I felt alienated and estranged from them, had no concept of belonging to them, and felt as if I were just using them as housing. It is quite possible that they discussed this matter between them, not in my presence, but I had no knowledge of it. I came back with the idea that I had to "get out of there" as soon as possible, but I had no idea how to go about this. So I lived there, but I did not feel I lived there.

Instead, I hung out with the Socialist Workers Party, not just with the youth group. The party seemed filled with young people at this time—a great place to hang out. They were headquartered on the second and third floor of an old loft building on University Ave near 13th Street, just below Union Square. One could go there and stuff envelopes and just socialize and be content. On Saturday nights they held dances where heavy drinking was the rule. It was an ideal place for a dislocated youngster who had "failed" at Oberlin. We all believed in Socialism and had a common antagonism to the Soviet Union and Stalinism at a time when, because of its sacrifices during World War II, glorification of that country was at its peak. The Yalta conference had given Stalin all of Eastern Europe, but the impact of this on those countries and on the world had not yet sunk into the consciousness of the general populace. What we meant by Socialism, however, was very vague. I remember one woman, perhaps in her thirties, dreamily speculating that "under Socialism, women will have one child after another." This shocked me, of course, coming from an ideological background that believed in the liberation of women by giving them reproductive freedom, so I enquired what she meant. "Just think of all the eggs you would save," she answered. It was at moments like this that I realized I was different and perhaps not as committed to these ideals. In fact, I had a fleeting feeling of contempt. A strong motive for forgetting my true feelings was, that I needed a sense of belonging. In this sense the Party was like a sect, a place where isolated people could find and be part of a cohesive group—as long as they adhere to the common ideal. The sense of 'group' then becomes so important that inklings of disagreement have to be suppressed into the unconscious or cynically set aside. There was a movie about a Hassidic Sect, shown in the 1990's, called "A Prize above Rubies." The heroine, an orphan, cannot suppress her disagreement and is expunged from the group, with all the difficulties and agonies that entails, while one of the male protagonists who contrary to all morality has sex with her, cynically can remain in the group.

It was not cynicism but a splitting of consciousness that permitted me to remain in the party. But as most of the people I associated with in the Party were of the working class (now called blue-collar class), I was often singled out as different because of my more middle-class background. The members in the party generally did not distinguish between the ultra-rich and the middle class. However, they had great contempt for the "petty bourgeoisie," joining in Marx's contempt for the "respectable" middle class—but also great contempt for the unemployed "Lumpen Proletariat." (This differs substantially from the later ideology of the "New Left" who defended the homeless and those on welfare.) So when my mother insisted that I join her for the obligatory weeks of her much-needed summer vacation, and chose as the location the ultra-rich Bar Harbor, I was roundly ridiculed and sneered at by my comrades. I had to deal with the split in my identity.

VACATION IN MAINE

Despite my general rebelliousness, I obeyed the one unbreakable rule of the joined vacation. When Mother was really determined, there was no contradicting her, and this she did so rarely that the compulsion never wore off. Having been kicked out of her newly found, but "restricted," mountain retreat in Randolph, New Hampshire, Mother now discovered Mt. Desert Island and Bar Harbor in Maine. The year was 1945. The war in Europe was over, and Japan surrendered during our stay in Bar Harbor. And it was three years before a huge fire destroyed much of the flora of Mt. Desert and ruined many of the mansions in Bar Harbor itself. Nowadays, Bar Harbor is a honky-tonk town loaded with tourists and cheap stores selling souvenirs and soft ice cream. But then Bar Harbor was an entrenched sanctuary for the very rich. There were posh stores and a fancy grocer, where the chauffeurs with their limousines would deliver an order from the cook. There were

227

huge mansions, on whose porches sat ladies rocking, wearing hats and white gloves, stockings and Cuban heeled shoes—we on the other hand rented a very modest house on the outskirts of town. At four o'clock in the afternoon these same ladies, dressed in their formal style, could be espied having tea and popovers with strawberry jam and bees on the lawn of the Jordan Pond House in Arcadia National Park. This style of dress seemed extremely strange to us in the middle of a National Park with the most wondrous trail system to climb the many mountains surrounding the pond. Many trails ended at the Jordan Pond House and, after a beautiful scenic climb, we would come in our hiking boots and blue jeans to join these ladies on the lawn for tea. What they thought of us I have no idea. But I do remember a couple of years later when Mother rented in Seal Harbor of the same island, receiving a handwritten invitation to tea which read in part, "My butler informs me that the daffodils will be in full bloom." Not having the proper attire, we could not attend this remarkable party. As before, despite my feelings of estrangements, there were always amusements which Mother offered and which I accepted as my due.

My sister and I found an unusual friendship growing between us on these vacations in Maine. In those days there were no crowds, no hordes of tourists clogging up Ocean drive. We would hop about on the pink rocks, sun ourselves, admire the many tidal pools with their fauna of sea urchin and anemones—the tidal pools are all gone now, picked lifeless by the tourists— eat boiled lobster on the beach by pounding them with rocks to open the shells, and actually swim in the arctic waters of the Atlantic Ocean. She was in medical school at the time. I admired her greatly for her intellect, her athletic prowess, and at the same time her rather subtle. rebellious attitude toward Mother. But there were lapses on her part into rivalry and hostility, sometimes overt and sometimes so hidden that they might have been accidental. We would be riding in a car and suddenly she would say: —in the same tone as she used in Vienna about "die Hexen kommen"—"You have mammary glands, you have mammary glands," implying an ugly mass of fatty tissue. If one asked her to stop, she would say, "I was merely saying you have mammary glands." That summer we went on our famous bicycle ride. Eva was more athletic than I and additionally owned a good bike. I had to rent one from a shop in Bar Harbor. We decided to visit some friends on Newberry Neck in Surrey Maine, over forty miles away. Every time nowadays that I drive upon that same route I marvel at our adventure. The road is at times a roller coaster of little hills, or at other places a steady 10-mile rise to Ellsworth. In a car one hardly notices this, but on a bike especially a rental one, without gears, it was murder. Drivers of cars took pity on me and told me to hang on and they would pull me, but that was too scary. My sister seemed fine and fit, but I was exhausted. When we got to Surrey and had seven more miles to go on a dirt road, I simply rebelled, sat down on the steps of a little grocery store and refused to budge. I no longer cared if I sat there forever. Luckily a truck came by and gave us a ride. My sister acted solicitous, and I have no idea whether she knew what she was getting me into. On the way home we shipped the bikes by Railroad Express.

Our visit was to a friend of the family, Annie Bergman, a woman just a few years older than we. She was a protégé of Mädi Olden, a sort of adopted daughter, whom Mädi much preferred to her own real daughter, who had remained in Europe during the war, had lost a leg, and was not enamored of her mother. Visiting with Annie Bergman and her child was a violinist of the newly formed Julliard String Quartet. As may be remembered, Mädi collected artists and musicians around her and ran a salon to which one was invited if one had the proper admiration for her. I did flirt with this musician who was young and handsome. The next morning the congenial atmosphere in the house was decidedly frosty and I felt definitely unwanted and excluded from the group. I could not understand this change, but it undermined my self-confidence. It was years later that my sister confessed that she had told Annie Bergman that the musician and I had retired to bed

229

together and were having sex. So there it was again, my sister's destructive jealousy and envy, and her need to extrude me from a group, ruining my mood and threatening our relationship.

POLITICS AT NEW YORK UNIVERSITY

That fall of 1945, I enrolled at NYU, a school of vast contrasts to Oberlin. NYU was a university with world-renowned professors in many fields, a huge student body, and an urban campus. Unfortunately, these famous professors taught small classes. As student registration gave priority to seniors, then juniors etc., I had to wait for my senior year before I could register for any of their classes, only to find that they were all taught from 10 to 11a.m. Monday, Wednesday and Friday. In the end one could attend only one of the eagerly awaited classes, taught by these renowned professors. Otherwise, there were huge lecture courses in tiered auditoria given by bored instructors. Nevertheless, as a history major, I had the opportunity to study with Professor Ferguson and that was very exciting. Into this milieu I entered with confidence. The first term I met many people, some I knew from before and many I met for the first time. I would attend AYD meetings (American Youth for Democracy), a Communist front organization which had huge numbers of adherents. I did this at the behest of the SWP, which always wished to infiltrate and then recruit from these mass student organizations. The Communists always ran huge youth organizations, changing the names over the years, without admitting to its members that they were Communist run. One did not "join" AYD. One simply attended. I was pretty busy that first semester at NYU.

At the same time the SWP had a contest of who could sell the most subscriptions to *The Militant*, their weekly newspaper. I think the subscription cost 25 cents. It is unbelievable now when I think back on it, but I would go into Harlem and canvas inside the tenement buildings, knocking on doors to sell my paper. Startled Black residents, often sleepy, wearing cloths wound about their heads, would open the door to this sole white teenager and generally would buy the paper. Was this a dangerous place for me to be? I don't know. In recent years, such an adventure would be most foolhardy. But perhaps Harlem was a different place then. I, on the other hand, got a glimpse of the crowded conditions of these tenements, and the rundown smelly aspects of their stairwells. When the contest came to an end, I had sold the most newspapers. *The Militant* proudly announced that I had won. But this created very unfortunate consequences for me. The leadership of AYD read *The Militant!* There followed a most bizarre confrontation. As was mentioned above, the AYD was not an acknowledged Communist organization, but I was hauled up on trial.

As far as I know, AYD had no formal structure, no membership requirements, and no by-laws; if it had had any of these, then I would never have joined the organization. Ostensibly it was not connected to the Communist Party, so that selling a Trotskyist newspaper should not have bothered them. Nevertheless, I was ordered to stand trial.

This was America in 1945, we had just won a war to "defend Democracy and Freedom" and we were about to spread this doctrine to the whole world. But this trial was out of the Moscow law books (a model of jurisprudence that Russia did not abandon till 2002). The judges were the prosecutors. There was no jury. The trial was held in a NYU classroom in front of perhaps 40 people. The prosecutors harangued me; I can no longer remember what they said. I asked to defend myself, but this was not allowed. This was not a trial with prosecution and defense, as we know it, this was just an accusation. I was kicked out of the organization. And then I was punished by "shunning." No one was allowed to speak to me, and no one did. Suddenly I was surrounded by silence, had no one to eat lunch with or hang out with. When once I was seen talking to someone, who incidentally later joined the Trotskyists, a person walked behind him and said, "You are known by whom you associate with." That is how I knew it was an organized shunning.

This was America, but these students obeyed a discipline foreign to us. Shunning, as many religious sects know, is a very effective means of punishment. Not only does it keep everyone else in line, but also it totally isolates and demolishes the offender. I became a waif at NYU, wandering the halls confused and dislocated. It was a truly shocking experience. How word got out about my "sentence" or how it influenced hundreds of students is still an amazing puzzle to me. What happened to me was not unique. The man I later married, also a Troskyist who had joined a previous Communist front organization, called the ASU (American Students for Democracy, a huge organization in the late thirties), while in high school, had the same experience. One day, after being discovered as an "enemy," he also was surrounded by silence and absolutely no one ever spoke to him again. Both of us remember these as a very traumatic experience. Of course, it drew each of us closer to the SWP. Furthermore, because I was a commuter student in an urban, mainly commuter school, I suddenly knew nobody. After I recovered from the shock for a term or two, I became totally focused on my studies instead of the social life of the school. As a result, I got all A's for a couple of years which helped me get into Medical School.

Feeling alienated from both my parents, and separated from my sister, who was living in Philadelphia, I turned to the SWP for family cum/ friendship support; but being totally wrapped up in this organization proved to have too many problems. Mostly I hung around with women in the party who were emancipated and self-supporting, something I desperately wanted to become. But these women also eventually disappointed. And the men I dated were definitely anti-intellectual so one could not have a proper conversation.

There were also problems for me with the ideology. All of us, of course, wanted to be "good" and "virtuous," but I no longer knew quite what "good" really meant. The working class in America was suddenly doing well, was unionized, patriotic, and seemingly happy. In fact, they started thinking of themselves, and still do, as truly middle class with the same ambitions for their children as other Americans. So, the Marxist division of classes seemed not to hold intellectually. There seemed to be no need for revolution and certainly no desire for it anywhere. A party preaching revolution was just out of date, a remnant of an earlier time. The truly downtrodden, the Bowery "bums," the few homeless, were relegated to the unsavory lumpen proletariat and not admired or defended. The only group that seemed oppressed were the Blacks, then called "Negroes." Herbert Hill, one of my friends from the party, made the plight of the Blacks his cause and fought valiantly to force the trade unions to admit Blacks. For this he was later made labor secretary of the NAACP, one of a group of very rare whites to work for that organization.

But the SWP did not make the cause of Blacks their main focus and it was not clear what we were fighting for. Fighting the Communists and their ubiquitous propaganda was worthwhile at the time, though later tarnished by Senator McCarthy as well as by a group of ex-radicals calling themselves Neo-Conservatives. History would soon prove that the Marxist-generated "dictatorship of the proletariat" was distinctly similar to Stalin's totalitarian society, no matter what country it was achieved in. The Soviet Union was not an aberration; it was the real Socialism.

It is ironic, as I write this to realize that America was ready for a revolution, but of a totally different type, never conceptualized or imagined by these Marxists. In the 60's and 70's, this revolution came with a huge, mass following of a size the SWP could only dream of. These revolutionaries concerned themselves with civil rights, the rights and place of minorities, the fate of the really downtrodden, the rights of women and created such a change in sexual mores that they destroyed the cult of virginity and the double standard. They got rid of most legal bans to birth control and abortion—a battle that is, unfortunately, not finished yet. There suddenly sprang up a "New Left" that bore no resemblance to the old Socialist and Communist Parties. These social changes in attitude in America encompassed a much wider population than any radical splinter group. Had I grown up in the 60's, what an enthusiastic experience I would have had!

The ideology of the "sexual revolution" owed much of its thinking, at least in the European version of this revolution, to the work my father had done in the 20's and 30's. It was he who had been the champion for freeing sexuality from its Victorian shackles, the rights for divorce, birth control, privacy, freedom to have orgasm and freedom to masturbate, if no partner was available. And it was he, who tied these existing sexual repressions to the authoritarian patriarchy and to capitalism. His Sex-Pol organization in Berlin reached many thousands of adherents. In the French student movement of 1968, Reich and his teachings were idealized. As a result, 15 years after his death the French psychoanalyst Chasseguet-Smirgel wrote a vicious book attacking Reich. (Grunberger, B. & Chasseguet Smirgel, J. [1970 French] [1986 English].) Her argument was that Reich was crazy and therefore should have no followers. I am sure she wrote this to counteract the ideology of the student movement. Apparently, Reich had again become a threat to the psychoanalysts. Uttermost in the minds of some psychoanalysts was still the fear of being tainted by his name. Even today, Reich's early political and sexual works are read and admired in much of Germany and Austria. It is not clear to me, however, that in the United States, the movement that led to the "sexual revolution" was aware of its intellectual antecedents. I don't think that Reich had any idea of where his sexual revolution would lead. He never envisioned the teenage pregnancy rate, AIDS, or rapid, random sexual encounters. Of these results he would have vigorously disapproved.

JULIE (JULIUS RUBIN)

My uncomfortable, dislocated adolescence finally came to an end. One day, one of the few interesting people in the SWP, Herbie Hill, invited me to a party given by his friend for a somewhat older group than I had been socializing with. I remember I brought as an escort the younger brother of a friend of mine. The party was held in Chelsea, then a working class, low rent neighborhood, in a third-floor dormered attic with slanting roof and casement windows—a very unusual setting for New York, reminiscent of Paris. There was much intense talk and drinking; the setting similar to scenes recently depicted in the movie, "Frieda." At one point a man went to the fire escape and threatened suicide. For some reason, I was unconcerned or could not grasp that he meant it. Someone talked him out of it and eventually he returned to the room. But what was memorable about the evening was our host. I had not seen him around or met him before. He was sitting with a slinky, black-dressed woman on his lap, but we made eye contact and flirted above her. He was 24 to my 17. His name was Julius Rubin, but everyone called him Julie—this was a time, when that name had not yet become exclusively feminine. I must have made an impression on him, because a week later he appeared at the Saturday night SWP dance and asked me to join him and a group of others for coffee after the dance. There were eight of us, four men and four women. I assumed I was his date, but during that night realized he had also asked another woman to be his date. She was offended; I was nonchalant, so somehow, I won out.

Our courtship had its ups and downs. First, he acted as my hero. I was handing out leaflets on the busy 14th Street, when a drunk accosted me. Suddenly Julie appeared, looking swashbuckling in a leather jacket and rescued me. After this we started to date regularly. One of the strangest events was the first time he came to my home to pick me up. As has been described, for years Mother had been abstracted, would withdraw after dinner to write her papers. The night Julie came to our house was the first time that Eva, Annie and I sat in her study mending and sewing: a real family scene. When he came in, his jaw dropped at the sight of this petty bourgeois togetherness. He himself, in rebellion, had left his family several years before and was turned off by what he misinterpreted as domesticity within the bosom of the family. Later he asked me to attend a Mozart concert. I shocked him by refusing his invitation because I associated classical music with my family's insistence on "Kultur." Nevertheless, he asked me out again.

Our dates were very different from anything that had gone before; his way of flirting was to impress me with his intellect. Finally, I had met someone who could express himself, read books, was knowledgeable, and wished to hold intelligent conversations. The flash in our courtship came when he told me, "If the revolution does not come in 10 years, I am leaving the party." I had found someone who could help me out of the narrow sect I had joined—though this took a couple of years. And I had found someone with whom I could connect and be my true self. He had dropped out of college at the behest of the Party, had worked at munitions and ship building—occupations exempt from the draft, as the party disapproved of the war—and then joined the merchant marine, a branch of the service, not under military control. Our first dating was brief as he was slated to ship out again for several months. While he was gone, we corresponded, one letter each, and I determined I was going to marry him. He seems to have had the same idea.

Julie returned in May of 1946, I had turned 18, and within a couple of days I had moved in with him. My family worried when I stayed out all night and, after the third night, hesitantly asked me, if it was Julie I was seeing. When Mother realized that the relationship was serious, she began to express a number of other worries. After learning that he could not get along with his mother, she worried that he was neurotic. It turned out, however, that he had been undergoing psychoanalysis for a couple of years prior to his shipping out. Mother was greatly relieved; what faith she had in her profession! Later, when it appeared that we were in a more permanent situation, she asked him "how do you intend to support my daughter?" Considering that she had had to support herself all her life, this question was rather amusing. Julie's answer is famous in our family lore. "I am a professional revolutionary, so I don't intend to support her." But I felt great. I had met a man who would not object to my developing my own career or call me "Miss Brain."

His lovely garret room was rented to someone else when he returned from sea, so we moved into furnished quarters in Chelsea. I remember that all night long we could hear rats gnawing at wood inside the walls. But after a couple of months his old room became available, and we moved onto 18th Street between 9th and 10th Avenue. (I recently returned there to see our first home, only to find that practically the whole street had been turned into warehouses.) We had one room, an alcove kitchenette and a bathroom with a door. If we were mad at each other, one had to go to the bathroom to be alone. Nevertheless, we lived there for four years. Being New Yorkers, we had cockroaches, and we also had mice. Julie woke one morning to find three baby mice on my pillow. He did not tell me about that at the time. Another time I opened the oven door and a mouse tumbled out. They had made a nest in the insulation.

Our neighborhood consisted of tenement apartment houses with railroad flats that had bathtubs in the kitchen. I believe that private toilets had been installed instead of the communal ones in the hallways. Ours was one of the few remaining three storied houses. Mostly our neighbors were dockworkers and their families. The men walked about with giant, evil-looking grappling hooks with which they would hoist the bales and crates. Some of the older women spent their entire days leaning on a pillow placed on the windowsills so they could lean out and watch the street. These women caused us to have a problem. One day there was a riot outside our house—but we were not home—as our neighbors accused the landlady that we were running a house of ill repute. They had seen me kissing Julie in front of the window, and they had seen me with male visitors, just visitors not undressed or kissing. The landlady staunchly defended us. Of course, we had visitors, many visitors, male and female, and not only when both of us were at home. We never thought anything of it; and of course, we kissed. Don't all couples? But we were not married, although the landlady did not know that. We did, however, observe a courting couple, who smooched in doorways across the street for several years, then had a big wedding to which practically the whole neighborhood was invited, and then never kissed or smooched or even hung out together again. So, naturally we called attention to ourselves, as we were obviously not married if we were kissing.

We continued to belong to the party and still were under the obligation to work in a proletarian setting. I dropped out of college and was a waitress, while Julie tried various proletarian careers. I would come home at night and drop huge bags of coins from tips on our bed and count my money. In those days, things were very cheap, and I was making what seemed like a fortune. What defeated me was having to iron uniforms. I had never ironed a thing in my life. In my home, after our maid had left, we sent things to a laundry. Julie and I felt we had to get into the skilled work force. He enrolled in a trade course to become an electrician—a skill that did not stick with him. Later he did not remember how to fix a lamp or splice a wire. I did not know what to become and this led to a fiasco experience with counseling.

I went to a social service agency for occupational counseling. A male social worker interviewed me. He was one of these self-possessed, emphatic young men, sure of his opinions. Of course, I did not tell him that the SWP required us to be proletarians and I wanted a skill. He asked me what my father did and what my husband did. I told him my father was a doctor and then I told him my husband was a house painter (I believe that was then his occupation). He was shocked. He was so impressed that my father was a doctor; how could I marry a house painter coming from such an important background. He sized me up as a rebellious daughter and exclaimed, "And I bet you didn't have a wedding either"!!! Being new to American culture, I misunderstood him completely. I thought he meant we were not legally married, but he meant the big party and ceremony that goes with marriage. I mumbled abashed, that we meant to do this but hadn't gotten around to it yet. But I did understand that this man was an idiot, a conclusion jumper, and thoroughly incompetent. He told me to come back next week, but I never returned.

My mother, recognizing that my relationship was ongoing, seriously worried about our future. She went on a campaign to get me back to school. Finally, she offered financial support. She would pay our $35/month rent (including utilities) and give us $10 a week for food, plus pay my tuition, if I would return to school. I was reluctant to have my independence undermined like this. But at the same time the proletarian life felt fake and the SWP was definitely palling on me. So, after six months together, Julie and I both returned to college—he to his tuition free, previous school, Brooklyn College, and I back to NYU.

Living together before marriage is so customary these days, that it has become the norm. In 1946 it was highly unusual. It is the rest of the country who have caught up to us. My family did not mind but they were worried about what might constitute "moral turpitude" in the eyes of NYU. Julie also did not have my European background and insisted that we get married legally. In February 1947 we decided we would wed, though I could not see the point. As my family was not much given to rites and ceremonies, having duly obtained a license, we trundled down alone to City Hall to get married. I remember I wore a bright orange wool suit, probably my best outfit. I was 18; he was 25. However, it turned out I was too young to get married at city hall, I should have been 21. So, as we stood befuddled and confused in the hall, a guard approached us and said he knew a judge who would marry us.

The judge was presiding over a trial. A man stood accused of stealing a roll of cloth off a garment truck. There was a six-paneled all women jury. There were spectators in the courtroom, probably people awaiting the following trials, a court stenographer and two lawyers. The judge asked the jury whether they would like to interrupt the trial to witness a wedding and they seemed agreeable. So we stood before the bench; the judge made a long philosophical speech about the meaning of marriage, and then had us say our vows. The jury cried, the defendant and both lawyers shook Julie's hand. Two guards acted as our witnesses. Julie always maintains that he wished to giggle but was afraid of being in contempt of court. Afterwards, we took the subway home and quarreled because he would not kiss me in public. In ensuing years, so many people have marveled at my getting married "so young," to have lasted in that marriage and to have still become educated and a professional, but there are two factors that people do not take into account. First in 1946 and 1947 as the men returned from war, everybody got married, young and old. People know about the baby boom, but never think that there was also a backlog of relationships. The other factor was personal to us. We knew about birth control, while other people either did not or just wanted large families. So getting married did not imply an immediate interruption of our youthful years.

Mother gave us a wedding reception. I remember we got a very formal china service, which I was much too young to appreciate, and we turned it in for pottery ware. Julie's family was not there, he had not been in touch with them for a few years. It only occurred years later to Mother, when we were about to have a child, that probably she should meet his mother before this event as they would be sharing grand-motherhood. But actually, by the time we had children, his mother was dead.

Chapter 15

SECTS

Much has been written on sects; what holds them together, what makes people join them, what makes it so hard to leave them? One does not usually think of a political party as a sect. It took me years to understand that this is exactly what the SWP was. A very small group of people, isolated from society, preaching revolution to the absent masses, talking to themselves. When they had "mass" meetings, in a dingy hall with hard uncomfortable wooden folding chairs, there might have been 200 people there. Nationally there were perhaps 1000 or 2000 members. Compared to the Communist Party, whose members and their fellow travelers could fill Madison Square Garden, our "mass" meetings were pitiful, even painful. We did not seem to notice this, or at least consciously, while we prated about the "coming revolution." I remember one memorable "mass" meeting. Tom Kerry, I think his name was, was joyfully introducing our leader, James P Cannon, when he made an unconscious slip and said, "Here comrades, is James P Morgan!" We all laughed, Tom was embarrassed, but even then, I understood what this slip meant. Tom did not want to be in this shabby hall, with this unsuccessful hopeless cause; he wanted to be associated with one of the great capitalists, a man he could admire and identify with.

Before the Cannonite-Shachtmanite split in the party, and also before my time, there had been a number of members of the intellectual elite in the party, who had various important ties to the New York intelligentsia and to academia. At the same time, before the U.S. government had sent some party leaders to the penitentiary for preaching "the overthrow" of the U.S. government, on the worker's side of the party, there had been a strong tie to the great union movements of the 30's and early 40's. Even if the party membership was small in number in those days, it was connected to the outer world. But in my time, it seems the party was in its death throes, no longer an influence on either the intellectual or the labor front, with a stale message of Marxism, held together more by an anti-Soviet, anti-Stalin stance, than by any message of hope or salvation. It was war time, the general public saw that the Soviet Union was fighting Hitler, Stalin was portrayed as a hero, the Red Army was engaging Hitler on the Eastern Front, and thus helping our war effort on the Western Front. The American public was no longer interested in the old fights between Trotsky and Stalin, or whether the Soviet Union was a "degenerated workers' state"—instead of the pure idealized true "workers' state" that Marx had predicted. To most people, these seemed like controversies similar to "how many angels are on a pin?" Employment was good during wartime; the American public did not want to change things. They certainly did not want a revolution. It was only several years after World War II, when the Cold War started, that the general public caught on to the evils and tricks of Stalin, something that the party members, both Shachtmanites and Cannonites, knew about in great detail. And it is ironic, now in our current situation of conservatism, that many of the more influential and intellectual Shachtmanites turned into "neo-cons," that is, old radicals turned conservative, anti-communist, defenders of free trade, which meant capitalism, and staunch supporters of our constitution. I believe they had no idea where the neo-con movement would eventually lead.

The SWP adhered strictly to the Marxist theory of the class struggle. They believed in a bourgeoisie, a petty bourgeoisie and the proletariat. But Marx also had described a "lumpen proletariat," a sort of underclass composed of drug addicts, alcoholics, the homeless, the mentally ill, prostitutes and pimps, petty criminals and the insane—in other words, those people who are currently called "the poor" as opposed to the "working poor." It is a remarkable description of ideological change that today workers are really thought to be part of the middle class and it is "the poor" who are now thought to be the "oppressed." But the SWP held tightly to the principle that only the working class was capable of making a revolution, so only workers were worthwhile. They scorned the middle class, calling it narrow minded, reactionary, holding on to what little they had, instead of thinking of the greater good. While the bourgeoisie were hated as "the capitalists," the exploiters of the working class, they were also secretly admired for their power. Like Marx, the SWP despised the "lumpen proletariat."

Because only the working class could make the revolution, party members had to be workers. One was supposed to learn a trade, join a union, and recruit from within. College education was despised as bourgeois. Apart from the prison sentences of six of the members, I am sure the basic reason for the split between the Cannonites and the Shachtmanites was related to this anti-education, anti-intellectual stance. Whatever theoretical differences they had avidly debated about—whether the Soviet Union was a degenerate workers' state or a failed revolution that had created a totalitarian, autocratic system—did not matter as much as the stance on education.

In a curious repetition of history both my father and my husband rebelled against the idea that only the working class could make a revolution. My father was actually expelled from the Communist party of Germany in 1934, not because of his highly visible opposition to the reproductive policies of the Stalinist regime, but because in his "Mass Psychology of Fascism" (Reich, W., 1933–2020 German, 1945 English), he averred that not only the middle class, but also the revered working class could turn fascist because of the authoritarian suppression of their sexual drives which would then turn into distorted, frustrated, sadism. This went against the communist doctrine

243

that the working class could never become fascist. Twenty-five years later, my husband shot across the Trotskyite bow with the pronouncement, that the Chinese Maoist revolution had been a *peasant* revolt and not a *working-class* revolt. In his case, too, it was obvious that he was on the way out of this association.

What made us join? What kept us there? I have already described that at a time of war, when I lost all the males of my social group to the draft, I discovered the SWP youth group, who were a wonderful and easygoing group. Later a series of personal reverses and trauma combined to make the SWP the only group that I still related to. Joining the party of adults was a more serious step, but the party also was full of young people, dances, and companionship. There were always men around as many of the members were merchant seamen and thus in and out of port. In fact, the party mixed up World War II with World War I, in averring that this was a capitalist war that had nothing to do with the working class. This was the reason that male party members preferred to join the merchant marine or munitions factory work, to joining or being drafted by the military. Another reason for joining the adult party was that there were also young women, while in the youth group there was only one other girl, and the rest were males.

There were also obvious reasons why I was bound to become a misfit in the party. The youth group had been made up of middle-class young people; the party was made up of working-class people. It must be clear by now, that I was not particularly impressed or carried away by Marxism, loyalty to the working class, or to Trotsky's theory, which I still don't quite understand, that there had to be a permanent revolution, by which, I think, he meant, it had to carry from country to country. I was more familiar from my own background with the severe anti-Stalinism of the party. I could recite huge instances of antidemocratic and nefarious activities that the Communists had committed: including the destruction of any reference to Trotsky in the holdings of the NY Public Library, the murder of anti-

Stalinists on foreign soil, the shunning and other devices to silence critics, the use of front organizations under false pretenses, and the infiltration of certain unions to the point of taking them over. But as already stated, the SWP was more a party against Stalin than a party for the future. Being surrounded by nice, but in certain ways uneducated people, meant that we never discussed any issues. I did fit in well enough as long as I suppressed or never voiced any intellectual ideas or questions. If I did say something out of their mainstream, I could see people pulling back and feeling uncomfortable with me.

There were also many odd people in the party who did make an indelible impression. There was the young man or probably teen-aged boy who came to our apartment every day and just sat silently and miserably, not interacting. I realize now he was seriously depressed, but I did not understand that at the time. There was also the very active and assertive man, called Irving, who could park in a tiny New York parking space by pushing backward with his car till he bumped and pushed the car behind, and then bumping and pushing the car in front till he had created a space. If someone was parking by pulling into a space backward, he was capable, without batting an eye, to pull quickly into the space forward, beating the other parker to it. He pushed Julie and me into joining a Lower East Side Social club, in a dingy cellar, in order to recruit its members into the party—but they later turned out to be Stalinists. Only Irving could have accomplished this. We were much too shy or inhibited.

The social club was happy to take us on and we became fast friends with about four people. As we had no money, I used a cookbook with guidelines from the Department of Agriculture. In it we were advised to mix a pound of hamburger with oatmeal to stretch the meat. I invited our new friends to dinner and served them the tiny hamburgers mixed with the oatmeal. What they thought of it, I do not know, but to me the patties looked and tasted like horse manure. This friendship lasted a few months. But then, as

245

I was dancing with one of the men, he mentioned that he could get hold of a copy of Trotsky's <u>History of the Russian Revolution.</u> This was a book that was out of print. I said I would be interested, whereupon we never saw the members of the social club again. I had been tricked into revealing our identity. The funny thing about this was, that I don't remember a single conversation with these people about politics.

At one point Irving asked me to open a bank account in my name but with his signature for entrée into the account. I agreed to this naively. Later I found out that he had put the money from his family's business into that account and then proceeded to donate it to the party. Had Irving committed a crime? I don't know. Perhaps he had a legal right, though not an ethical one, to draw money from the family business. What I do know is that he endangered me without a second thought for my safety. Everything was legitimate to him for the cause.

As I returned to school and even talked vaguely of going to Medical School, he advised me strongly against this. He said I would "alienate" myself from the proletariat. Our friendship with Irving broke up, after he made a pass at me, which I rejected. He then lost interest in our connection.

We all knew that the FBI had agents that had infiltrated our group. These were still the days of J. Edgar Hoover and his preoccupation with subversive groups. After Churchill's "Iron Curtain" speech, there was great concern in this country with loyalty to the government. I remember one person who could be identified as an FBI agent with certainty. One night a man appeared at one of the dances, straight posture, dressed in "proper" clothes and a tie, hair cut just so, and one of those very American faces with even features and proper expression. (A younger physical version of what presidential candidate John Edwards looked like). He stood out, being as different from everyone else as one could imagine; nor was he interested in the women who swarmed about him and made sexual advances. This clean-cut young man finally accepted the invitation to hook up with my friend

Carmen and moved in with her. This infiltration of our organization came apart when Carmen a few months later found Broadway theater ticket stubs in his jacket pocket. Party members had no interest and no money for the Broadway stage.

Just like the Communists, the party seems to have had strict discipline about the party line. A more intellectual member had made some critical comments to me, which I unknowingly, or rather unconsciously, let slip to someone else. Reminiscent of the "trial" I had suffered at NYU, this man later told me that he, also, had been hauled before a disciplinary committee, and severely reprimanded. Julie and I became suspect as we returned to school and started thinking of graduate training. It was considered an act of rebellion to give up our "working class" occupations and to return to school. We noticed increasing unfriendliness and frowns directed toward us by our "comrades." Julie reacted by withdrawing and stopped attending meetings. I hung around a little longer. At the same time that the party members began to distrust us, they showed an inability to cope with regular society. They were so cut off from ordinary middle-class connections. One day they called me up in a panic because one member had become catatonic, unable to speak or react to people. The comrades knew my mother was an analyst and they wanted me to call her to find out what to do. They had no conception that an analyst did not treat catatonic patients. They had no conception of the vast free hospital system that New York City provided at that time. So I had to call Mother and get her to recommend a psychiatrist.

One day when I appeared at the party headquarters, George, the head of the New York branch of the SWP, came up to me and sneered in my face, "How is the petty bourgeois Julie doing?" A sudden rage overcame me, and I snarled back before I could think. "I am a petty bourgeois, and always have been, and I am proud of it!" George turned white as a sheet, and I stalked out. That was the end of our party affiliation. I must confess, I have been proud of that outburst to this day. It was as if I finally found my "true self."

What took us so long to leave? As I have mentioned the party was a sect. A sect means that one associates only with the members of the sect, as all others might misunderstand one or corrupt one's ideology. We had cut ourselves off from other acquaintances and almost completely from our families. We only knew party members. And now, what we most feared, happened. We were subjected to the same type of shunning as we had already experienced with the Communists. If we passed one of our ex-comrades on the street, they refused to greet us. If we accosted them, they snubbed us. We did not mind these snubs, we did not care for these people, had no respect or admiration. The people we did care for were themselves withdrawing from the party in their own quiet way, and these friendships endured in the end. But for a couple of years we were not in touch.

There ensued a period—I tend to think of it as lasting a couple of years, but perhaps it was much shorter—when we were entirely alone as if we had moved to a strange city. We engrossed ourselves in our studies, and we saw no one. It is true, we were going to school, but they were commuter schools. Here and there we got acquainted with someone in a class, but we never brought them home or saw them outside of school. Why it was suddenly so hard to connect with people at school, I don't know, it felt different from before. Perhaps it was because our high school cohort had moved on. Julie had been out of school since 1937 and this was perhaps 1947 or1948. Our classes were large and impersonal; we did not join any clubs. It was only later that Julie made some friends in school. In the beginning of our self-exile from the party we saw no one.

Julie and I lived in a one-room apartment. We had two desks in the room, and there we sat and worked. I can't remember now whether we shared a portable typewriter I had received as a graduation present from high school. We had so little money, that we did not partake of the cultural life of the city, certainly not the movies. We may have had a radio, but I do not remember it. My memory is of us sitting in our garret, painted dark blue, with sloping ceilings over the dormer windows and studying or typing papers. I had the feeling that we would never enter a social life again. It resonated for me with all the moves to strange cities that I had made in childhood.

Under these circumstances we got to know each other very well. We ironed out the kinks in our marriage, softened idealizations and accepted faults. Julie has described this as "two square pegs rubbing against each other till they became round." If we quarreled one had to retreat to the bathroom to close a door between us and have some privacy. We had so much in common and our basic bond was strong. Not only did we share the seriousness of our studies and later many cultural interests and seem to have had a common sense of aesthetics, but we also shared both the party experience, our previous "shunning" by the Communists, and our interest in history and current events. Above all we shared the alienation from our families and the need to "go it alone."

It is true our alienation was not complete. Julie had left home after a year of college to become a "worker" as was required by the SWP. This was a total shock to his uneducated Jewish immigrant family. One did not leave home and live on one's own, no matter how old, till one was married. Unfortunately, a year or so after Julie left, his father, aged 49, died of a heart attack. His mother, in a hysterical outburst at the funeral, accused Julie of "murdering" the father. After this, he walked out and had no intention of any further contact. He did keep in touch with one younger sister. I kept in touch with my sister, but she was in Philadelphia going to medical school. My mother, to her credit, would not accept our alienation and kept at us with some invitations, the obligatory two weeks in summer, and especially her insistence that she help us financially so we would complete school. At some point she also insisted that I should go into analysis. Her insistence paid off eventually, as I grew up and recognized her value in many aspects and could accept that she was not skilled at mothering.

We were rescued from our social isolation by the owner of a small grocery store in the middle of the block where we lived. The block between 9th and 10th Avenue on 18th Street was very long, and, amongst the tenements in the middle of the block was a very small grocery store, the type that extended credit to its known customers. The owner therefore knew everybody in the neighborhood. One day, I remember it exactly, I went there to buy a stick of butter. The grocer told me there was another couple living on the block, who were students, and he thought we should meet. It was a huge block of tenements, filled mostly with dockworkers and their families. We lived in one of the few left-over private houses, now converted to apartments. This grocer knew all the thousands of inhabitants and recognized our "differentness." He said, this other couple were students, but perhaps he also recognized that both the husbands were Jewish, in this Irish conclave, and even odder that both the wives were half Jewish with Jewish fathers and Protestant mothers. The store owner was also different because he was a Greek in an Irish neighborhood. In any case he left a note for us with a phone number and so we met Gideon and Shirley Nachumi. They lived in a tenement with a bathtub in the kitchen, usually covered by a metal plate. We made an instant friendship, becoming very close. Gideon was premed at school, but Shirley was already working as a teacher. Through them we met a whole group of people, intellectual and interesting, vaguely liberal, but in no way political. And thus, our life in the real New York began.

CHOOSING A PROFESSION

Having given up the SWP and the need to become a worker, I now had to seriously consider what my future professional goals were to be. Unwittingly I was influenced by my family background.

My Opa, Grandfather Alfred Pink, was in *trade.* He imported cocoa. Mother explained a few times, that he wanted to study biology, or even be a concert pianist, but that circumstances had forced him into trade. Trade was not acceptable; it was not intellectual; it was not cultured. Mother had some very definite ideas of what was acceptable. The cocoa business, a comfortably lucrative endeavor, was an unfortunate condition for Opa. But he accepted it. She did not. Was her attitude influenced by the ubiquitous nobility of Austria, who would not mingle or meld with the bourgeoisie? However, one was not interested with mingling with the aristocracy either; cultureless "barbarians," only interested in fashion, being seen, or in the country riding and hunting. As a reaction, one was to be more interesting than they. And at the beginning of the 20th century, Vienna was a very interesting place. Artists and musicians flourished, so did philosophers, scientists and writers. And Viennese medical knowledge was world famous, or so we were given to understand. However, after World War I, starvation and deprivation, one was to *earn a living.* Indeed, there were many beggars, and many of the intelligentsia were starving.

These attitudes were subtly infused into my sister and my consciousness with our "Griesbrei" and our cocoa. We also knew that to marry and become a "Hausfrau" was anathema, not worthy of a modern liberated woman. We were to earn our living and hire a country girl, fresh off the farm as a "Dienstmädchen" to do the housework and cooking, perhaps also child raising.

As we entered college, our future became of grave concern to our mother. As my sister and I would be enthused and stimulated by one field or another, my mother would become anxious. Her face still and serious, a slight frown on her brow, she would try to dampen our interest in becoming an artist, a scientist, a mathematician, by saying: "But you can't make a living with that." I was most interest in studying history, my sister mathematics. How was my mother to know, that soon after our graduations, the academic world exploded, and all these fields opened up? At the time we were talking she thought with "that" one could only become a teacher and there was no money in that. Even about the money question she was mistaken as the colleges and universities expanded to accommodate the discharged GI's, salaries expanded in lock step.

There was only one avenue that would fit her idea of respectability, interest, and ability to earn a living and that was medicine. We were to become doctors. Secretly she hoped we would choose to become psychoanalysts, but that she did not pressure us about. Nor was my mother alone in her attitudes. I am told, for instance, that the Loewenfelds were upset when their son Andreas chose Law instead of Medicine.

At the same time my father's only wish seemed to be that we would show greatness and fame. If we played the piano, we were to be concert pianists, if we wrote something, we were to become writers, if we looked in a microscope, we were to become scientists. But, while my mother was steadfast in her beliefs, he showed contradictory attitudes. Early on, we were to be revolutionaries or workers and artisans. Later my sister, when I was no longer part of his life, was to become his assistant, to my mind his slave. He did not object to our becoming doctors, but when my sister chose an impoverished area of Maine in which to practice medicine, he showed contempt. It was not grand enough. He was not opposed to country living. He had been raised in a small village and he liked hunting and riding, but his idea was more of the "master of the manor," than seeing himself live in poverty. When he was able, he bought a large tract of land in Rangeley, Maine and there he wished to found a scientific study center. He sported the heavy plaid jackets of the simple Maine woodsman and hunter. He imbued in my sister and my brother the love of country living, and of raising vegetables in one's garden. Not that my father ever dirtied his hands in the soil. It was his wife, Ilse, who gardened and canned her produce. My sister, before she turned vegetarian, went on to raise her own beef cow and to eat her calf every year. My brother raised bees and chickens. How Father felt about himself is best illustrated from his remark to my sister about Annie, his first wife and our mother. He referred to her as "that petty bourgeois from Vienna."

My mother, instead, was strictly urban. True she loved vacationing in beautiful scenic places and would go skiing and mountain hiking, but *real* life was to be lived in the big city, not a rural or provincial town, but the capital and cultural center of a country.

While Father's snobbery was based on class and Mother's on culture, both wanted us to become rich and successful. My sister's rebellion was to espouse poverty. Pressured by Mother's insistence that all her enthusiastic interests would not "earn a living," she did go to medical school. But eventually she chose, what at that time, was an uncultured area of Maine. Her rebellion against her father was to choose the poorest area she could find, where people, if they paid the doctor at all, paid in chickens or other produce.

My own rebellion was short lived, as I could not but see the humor and stupidity in my revolutionary, Trotskyite past. Thus, I was forced to consider my professional future.

Having majored in History and minored in Psychology, I neared graduation with no idea how to get a job and earn a living. Graduate school in History never occurred to me, though I had loved my major. What is odd about my oblivion, like a blank, that I could choose this road, is that Julie, who was finishing college at the same time, having been delayed by World War II, went on to graduate school. However, we decided that History "had no future," so he chose to study Economics with an emphasis on Economic History.

I must have been impressed by Mother's anxiety about "earning a living," but somehow this anxiety I failed to apply to my husband.

My indecision about my future was more like a paralysis; more like the identity crisis about choosing a profession described by Erik Erikson in

"Young Man Luther." It was reminiscent of my baffled question at age six about whether there were any other fields of work besides psychoanalysis, which led my father into having a temper tantrum, I assume because I did not know of the working class. But it was also a result of ignorance, because of our immigration, about the mechanisms of developing one's future in America. I decided for the second time to get professional help about what direction I should take. This time I asked help from the Psychology Department at NYU. I underwent a huge battery of tests, and then intensive interviews, and then heard nothing, no advice, no follow-up appointment, no closure. When I pressed the service for a follow-up, I was given an appointment with one of the junior faculty. The man looked perplexed, but then, when he found out I was married he exclaimed "married!! You could become a salesgirl." I was outraged.

Eventually, through some friends of mine, I obtained a job as an assistant nursery schoolteacher in a settlement house. But I soon found out that this was not a suitable profession for me. There is a certain knack for teachers to both love their children and at the same time to exude such an air of authority, that they have no disciplinary problems. I was totally inept on both counts. The work did not enthuse me, it was more like a chore. At the same time the pay was exceedingly low, and I believe, contrary to academia, it remained that way in the post war boom. I therefore gave in to my mother and applied to Medical School. Because I needed extra science courses, it took two years to start that training. During this time I remained a teacher and therefore had ample evidence that I had made the right decision.

Eventually, after a little pressure from my mother, I chose the Medical-school route in order to become a psychoanalyst. There was a definite comfort in finding a road, but no excitement. This led to friction with Mother who could not understand why I wasn't reading Freud with great enthusiasm. It is amazing to me that with this inauspicious beginning, I eventually found my field and found great interest, stimulation, and satisfaction in this field. I had made the right choice!!

Chapter 16

FATHER'S TRAGIC END

I had not spoken to my father since my last contact with Ilse, when she told me that my father did not wish to see me. Nor had I thought of him since then, but his presence hung around my unconscious and expressed itself in various disguised forms. For instance, when I was in trouble with my college grades at NYU, I thought it was due to the shunning by the Communists on campus, but when I was asked about this by a committee of professors, I "lied" and said it was because my father refused to pay my tuition and I had to work to support myself. I was so proud about my invention, I had absolutely no knowledge that I was telling the emotional truth.

I was therefore surprised when a gangly, ugly young man with a huge cold sore on his lip, approached me as I was crossing Washington Square Park on my way to NYU. He said, in a diffident perhaps embarrassed voice, I am an Assistant Professor of Philosophy and a patient of your father's. I was annoyed and puzzled, what did this horrid man want from me? It never occurred to me that this was another unfortunate patient ordered by my father to approach me. We had no further conversation and parted at the entrance to NYU.

It is also odd that my memory, which seems so sharp and precise about my past, gets extremely vague in relation to my father. At some point my sister must have effected another reconciliation, because I have an image of a scene involving my brother, when he was a toddler, so it must have been within a year or two after I returned from Oberlin. The story about my brother has always struck me as funny and so I do remember that quite well. My father had developed the idea that children should be raised by "self-regulation." If one did not impose authoritarian rule, they would develop naturally and without character distortions and armor. So my toddler brother is running about in my father's study with an open bottle of club soda, which he proceeds to sprinkle upon the carpet. Ilse runs after him and tries to stop him. My father says something to the effect of "leave him alone;" meaning that Peter should self-regulate himself. Ilse immediately stops interfering but looks worried. Then Peter goes to my father's desk in order to sprinkle it. At this moment Willi firmly tells him to stop. I am amused. Willi sees no contradiction in the message he is sending.

My amusement points to the cynicism with which I viewed my father by this time. He had ejected me one too many times. This last reconciliation was totally false. He avoided sharing any of his ideas or work with me. In the past he had burdened me with trying to interest me in his research, which was way beyond my comprehension, as if I were an intellectual equal. Now we talked in the most artificial manner. He decided that I was going to be a writer because I had written some short stories at Oberlin. It was assumed that I would be famous. But otherwise, we had no topic in common. At the same time, I believe, he was becoming renowned in some places and had quite a following. He was developing his "Orgone Box," and was being taken up by avant-garde circles as a great therapist and had many students wishing to learn his technique. This spreading fame eventually led to his undoing.

We danced about each other with extreme care, not voicing any true emotions. It should be remembered that my father had no tolerance for hidden, veiled feelings, and unvoiced emotions. He was being completely unnatural to his true self. He tolerated my evasiveness for quite a while. Eventually he accused me of accepting money, the occasional twenty-dollar bill, without showing that I cared for him at all. I don't think I answered this and probably just saw him less often. He started to make critical comments. At some point he told me that he could not stand people with small eyes—he liked an open look. I did not understand at the time that he meant that I was armored and not open with him. I was very insulted by this as my small eyes were due to edema of my face, which was plaguing me though I had no concept why it was happening to me. Much later I came to learn that I was allergic to tyrosine rich foods. But it shows that he was not able to continue our non-aggression pact. It can be no surprise that our contacts were rare and spaced out.

I introduced him to Julie and found my father able to accept our relationship without any of the worries about our future as expressed by my mother. But his conversations with Julie were as stilted and careful as the ones with me. It has already been described how tenuous and superficial our relationship had become. Julie could not stand him. He found his social theories about "work democracy" childish and naïve and he could sense the underlying tendency to pressure people into becoming his disciples. When we were married my father gave us a set of five books he had written, which were now translated into English and recently released. No one in my family believed in ceremony or celebration but giving us his books seemed to me a sign of true self-involvement, a lack of thinking of what we needed in our new life, and only thinking how important he was. Eventually, we just "dropped out" of his life. There was no quarrel or disagreement, we just stopped calling. My father was not one to pursue us or invite us. So we just drifted apart.

A few years passed. During this time, I continued with my life without much thought about him. But his rising fame did intrude upon my life. I found myself the object of intense interest to people who pursue contact with celebrity. I began to become ashamed of the relationship and started to hide behind my married name. At one time, I was invited to a party and our host suddenly turned to me and said, "I understand that the daughter of Wilhelm Reich is a guest here today" and I pretended it was someone else. Most people did not associate the name Rubin with Reich, so I was relatively safe. There were, however, associates of my mother, who pressured me to renew my contact, which I angrily rejected. Somehow, I seem to have heard this advice as accusation of guilt. For one day while passing by my father's house in my car, I decided to drop in, unannounced, just to say hello. Ilse was in the kitchen and greeted me with worried restraint. We were chatting politely when my father suddenly entered the kitchen to ask Ilse something. He looked right through me as if I were not there, talked to Ilse and left. At first, I thought is it possible he did not recognize me, but I knew this was not correct. To pretend nothing had happened and to suppress any feelings was my first urge. Therefore, I asked Ilse, as if to suggest she was not a good hostess, for a cup of coffee. This she reluctantly made. Then she started to explain that my father had had some kind of dental procedure and was in great pain, as if to imply that he truly had not noticed me. We left it at that, and I departed as quickly as I could without showing any outward affect. I knew that there was going to be no further relationship. This was the end. Truly, I never did speak to him again. And as before, I pushed the experience away into the subterranean recesses of my mind.

Totally separated from my father, I became closer and closer to Mother's orbit. I was still feeling fairly alienated from her; but she was skilled in offering us more and more "perks" which we could not afford, and we went along with these bribes. At the same time, I was following her path into medicine, then psychiatry, and then psychoanalysis, which in spite of me, I was enjoying very much. While I was entangled with my mother, my sister entered my father's life with stern determination. She left her husband at Reich's request and joined him in Rangeley Maine, becoming his assistant. A few weeks later, she sent a letter to Mother, dictated by my father, which stated categorically that she did not wish to have any further contact with her. Her contacts with me were confined to the few times she was separated from Father. But at no time did she ever discuss her work, friendships, or events affecting my father; and the last four years of my father's life my sister and I had no contact at all. She dropped out and disappeared together with him.

One day I was perusing the New York Times, when on a back page I came upon an article of about two and a half inches with a headline saying something like "Scientist Sent to Prison." With total surprise, I read the prisoner's name, it was Wilhelm Reich!!! The article gave no details of what had happened, or what he was arrested for. A wave of shock flowed over me and then shame. My father was a prisoner, how could I possibly face the world; what would my fellow residents think of me. This emotion was intense, but I don't remember feeling any worry about him or his welfare. It was probably thirty years later before I knew the whole story—because people did so much research, wrote articles, and obtained records under the freedom of information act—of his persecution by the FDA, accusing him of being a charlatan out for money, using a fake medical device called the Orgone box and pretending he could cure cancer. There followed the burning of all his books, because they were considered advertisements, reminiscent of the earlier burning of his books in Nazi Berlin. I learned of his refusal to accept help from the ACLU and defending himself in court by maintaining that a court could not judge science. I saw photos of his arrest, the expression on his face of anxious terror. But when I first read about his arrest, I had been completely isolated from him and my sister, there was no public outcry yet, no movies, no protests known to the general population, and so my ignorance was complete, and embarrassment and shame were my emotions.

The hospital, where I was undertaking my psychiatric residency was located at the furthest northeast corner of the Bronx. We lived in the West Village in Manhattan. To get to work I usually drove our only car by highways, going in the opposite direction from rush hour traffic. One could get there by a very long subway ride and then walk almost a mile, something I once did when the city was layered in ice. The walk was so slippery, that I accepted a ride from a complete stranger. Given the difficulty getting there, I was puzzled and surprised when my husband appeared one day at the hospital. He explained that my sister had called and said that my father had died—in prison—and if I wanted, I could come to the funeral and then hung up without further information. Julie did not know what to do so he thought he'd better come and tell me. My initial reaction was to feel very strange and not in touch with myself, and very grateful to Julie for taking the trouble to come get me. Then I got into a dither about whether I should attend the funeral. I pondered this for a few days, unable to make up my mind. I had no idea when or where the funeral would take place, and also no address or phone number for my sister. It was an odd predicament and led to a lot of work to gather relevant information. I decided to call the warden of the penitentiary where my father had been imprisoned. I wanted to know whether he had committed suicide, or how he had died. The warden was stiff and formal, did not express any sympathy, but did inform me that my father had not committed suicide but died of heart failure in his sleep. He also honored my request to tell me what funeral company was handling the body. (Years later I received a gift of the copy of the prison record, obtained under the freedom of information act, where I found out that the warden did not know of any daughter called LORE, as she was not in the permitted list of visitors and correspondents. Under this constraint he certainly was polite and helpful.) I was now able to obtain the information that the funeral would be held at Orgonon in Maine and on what date. Furthermore, the funeral company told me the name of the Motel in Rangeley and the room number where my sister was staying. After further indecisiveness, I decided it would be better to attend the funeral, even if I later regretted it, than not attend and regret something that cannot be undone.

We arrived in Portland on a dark November afternoon and rented a car to drive to Rangeley at the northern edge of Maine. We chose the straightest route, which however covered the back roads. Never had I witnessed such a bleak landscape; bare trees with thin branches, brown plowed fields empty of any crop, rare houses without lights in the window, no other cars on the road, no people, it looked like a nightmare winter desert. I had only visited Maine in the summer, and then only the much more populated coastal areas. This landscape was depressing, even frightening. It was a very lengthy road trip and we only arrived around eleven o'clock that night. We found our motel and knocked on the door to my sister's room. But it was William Steig, the cartoonist and disciple of my father's, whom we roused out of bed. We had been given the wrong room number. His book of cartoons had come out fairly recently and had made a big splash in the book world. I found the cartoons offensive and condescending. The most unpleasant one was of a miserable young man saying: "My mother loved me, but she died." This was supposed to be funny, but I thought it showed contempt for someone's suffering. Steig met us in the parking lot. I asked where my sister was. He said that my sister was sitting vigil up at the observatory at Orgonon, but that—as an outsider—I was forbidden to go there. I said, "But I am family," Steig answered in a low growling voice: "You should have thought of that before!!" I was incensed. I said, or rather shouted: "How dare you, you have no idea about it!" My husband became nervous and made me hush up. And to this day I feel deprived of giving this judgmental man a piece of my mind.

Ilse and the thirteen-year-old Peter found us in the parking lot. Ilse had left my father about 4 years earlier and was considered as much of an outsider as I. She came to the funeral as Peter's mother. Peter looked sad and also sleepy, but he greeted me very warmly as if nine years had not passed, since I last saw him. As a keepsake he handed me a spent shell casing from my father's rifle. I was very touched by this gesture, and I think from then on we formed an instant bond that has lasted all our lives. The next day we met up with my sister, who surprisingly, also greeted me with warmth and great relief. I only realized later that she was all alone there, isolated from the disciples, bereft of her second husband who had been a close disciple to Reich, who either had to remain at home to take care of their livestock, or was avoiding the disciples because he had become persona-non-grata to Reich over some minor misunderstanding. Nor was Eva that close to Ilse.

The funeral was held on a hillside at Orgonon. A grave had been dug and above it was a large sculpture of my father's head. There were at least fifty people there. My greatest wound of that day came when a group of disciples, who had chartered an airplane from New York, arrived; they included at least three fellow psychiatric residents from my own hospital. What a mockery, they had never mentioned my father to me or told me about their hidden beliefs, but of course they knew exactly who I was. They did not acknowledge me at the funeral, not even with a nod. I wondered, why they did not invite me onto their flight, when instead we had had a long and tortuous journey. But then I also observed that none of the disciples greeted or acknowledged my sister or Ilse and Peter. It was clear that the family were the outsiders at this funeral. One of the older disciples gave a graveside eulogy. The words that stick in my mind are: "Not in a thousand nay two thousand years… [has someone like Reich arisen.]" They were comparing him to the second coming of the Messiah. I was visiting the funeral of a cult leader. At lunch Eva and Julie and I ate in a restaurant, where several disciples were eating. Eva told me that we have nothing to do with *them*. She gave no details about this situation. But we were at peace and friendly with each other. It was obvious that she was very happy I came. Then she suddenly started to tickle me aggressively, I had a very hard time to make her stop. She was showing her other side, her ambivalence toward me, but also her lack of self-control. It was a warning to me that the old sister was still buried in the new one.

The behavior of the disciples toward us was made graphically clear to me in my late seventies. I was invited to drinks and dinner by friends, who had also invited another couple. I forget their last name, but the wife was called Penny. I remembered her vaguely as someone who was a well-liked assistant to my father in my very early teens and then mysteriously disappeared and was never mentioned again. As soon as Penny saw me, she launched into a long frustrated major complaint, which she had had no prior opportunity to voice, or so I guessed. She was not hostile to me but needed to be heard. While she was a lab assistant, Penny married a man, who soon had a negative reaction to my father, I think fearing his insistent dominant personality. My father became belligerent and kicked him out of the summer job the man had assumed. My father declared him an enemy, then roused all his disciples against the man, forbade them to treat him in their practice even though he was already a patient of one of the disciples, and forbade anyone to talk to him. Huge pressure was put on Penny to get a divorce, when this did not happen, Penny was also let go from her job, under the same indictment. The young couple had no money and suffered the immense loss of two jobs, as well as the loss of the community she had been a part of.

My sister and Bill her husband, had been accused of something during Father's year in prison and were now suspect enemies. This was a deep pain to my sister, who had sacrificed so much of her own life for her father. I had been declared an enemy in prior years. This was evident as I was cut out of the will, though Peter and Eva received precious little money, all else was willed to the Wilhelm Reich Infant Trust Fund. The disciples had obviously been told not to speak to us. My fellow residents were obeying this dictum at the funeral, but at the hospital, unseen by the faithful, they had always been cordial. After the funeral they acted as if the whole event had never happened.

My father's death had a remarkable effect on my family. It was as if an evil genie had been eliminated. My sister and Mother slowly reunited. My mother, who had been widowed some two years earlier, became a sort of family matriarch. She started having large family parties on holiday occasions, which were not only attended by my sister and me, our husbands, and then children, but also amazingly included Ilse and Peter. It was now since Willi was dead, that they could become friendly. And since Ilse and Peter had no other family, at least in the United States, it was wonderful that they could be included. When my mother became too ill to continue our festivities, Ilse took over as the family matriarch. For many years she held our now dispersed family together and made us feel like a unit. She also took a great interest in the grandchildren and was often very helpful. By coming to the funeral, I had not only gained a sister, but also a new brother and Ilse. It was from Peter that I derived the most pleasure. He was in boarding school located nearer to me than to his mother. Peter started to visit us regularly on weekends. He brought numerous friends with him who all slept on the floor, ate spaghetti and meatballs with tomato sauce on Friday night and blueberry pancakes in the morning. They were a delightful bunch of kids, who enjoyed the benefit of having free accommodation while they rambled through New York City. It was only when Peter entered college that we lost the pleasure of his weekly company.

My relationship to my mother had improved markedly. I realized, she had not been very maternal, but she had always seen to our welfare in the best way she could, had arranged who would take care of us, had supported us financially and had made sure we were self-supporting adults. I found out she was a very well-read cultured woman with a wide range of intellectual interests, knowledgeable about literature old and new, music old and new, and art. She was well known in her profession and had written some very good articles. I began to admire her achievements. Contrary to my father, whose diaries are a very substantial record of his life, my mother never talked about her past. All I can remember are one or two sentences about her mother. Despite being a suffragette and raising my mother not to be a housewife, her mother was a compulsive housewife and overly thrifty. So I believe she was raised in a very strict manner without warmth, and I began to see that her own past and upbringing had interfered with her maternal instincts

My view of my father also changed. I understood that my defensive attitude had been necessary to defend against his demanding, intrusive, and engulfing personality; but I also began to understand his own development and basically the tragedy of his life. So many books came out about him that I saw that he had been a victim in more than one sense. After a very traumatic childhood, he had been a victim first to Anna Freud, then to the Nazis and then to the FDA. His tendency to be "in your face" provocative had contributed to his troubles, but the situations he was in were not caused by him. His increasing grandiosity was his response to the frequent reversals in his life. I began to meet Reichians, who were not cultish disciples, and to understand that he had made a number of great contributions, for which he often gets no credit—for instance his working with the eyes produced the same traumatic memory reaction as is now found in the practice of EMDR. In Psychoanalysis he identified the nature of character traits and how they arose, in a much more complex way than Anna Freud's mechanisms of defense. He understood that trauma was a very important contributor to these character traits, while for many years the psychoanalysts paid little attention to the importance of trauma. He understood characterological resistance in the transference, though his methods to analyze them were perhaps too autocratic. His vegetative streaming body therapy seems to have effects, even if his underlying theory is not quite correct. The Psychoanalysts were strictly opposed to touching a patient and feared that it would lead to sexual acting out, which of course is a danger. However, many professionals touch the body, e.g., doctors, physical therapists. Their treatments are beneficial, though there are sexual transgressions by some disreputable practitioners. And finally, Reich's contributions to sociologic matters should not be underestimated. These include his insight into the psychological underpinning of fascism as well as his thoughts about sexuality. I have come to understand why his fame has not died especially in Europe. And I am glad that I have come to be at peace with him and am no longer ashamed to be his daughter.

In my view growing up consists of seeing one's parents as people with good points and with flaws, and to appreciate them for who they are. Understanding their own struggles and life history makes it possible to get a more equitable perspective. This is not quite the same thing as the religious command "to forgive." It is a parallel process, in which by understanding, one is suddenly able to relinquish the many negative emotions that were created in one's childhood; feelings of abandonment, low self-esteem for being unlovable, anger and rage, and rejection of the parents altogether. Even better, for some unfathomable reason, writing down one's story seems to make these feelings recede into oblivion.

Wilhelm and Ilse, 1944

Lore at Oberlin, 1944

Ilse with Peter, 1944

Wilhelm and Peter 1944

Wilhelm holding Baby Peter 1944

Wilhelm Teaching at Orgonon, c. 1950

1955 The Happy Annie, Late 1950s

Lore and Annie, 1960

Peter, Mid 1960s

BIBLIOGRAPHY

Bergman, M. (1997). The historical roots of psychoanalytic orthodoxy. *Int J Psychoanal, 78*(1), 69–86.

Burlingham, M. (1989). *The last Tiffany: A biography of Dorothy Tiffany*. New York: Atheneum.

Deutsch, H. (1944). *The psychology of women; a psychoanalytic interpretation. Vol. 1*. Oxford, England: Grune & Stratton.

Etkind, A. (1997). *Eros of the Impossible: The History of Psychoanalysis in Russia*. Boulder, CO: Westview Press.

Fallend K. (1988). *Wilhelm Reich in Wien: Psychoanalyse und Politik*. Wien: Geyer Edition.

Fallend K. & Nitzschke B. (Hrsg.). (1997). *Der Fall Wilhelm Reich: Beiträge Zum Verhältniss von Psychoanalyse und Politik*. Frankfurt a. M.: Suhrkamp.

Fenichel, O. (1998). *119 Rundbriefe: (1934–1945)*. 2 Bde. Hrsg. v. J. Reichmayr & E. Mühlleitner. Frankfut a. M. u. Basel: Stroemfeld.

Freud, A. (1934). Letter to Eitingon. Library of Congress archives: Anna Freud papers.

Gardiner, M. (1983). *Code Name »Mary«: Memoirs of an American Woman in the Austrian Underground*. New Haven: Yale University Press.

Grunberger, B. & Chasseguet-Smirgel, J. (1986) *Freud or Reich: Psychoanalysis or Illusion*, published in 1970 in French, republished 1986 Yale University Press, New Haven.

Heller, P. (1990). *A Child Analysis with Anna Freud*. Madison, CT: International Universities Press.

Martin, J. (2000). *Wilhelm Reich and the Cold War*. Fort Bragg, CA: Flatland Books.

May, U. & Mühlleitner, E. (Hrsg.). (2005). *Edith Jacobson. Sie selbst und die Welt ihrer Objekte.*

Leben, Werk, Erinnerungen. Gießen: Psychosozial-Verlag.

Peglau, A. (2013): *Unpolitische Wissenschaft? Wilhelm Reich und die Psychoanalyse im Nationalsozialismus.* Gießen: Psychosozial-Verlag.

Reich, A. (1973): *Psychoanalytic Contributions.* New York: International Universities Press.

Reich Rubin, L. (2003). Wilhelm Reich and Anna Freud: His Expulsion from Psychoanalysis.

International Forum of Psychoanalysis, 12, 109–117.

[Dt. 2007: Wilhelm Reich und Anna Freud, S. Reichs Vertreibung aus der Psychoanalyse. *Bukumatula* [Zeitschrift des Wiener Wilhelm Reich-Instituts], *1/07,* 5–26.

Reich Rubin, L. (2008). Wilhelm Reichs wechselnde Theorien über Kindererziehung. *Werkblatt,* 61, 3–21.

Reich, W. (1933 German, 1979 English). *Character Analysis,* translated by Theodore Wolfe. New York Orgone Institute Press.

Reich, W. (1933 German, 1947 English, 2020 reprint German). *Mass Psychology of Fascism,* translated Theodore Wolfe. New York: Orgone Institute Press.

Rubin, L. (2005) pp. 313–328 in May, U & Mühlleitner, E. (hrsg).

Schröter, M. (1997). Max Eitingon ein Geheimagent Stalins? Erneuter Protest gegen eine zählebige Legende. Veröffentlicht in: Psyche, 51. Jg. (1997), pp. 457–470; gegenüber der Druckfassung leicht korrigiert

Steiner, R. (1989). It is a new kind of diaspora. *Int. R. Psycho-Anal.* 16, 35–72.

Sterba, R. (1985). *Erinnerungen eines Wiener Psychoanalytikers.* Frankfurt a. M.: Fischer.